Steven Curtis Lance

LOVE
By +Steven Curtis Lance
Published through Lulu Enterprises, Inc.

All rights reserved
Copyright © 2009 by +Steven Curtis Lance
Cover photo by Matt Vulcan

Interior Book Design and Layout by
www.integrativeink.com

ISBN: 978-0-578-00658-1

No part of this publication may be reproduced, stored in a retrieval system, or transmitted in any form or by any means electronic, mechanical, photocopying, recording, or otherwise, without the written permission of the author or publisher.

LOVE

by love I came to be

Through a thousand nights of love into a thousand days of poetry, love came to me wearing its thousand faces and thrillingly whispering words into my heart. I wanted to remember them and to share them with you so I wrote them all down with the uttermost care as my uttermost offering, by love and for love with all of my heart.

Those words were these poems which are this book of a thousand nights of love into a thousand days of poetry, written down with the uttermost care, to remember and to share.

And even and especially when it might not seem so, all these words in all their thousand ways share as their source and destination love, wearing its thousand faces and thrillingly whispering words, these words, into your heart through mine.

I made this book for you and it is yours now. It had to be called LOVE because it is.

Take it.

Love,

+Steven

Contents

Pigeons	1
A Little Help from Angels Here and There	2
Mutual Respect	3
Dying to Find Out	4
Beyond	5
Instrument of Grace	6
Road	7
Shadow of Despair	8
To Someone Somehow	9
Into the Night	10
Pieces of Us Both	11
Becoming	12
Selfmade Unmade	13
The Point of It	14
Questions in a Quiet Voice	15
Love's Lightning	16
Paint Plaster and Pandemonium	17
As the Cow Jumps Over the Moon	18
Come Back to Me	19
Stupor Mundi	20
Little Big Man	21
Sucker	22
Through Me	23
Late Birds	24
Out	25
Friday Afternoon	26
The Time of Our Lives	27
Glimmer	28
Parallel	29
Curling Up With Cats	30
Grandpa!	31
Handyman Keep Your Hands to Yourself	32
As the Sun Rises	33
Familiar Company	34

Forever Free	35
Tube a Tuba	36
To Care and Care Not	37
My Religion is Kindness	38
Rose Red	39
This Gift We Live	40
Broken: Free	41
Rind of Reality	42
Reflection	43
Smokey Joe the Extra Cat	44
As the Night Gives to the Day	45
Harvest Moon of Saturday	46
The Man in the Moon	47
Fresh-Baked and Only for Today	48
Reality's Ledge	49
My Special Relativity	50
Feeling Time a Pinwheel	51
Back Home to the Dark	52
Second Saturday	53
Right Here	54
The Only Cure	55
The Rest Remains	56
Midnight Song	57
Pickled Hell	58
Quiet and Cool	59
Robots Calling	60
A Rice Day	61
Because of You	62
Mr. Hot Dog Head	63
Mr. Hot Dog Head Hits the Road	64
Mr. Hot Dog Head is Gone	65
The Rose Within the Flame	66
Uncertain Raven	67
Autumn Leaves and Commonday Miracles	68
If You Want To	69
Tomorrow Never Comes	70
Heaven on Wheels	71
Heading Home to You	72
This Rambling Road	73
Enjoying the View from the Carousel	74
Completion	75

Come Night	76
Hypocrisy	77
Nightmares	78
Full Moon Beckoning	79
Decision 2006	80
Two	81
Flight	82
8 November 2006	83
These Improbable Wings	84
Never Know Until	85
Success	86
These November Evenings	87
Fragments of the Whole	88
A Song to the Dust	89
It Was Always You	90
My Fall My Rise	91
Do Not Disturb	92
Sweet Bread	93
Respect and Solidarity	94
The Veil Withdrawn	95
Coming Home	96
Sheltering Shadows	97
Slugabed	98
Her Name Was Patricia	99
My Providential You	100
These Autumn Stars	101
Midnight Consolation	102
My Brother Bee	103
To Be Lonely	104
It Was You	105
Star	106
Snow	107
Survival Sonnet	108
Love is Free	109
Life Instead	110
One Hell of a Ride	111
Got What He Wanted	112
Apple-Crisp Moments	113
Christmas Carol	114
More	115
Orderly Retreat	116

3:53	117
The Game Itself	118
Fortune Cookie	119
Where Old Sailors Go to Die	120
Wrong Turn Eternity	121
Tragicomedy	122
Without Me	123
Never Been the Burying Kind	124
"Love"	125
HumanKIND	126
Making Homemade Poetry	127
Sonnet at the Winter Solstice	128
The Constancy of Change	129
Embraced by the Moon	130
What She Meant After All	131
Soil and Sky	132
Two by Two	133
Delighted to be Invited	134
Of Higher Choice	135
Christmas 2006: Absolute Aloneness	137
War Sonnet	138
A Set of Three on Christmas Eve	139
This Mischief I Make in the Night	141
The Hopeful Heart Knows	142
Through Bamboo	143
For Her	144
Ars Longa	145
Birthday Contemplation	146
Human After All?	148
New Year's Resolution	149
The Stubbornness of Self-Sacrifice	150
On a Blue Cloud of Dreams	152
Curiosity and Me	153
And Two Stars: Free	154
Pigs of the Sky!	155
Refraction	156
Secret	157
Infinitude	158
Another Loser of the Human Race	159
Night Ravens	160
Defiance	161

Lonely Eyes	162
As If This Were It	163
My Last Refuge	164
The Diet of Worms	165
Franziska and Me and World War III	166
Brazil Nuts Over the BBC	167
Street Sonnet	168
Living the Good Life Badly	169
My Hiding Place	170
Sinus Sonnet: An Independent Nose	171
The Plaza in Orange California	172
Down	173
Recognition	174
Nocturne	175
No Greater Love	176
Just About	177
A Rising and a Reaching	178
Shenanigans	179
Playing Chess with My Cat	180
Eternity	181
Geocentricity	182
Regret	183
Out of Our Hands	184
The Ring	185
Yesterday's Elephants	186
Magical Morning	187
Eccentric	188
Like it or Not	189
Chances Are	190
Why We Wander	191
Answered	192
Dry Flowers	193
Stop	195
For Right Now	196
Shot by Cupid	197
The Art of Poetry	198
Sick Enough	199
Old Soldier	200
The Learning Curve	201
I Wish I Could Write a Poem Today	203
I Hope	204

Gone	205
New Pants in a Spacetime Anomaly	206
Existential Baseball	207
Suddenly Now	208
Broken	209
Visual Reality	210
Little Big Boy!	211
Come Turn the Key	212
Drifting	213
To Us	214
Redeeming the Time	215
Still Way Too Tough to Die	216
Volunteers in Waste Places	217
Electric Freefall	218
Rise	219
Blood	221
At Last	223
Fast Cars and Slow-Walking Men	224
Like a Kiss	225
Thump-Thump-Thump	226
Nirvana	228
Under the Moon by the Railroad Track	229
Curious Canyons	230
The Meaning of It	231
Two for One: Bagel and Coffee	232
Broken Veterans	234
The Mirror and the Window	235
Rather Like Rhymes	236
Orphan	237
The Gift We Keep	238
The Thing I Like Best About You	239
Etude: Thirteen by Thirteen	240
Surprised	241
Easter Before I Go	242
Exacta	243
Circus Train	244
Shy Little Love Song	245
A Sonnet in Solidarity	246
Possibility	247
Cigarettes and Kisses	248
Rite of Passage	249

Jim	251
Black-eyed Peas	252
Up Up and Away!	253
Outside Inside	254
Consecration	255
In Utero	256
Just Poetry	257
Surprised by Dawn	258
Showtime	259
The Visitation	260
Your Steppenwolf	261
Crystal Blue Sun Sky	263
Mother's Day Meditation	264
Or	265
Return to the Garden	266
Lonely	267
Walk Softly	268
Cats on Two and Four Legs	269
Fair Trade Forgiveness	270
Night's Answers to Day's Questions	271
Beautiful Complex Humanity	272
I Believe in You	273
In the Firmament Between Always and Never	274
Whole	275
Anticipated Reality	276
When My Cat and I Have Tea	277
Credo	278
The Queen of Spades in Exile	279
For Grandma	280
Paris Moon	281
Oral Fixation	282
If This is Sociopathy Then Sign Me Up	283
Life Lives Belief	284
Poets' Corner	285
Life's Tender Kiss	286
Specific Leaves	287
A Sonnet Upon It	288
My Misplaced Destiny	289
Meeting at Spiro's for Dinner	290
Farewell My Child	291
Faith	292

Beyond the Illusion	293
Dark Mirror	294
Stay Hungry	295
One of Those Places	297
Friends and Lovers	298
The Veil and the Vision	300
Somebody Worth Loving?	301
Acceptance	302
The Heart Knows Better	303
Freedom of Thought Would Give You Wings	304
Essence	306
For You	307
My Mother the Moon and Me	308
An Erstwhile Undiscovered Part of Me	309
Anything	311
Shadow	312
From the Leading Edge of Always	313
The Fall of the House of No	314
Left Unknown	315
Between Now and Never	316
Family Skeleton	317
Fiat Lux (if just a little for now)!	318
For Natasha	319
One Summer Moment	320
A Convicted Man Confesses	321
Love Song	322
Going Your Way	323
Within the Rose	324
She	325
Plausible Deniability	326
Good Enough	327
Chance	328
Here We Are	329
Birthday Song for Teddy	330
Each One a Star	331
Sibling Rivalry	332
My Own Universe	333
Nightfall in the Garden	334
Because Because Is	335
Cruciform	336
I Chose to Live	337

Specificities	338
Invincible	339
Hope	340
An Obscure Eccentric Poet Wonders About Being Discovered	341
Butts on my Butt	342
These Snorting Snouts	343
Thank You for Being Friends with Me	344
Among Friends	345
Along the Way	346
The Dance of Life	347
A Misfit Born and Bred	348
Threshold	349
One Love	350
Matchsticks	351
Phone Home From the Twilight Zone	352
Now and Then	354
Success	355
I Too	356
Dark Angel	358
(I simply cannot tell you...)	359
Straightening My Cigarette	360
With Salem Far Behind Me	362
For Shelby Cundiff: My Poetry Pal	364
Will	365
Mattie and Me in High Society	366
The Other Side of the Mirror	368
Beachcombing in Autumn	370
Lunchtime in the Plaza	372
Mackerel Sky	374
Could Be	377
Sweet Addiction	378
Wings	379
The Boy is Father to the Man	381
Answered by Silence	383
To Have a Because	384
Alone with God ...and You	385
De Rerum Natura	387
Pick a Star	388
What Fred Said	389
Night Rain After Disappointment	390
The Bubble Now	391

Iron Grey	392
The Bifocal Perspective of Being	393
Not Until	394
The Golden Frame	395
Our Time Will Come	396
Never Quite	397
Inside	398
Sickbed with Cat	399
Promise the Dust	401
Still Free	402
November	403
Autumnal People	404
The Most Beautiful Thing on Earth	405
Blood Red Rose	406
Like Birds Waiting for the Rain	407
Hard Knocks and Soft Answers	408
Moon and Sea	409
Raindrops for the Rain	410
The Rest of Me	411
Thoughts on Thanksgiving Day MMVII	412
Of All Places	413
Caravan	414
Souvenirs of Ecstasy	415
Two-Part Invention	417
Countdown	418
Among My Souvenirs	419
To Spend the Evening Quietly	420
A Mystery Which No One Need Explain	421
Winter	423
Tough Guy (Not Enough Guy)	424
The Dow and the Tao	425
Still Open	426
Lonely Street	427
The Quest	429
Oops!	431
Because We Share This	432
Suicide Note	434
Evolution Revolution	435
Yes	436
Being Me	437
I Finally Wept for My Father Today	439

Right Where You Are	440
Healing Waters	441
Son of a Gun	442
Water Music	444
Birthday Meditation	446
Compassion Fatigue	448
Paradox	450
Without into Within	452
Poetic License	453
This Quixotic Quest Called Poetry	454
Oh God (Are You Still There?)	455
A Curious Heart in the Sunshine	456
Within the Labyrinth	458
Breadline Blues	460
Sunday Morning Veterans	462
Butterflies	463
Clarity	465
Cookies and Pink Propinquity	467
Lotus	468
Twice Winner of the Breadline Milk Lottery	469
Past the Puppet Show	470
Running in Place	472
Nothing Less Than Everything	474
The Unanswered Question	476
A Silent Song of Solidarity	477
Shrapnel	479
Dust	480
Breadline Solidarity	481
Hear it Ring	482
Having Come This Far	483
The Finding of Easter Eggs	485
Four for Four	487
Our Own Reality	490
Happy Birthday	491
Strawberry	492
Everywhere	493
Forgotten Awhile	494
Out Here	496
Two-for-a-Dollar and One Free Song	498
Private Mass	500
Lisa	502

Finish Line Blues 504
Emblem and Anthem 505
The Brink of Never 507
Trajectory of Tragedy 508
This Fountain of Us 509
She Was a Star 510
Existence Without an Apology 511
The Secret 513
Breakthrough 514
Then and When and Now 515
Good-Looking People 516
Embraced 517
Epitaph 518
The Hand You Feel Within Yours 519
Incarnation 521
Someday When We Look Back 522
Stardust 524
Night Lights 525
Circles 527
Change Your Mind 528
Close Encounter 530
Soul 532
Stranger 533
Sparrow 535
And Yes: When Broken Too 537
You 538
Imagining the Unimaginable In 540
Bad Hair Day? 541
Heaven Knows 542
Confluence 543
Mirrors 544
Robert Frost and Me (Like a Chimpanzee) 545
Could it Be? 546
Up in the Trunks of Elephants 548
Human Being 549
Wake Up and Scream 551
Just So 553
Falling Stars Mistaken for Landing Airliners 554
A Call to Revolution 556
Franziska's Song: The Return 558
Grandma 559

Start at the End	560
Lucky	562
Keep on Dreaming	563
Captain Fantastic	564
Egg and Stone	565
The Question of Destiny	566
Interior Spacescape	568
The Consequences of Resurrection	569
A Love Song Actually	570
Hummingbird Reality	571
Let Me Know	572
Twilight	573
The Unruined Movie	574
Spell (for You)	576
Karen Smith	577
Our Flexible Selves	578
Empathy in the Afternoon	579
Wait	581
Existential Magic Show	582
The Time of My Life	583
Maybe	584
Manifesto	585
Thanks	586
Lonely if Only	587
One Spark of Happiness	588
Existential Satisfaction	589
I Mean to Find Some Meaning	590
Found Meaning	591
Snakes on a Bus	592
Only Love	594
Eating the Moon	595
Just Sitting Here with Fred	597
Sister on the Line	598
O Mother Soul	599
The Lotus Unfolds	600
Lucky	601
In	602
The Love Revolution	603
The Existentialist	604
Alia	605
Without from Within	606

I Love You More	607
Bubbles in Traffic	608
Freddie's Song	609
Unreturnable Now	611
Like a Knife	612
Thin Green Line	613
Passageway	615
Forget About You	616
This Hand Which Meets Me Rising	617
The Lucky Ones	618
Turns Out	619
(True)	620
The Family Goes On	621
Rebellion	622
And Along with These to Sniff Beneath Trees	623
Choristers Assembling at Evensong	624
Say Good Night Little Hitler	625
My Magical Life	626
Perspective	627
Admitting It	628
Parallel	629
Someday When You Remember	630
In the House of the Dead	631
See	632
Not for Me	633
One Bright Star	634
Like Living Until	635
These Steps of My Own	636
To the One I Love	637
The Other	638
E is for Empathy	639
A Lot Like Being Born	640
Fall	641
Pink Pets and Pills	642
At Present	643
When I Awaken	644
Platinum Diamonds on Black Velvet Sky	645
Just a Little Dream Away	646
Be	647
How it Hurts to Heal	648
Somebody	649

Throughout the Velvet Universe 650
To Journey Mindfully 651
Like Birds 652
Paradise 653
For Now 654
This 655
Tragic Magic 656
Your Other 657
All Right with Me 659
Keep 660

Pigeons

Like Skinner's superstitious pigeon we
Repeat strange patterns in the hope of love
Wasting life waiting for eternity
Hopping foot to foot while glancing above
Anxiously this way and that faithfully
In pursuit of the utterly opaque
Pecking each other when we disagree
Worrying lest we might make some mistake

Wise pigeons say we never know until
Someday when the box is opened at last
But as things stand now it looks like we will
Ignore our present to play out our past
Hopping and hoping for bits of birdseed
Watching the feathers fly as pigeons die
Pecking each other in need or in greed
And flapping our clipped wings as life flies by

At night we dream that when the box is gone
A pigeon might transfigure to a swan

A Little Help from Angels Here and There

I have decided to give up worry
As Lenten sacrifice though in July
And I firmly resolve not to hurry
But take life as it comes as time goes by
I mean to mosey to cease to scurry
And live all I can until I must die

Since nothing can be helped by worrying
Except turning whiskers white on my chin
I will not worry about anything
Just let this summer sun come streaming in
Triumphantly into my darkened room
Rejecting death unready for the tomb

Under this brilliant blue high summer sky
Where hummingbirds and butterflies abound
I cherish the simple belief that I
Though I had lost my way have now been found
By life itself and rescued from despair
My night washed away by the light of day

Hope falls gently like snow without a sound
Here in July through bright blue summer air
Falling like manna to me on the ground
Which when I gather it blooms in my hand
And I need not question nor understand
A little help from angels here and there

MUTUAL RESPECT

We need each other but need ourselves more
The self must be in good repair to share
To be we need to know what to be for
To "be there" for you I must first "be there"

If there exists among us an elect
Election is by mutual respect
To love my neighbor as myself I must
First love myself in order to love you
How can I trust you if I cannot trust
My own word when I give it you as true?

We are spirit as sure as we are dust
If "hell is other people" heaven too
I watch your back because I watch my own
We live together but we die alone

DYING TO FIND OUT

two roads to nowhere

Back in the day they all used to say
"You want to live forever?" "Hell no!"
But it is hell to go the hard way
To be falling apart as you go

Now they are more genteel in their ways
They "live right" up to a point right up
To the moment of the hemlock cup
Twisting the end of the end of days
This could be because death takes longer
When practiced by cigarettes and booze

Old-fashioned patience might seem stronger
People preach and argue pray and shout
Modern self-destroyers like to choose
Yet both still have to die to find out

Both live all they can and then they die
One slow one fast both wondering: "Why?"

Beyond

When I sold my grave back to the mortician
He said "Mr. Lance you will need it someday"
For him it was a grave breach of tradition
To leave the family plot and move away
He may be a slave to a grave but not me

If I want to join my loved ones I know where
To find them where they always wanted to be
In the water the fire the earth and the air

When I pass from earth through fire then I will see
The glory they taught me and we will be there
With our mortal eyes opened immortally
Together forever together again
Past graves and morticians beyond death and pain

INSTRUMENT OF GRACE

Your telephone knows and tells you it is time
Mine knows nothing never tells me anything
But thinking of you I feel this poem rhyme
And hope you will tell my telephone to ring
It will only waken when you tell it to

This squatting black slab-like unglamorous thing
Inertly waits here for a signal from you
It knows no tunes no tricks does not dance nor sing
Knows but one bright ring but one right thing to do
When you call it as an instrument of grace

Until you come home when we come face to face

ROAD

Having rather been a has-been than a never-was
I am grateful to have once believed in Santa Claus

And I look back now with no regrets at all because
It all went down according to how it had to be
For the pieces of the puzzle to become this me
You see today the only me which ever could have been
Because of what I do and did what I see and have seen

For better or worse this is life and I am used to it
The pieces of the puzzle come together and they fit
Just as they are and having come as far as I have now
All I can do is move along and muddle through somehow
So I will see where I will be when this road ends somewhere

We never know until we go and get from here to there
Where we will finally end up but until we arrive

The journey is the destination: on the road ...alive

Shadow of Despair

There suspended in the air
With its unanswered question
Waits the shadow of despair
Immune to all suggestion
Night might pass light might return

If you have not yet felt this
Welcome to your turn to learn
To receive your virgin kiss
Of that chill which gnaws the soul
Snaking softly night and day
Of that dark which swallows whole
Lives which have been sucked away
By the shadow of despair
Which with patience questions for
All you have and then some more

There suspended in the air
Immune to all suggestion
Waiting for us me and you
With its unanswered question
Where the nightmares all come true

As it waits so too can we
Hold my hand and stay with me

To Someone Somehow

A fear to freeze the blood within the veins
In which it runs in panic through the night
A deadly dread's ironic labor pains
Where people all say it will be all right
But it will not because it cannot be
While reason sleeps where rulers have gone blind

In the "New American Century"
My country lost its way then lost its mind
What little light is left is scarcely seen
And if it shines it seldom shines on me
So you might never know now what I mean

You reading this might wonder who I was
Who questioned in an unquestioning age
Might even seek yet not find me because
As a wanderer on a pilgrimage
I was once here but I am long gone now

May my words matter to someone somehow

INTO THE NIGHT

I felt a chill and looked within today
To find that my heart has been gnawed away

Though I had felt a growing emptiness
And bit by bit an increasing distress
As if I were losing myself somehow
I find that I have been hollowed-out now

A hole in my soul and nothing I say
None of those clever things I used to do
Can make it any better anymore
Since from this open sore my life leaks too

As if someone forgot to close the door
Let in a chill wind which blew out the light

And what I was slipped out into the night

PIECES OF US BOTH

Whatever ends up happening to me
I might as well look fate square in the face
No matter where the pieces come to rest

The puzzle will be finished finally
The way it will and that way will be best
Because that way is the way it will be
However the pieces fall into place

That configuration of destiny
Can only be accepted then with grace
Since there will be nothing else I can do
But inhabit my place in time and space

I only hope that I will be with you
And that together someday we might see
The pieces of us both fit in embrace

Becoming

on the eve of the birth of a book

Oddly classical and formal
A fastidious fellow I
Am definitely not normal
(If such a thing exists these days)
A solitary simple soul
And a little set in my ways

As unrelentingly I try
To achieve whatever my goal
Might be with cunning courtesy
Like getting good at poetry
Perhaps becoming somebody
Before (maybe after) I die

Believing the dream becomes me
Becoming and coming to be

Selfmade Unmade

In a voice roughened by regret
I can hear what he has hoped for
And that it has not happened yet
That he has always been so strong
But now he wonders how much more
Disappointment he can endure
Before he leaves it all behind

When he was young he was so sure
He knew the answers or could find
Them if he asked the questions long
Enough or maybe loud enough
But he got lost and things went wrong
He bet it all and lost the bet
And now it hurts inside his mind

So when he talks his voice is rough
Since he is fighting not to cry

How do you live when your dreams die?

The Point of It

One extreme reflects the other
Just as sister is to brother
The bloom of triumph bears the seed
Of its defeat as greed bears need

An alcoholic wet or dry
And addict felled or flying high
Saved from the sin of living die
While yin and yang eternity
Leaves behind raptured you and me
As crusader and jihadi
Find freedom to be slavery
And seek to do wrong to do right

I only seek to kiss your face
And neither slave nor master be
Not black nor white but human race
Past reason and insanity

Sunset moonrise day follows night
As we are complementary
We face each other and we fit
Which seems to me the point of it

QUESTIONS IN A QUIET VOICE

Standard answers and sophistry
That certain sense of certainty
Prevent me from the ministry
Faith is a gift which I have but
One wonders still no matter what

The freedom of thought to cherish
Intellectual honesty
Albeit at the cost of all
My heritage this heresy
Keeps me from serving a parish

I live by faith and rise or fall
I have to do it honestly
To serve the God who gives me choice
Some questions in a quiet voice
And these nine books of poetry

Love's Lightning

Tomorrow is not clear to be
Foreknown while fortune's storm winds blow
But I know you are dear to me
And never mind what comes I know
That I would like you near to me
And side by side ride out the storm

Together whether come or go
We two can come through anything
Or go as we have and we will
Because we share the certainty
Though winds rage love stays rooted still
Down deep in hearts held safe and warm

Despite the storm's intensity
Believe and feel steadfast and real
Above the night beyond the norm
Love spark the dark cloud clear to see
A rainbow bridge of light take form
From you to me and back again

Love's lightning never strikes in vain

Paint Plaster and Pandemonium

The relentless rush of renovation
Of my house has crushed my innovation
Grinding my mind to that of a zombie
Or drudge beyond the nudge of poetry

As all summer long my back has been bent
By soulsucking chores which never relent
I finish one and then another one
Or two or three or four must be begun
The past still holding a grudge against me

Miraculously I finished a book
But have scarcely seen time to sneak a look
Or even begin to savor what I
Am adequate at and what I live by

Harnessed to trudge to inadequacy
Instead I have to paint high ceilings blue
Or porch floors green or whatever I do
All a blur and bore I would do no more
Than write poems and seek a little peace

My employee believes he employs me
As he lectures me on the ebb and flow
Of pipes and the truth of the two-by-four
Sore-trying my passive diplomacy

Exhausted heatstricken now stricken dumb
I look forward to locking my front door
On paint plaster and pandemonium
When autumn falls and sacrifices cease
And renovated rise again to soar

As the Cow Jumps Over the Moon

That know-it-alls know nothing is well-known
What can be known is known unknown alone
And most of what can be is not for me
To know in any case and not my place
Because the more I know the less I know

Once certain I become less so with time
Which shadows me the faster as I slow
Robbing the reason while leaving the rhyme
The dialectic of form and function
Made moot as the cow jumps over the moon

All in a circle joins into junction
The spacetime fabric shrinking small and soon
To form a pinpoint only of the now
Soon to know nothing this suits me somehow
Satisfied to everlastingly be

And to take my turn at eternity

Come Back to Me

You turn your head and turn away
From what you dare not understand
As darkness overcomes the day

I turn my heart and turn my hand
To reach out in a gesture of
Defiant hope and stubborn love

Believing that you still might see
If through the gloom and fleetingly
My hand extended reaching to
Find yours tonight that we might touch
Across the darkness me and you

To arc the spark of life again
The hope of love we need so much
To get us through this night of pain

We feel the light no longer seen
And I know you know what I mean
By touch we see: come back to me

STUPOR MUNDI

The effect of yesterday on the hands
Of tomorrow's clock on this day before
Is that "the war" has always been "the war"

What I call "Vietnam" you call "Iraq"
The present of the past forward and back

I wonder if anyone understands

LITTLE BIG MAN

I sing of Little Big Man and you know who I mean
Our false unworthy emperor of what might have been
On whose mad unreasoning the earth is forced to hang
Mispronouncing grave pronouncements in his tangled twang

And if we disagree we are "fascists" you and me
Disloyal to royal and imperial decree
Freedom of speech is relative now as we have seen
Completely unrelated to the Bush family
Democracy seems to be a matter of degree
Good for Iraq but back at home he is not so sure
Especially if our politics are deemed impure

As democracy devolves into theocracy
We evolve into "the enemy" it seems to me

But he is "the decider" and only he knows best
In his brave new world only Little Big Man is free
To say and do what he pleases never mind the rest
Of what is left of what we once called "humanity"

Sucker

I thought someone loved me but she forgot
To tell me how trust had led me astray
Or mention how faithfulness steered me wrong

What I had mistaken for love was not
And she let me dream a little too long
She played me for a sucker all the way

So to hell with love and to hell with her
To hell with lovely dreams which never were
The longer I live the clearer I see
The world is all a lie to her to me
To everyone that we are all deceived
Looking for lovely dreams to be believed
To be treasured and to be tortured by
We die by our dreams as we live a lie

She never loved me nor did she explain
How my wholehearted love had been misplaced
And now I can never find it again

My dream dried to dust and I feel disgraced
To have been ensnared by this world of lies
Where hate only lives and love only dies

THROUGH ME

My poems write themselves
Their origins unknown
My fingers scheming elves
With ideas of their own
And what they have to say
Seems up to them alone

I feel them trace their way
In patterns on the page
At midnight and noonday
Plying their pilgrimage
Both whimsical and stern
Doing their daily rounds

And night by day I learn
To touch becomes to see
How life outside the bounds
Of ordinary things
Is fanciful and free
How an opened heart brings
What once was closed to be
As an opened heart sings
Through life to light through me

LATE BIRDS

Late birds soaring solitary
Sailing sunset on their unknown
Missions seem to race the very
Sun as they run their course alone

Called away with the close of day
To destinies which only they
Will ever know and as they go
I dream of sky of you and I
Can see that we are late birds too

Out

I stacked chords by thirds
Stacked nine books of words
And fat lot o' good it did me

Finding fame and shame
Two sides of the same
Bid for fame and life outbid me

Was too young to die
But the years slid by
And sliding home death outslid me

Friday Afternoon

renovation rumination

Friday afternoon and I await brown rice
Which takes awhile but is well worth waiting for
The mail came and went and it would have been nice
To get my Vanity Fair or something more
Than advertisements not really meant for me

Or better still I could have gotten a book
That hardcover edition I want to see
And have handy that my guests might have a look
At what I do here while time flies as it lies
Couched upon the coffee table casually

Tonight a new student will ring at my door
But at least he is not coming by surprise
I suppose a softcover will have to do
Autographed yet presented with modesty
I hope he rents a room but wish he were you
I have a secret new telephone number
Which only you and a chosen few may know

The garage is stacked with all sorts of lumber
And we make daily progress however slow
Toward building a stairway to heaven that we
Can use to escape to our sanctuary
High up in the ghost rooms above everyone
From the university down here below
We two can play up there when our work is done

Leave the students and their cares behind downstairs
Having done our homework now let them do theirs

The Time of Our Lives

Time flows away like water down the drain
Life flows too yet without unseemly haste
Not only down but up to live again
Life goes on flows on never goes to waste
Knowing no past nor future only now
Its destination always here somehow

So much to live! Such promises to keep!
May life through the dining room ceiling come
And from the floor raise steps up to the stars

As feeling tingles back to rooms gone numb
In new days more of Venus less of Mars
May singing start where all was deaf and dumb
Keyboards and drums and electric guitars
Meaningful silence of study and sleep
All things in season ripe and full and sweet
Life over time and triumph past defeat

Our time is the relative measure of
Life as we live it in the day-to-day
Made up of things like hope and faith and love

The time of our lives never goes away
Along the way somebody remembers
That which is truly us is us to stay
Decembers bear Mays which bear Decembers
As life flows yet without unseemly haste
Life goes on flows on never goes to waste

Glimmer

A glimmer of hope in a glimpse of light
At the tunnel's end at the edge of sight
Appears through my tunnel-vision tonight
Dim in the distant darkness as I grope
Toward what could be a heartbreak but I hope
Since were it not for hope the heart would break

So I believe tonight and I will take
This spark across the shadows as a sign
Despite what clock and calendar may say
That someday some peace of mind might be mine
If not right now in the future somehow
If not today at least not far away

As those who judge such things give second looks
Beyond what clock and calendar allow
At me like what they see and buy my books

Parallel

Reality is relative and specific
To each participant just as each perceives it
Bright and beatific hellish and horrific
An elastic state which is as one believes it
To be
So your reality is unreality
To me

Indeed we live in parallel realities
You there in your dimension and I here in mine
While at the same time there are billions more of these
Glorious unbearable demonic divine
Yet each like its own star in a grand galaxy
We see each other sparkle in propinquity
And other galaxies to great infinity

I sparkle you this greeting across this fleeting
Moment bridging time and space from my to your place
I see you sparkle back a smile and know
We are parallel wherever we go

Curling Up With Cats

The cats are asleep curled up in chairs
I curl up in mine and they in theirs
And no one has bothered us today
Just as we like (may it stay that way)
The cleaning lady comes tomorrow
(A cleaning lady! Imagine that)
I inherited an extra cat
Friends give me things or let me borrow
Whatever I need: thanks be to God

People are reading my poetry
In faraway places across the sea
And though it is strange and I am odd
Some seem very fond of it and of me

The cats are asleep but I will be
Awake for awhile before I sleep
To savor the unaccustomed sight
Of hope as it dawns on me tonight
A light which is warm and soft and deep
Beckons me join in the cosmic dance
For fate has decided to take a chance
On poetry spelled L - A - N - C - E
Curling up with cats at Studio Lance

GRANDPA!

My Grandpa wasn't my grandfather
Whereas one who was wouldn't bother
While the other one was decades dead
And so I had Chief Graham instead

It was "national security"
My father said which kept him from me
So when I appeared on CBS
Who was proudest of me? You can guess

I made books for him even back then
As a troubled child but he died when
I had turned thirteen because he was
The angel of my childhood to cause
Me to know what it felt like to be
One who is loved and I hope to see
This best man this lost boy ever knew
Who loved me unconditionally
Chief Al W. Graham again
In the next world but until I do:

Grandpa! I'm still making books for you

HANDYMAN KEEP YOUR HANDS TO YOURSELF

A hobo handyman a tiny tyrant
Blew in on the wind a tumbleweed my way
As fixed in mind as in form itinerant
To work for free but I could not afford it
To suck my soul away while I ignored it
And I had to let him go for good today

Hobo handyman your handymanity
Is just not worth your unworthy vanity
On the one hand you preach at me and you say
That I am no Christian at least not like you
While on the other hand you ask about sex

Well go to hell alone whatever you do
Stay well the hell away from my house and me
Keep the stink of your hobo handyman hex
Far from me and keep your hypocrisy too
My soul and faith are mine nor can you budge me
How dare you order me about and judge me

O Lord from fundamentalists and handymen
Especially both in one save us now and then

As the Sun Rises

So many pages through so many years
Of my life's ages through laughter and tears
Phases and stages of hopes and of fears
Waxing and waning cycling with the moon
Just out of reach and the sun rising soon

Stones on the beach ride the tide to my hand
I hold them and begin to understand
Nothing is in vain nothing is wasted
Each sight I've seen each flavor I've tasted
Bittersweet savored becomes part of me
Everything I live becomes poetry

Love on my lips curls a smile makes me say
I'm happy to be here glad just to be
My life is as it is this is my way
Fresh flavors to taste and new sights to see
As the sun rises on a fresh new day

Familiar Company

Observed as anorexic seen as socialist
Survivor of abuse yet still an optimist
Because it would have been worse had I known my dad
The Bush administration has me on their list
To me my greatest literary feat so far

Liberal Lutheran existentialist lad
And overall a human being as you are
Some good some mediocre blended with the bad
Intelligence has been fun if rather lonely
Just be glad this life was mine not the one you had

Now dried-up and alone I see it is only

Me

But I remain and in familiar company

Forever Free

I would rather be alone than wrongly paired
As I have been before with one who cared
But little if she ever cared at all

Far better in my solitude to be
A leaf flying free on the wind of the fall
Complete in perfect singularity

With no one yet with everyone on earth
If I know loss I also know new love
And as I know death I also know new birth

The grave beneath my feet the sky above
Now lifts my heart so high that I can see
The grave beneath outgrown a size too small

And my heart forever young forever free
Invites you soar along here by my side
The sun itself our groom the moon our bride

TUBE A TUBA

A tube a tuba toothpaste
A train a thought in vain
Wasted through unseemly haste
To squeeze away the stain
Ran off the rails with madness
While toothless tuba-mouth
Oom-pah-pah-ing with gladness
Laughed roses from the south

Squeeze not your tuba top-down
Lest toothpaste never come
Before you see a cop frown
Then feel his kettledrum-
Stick beat dissatisfaction
Behind the lower brass
Squeeze in an upward action
Or take it in the ass

To Care and Care Not

A shadow fell between my friend and me
So dark so cold no light nor warmth between
Could pass one to the other either way
Where once we two had been as family
A wall impenetrable though unseen
Rose to divide between as night from day
An absence and a presence equally
A two-faced wraith which haunts us everywhere
It prisons us that neither one is free
From grave-deep trench and head-high thorny hedge

As love and hate dance on this razor's edge
The more we care not is the more we care

MY RELIGION IS KINDNESS

My poems are written as therapy
I send them to my doctor every day
Only he knows what might be wrong with me
Or right so it is not for me to say

I just know I like to write and drink tea
And I hope that handyman stays away
Since he was altogether too handy
I did all the work myself anyway
But my tenants could crush him easily
Defending their landlord muscularly

I may be strange yet there are still stranger
People out there who cannot even write
I use my charm to stay out of danger
As the angels watch over me all night

I am a blend of English and German
Cultures and something of a hothouse flower
An extremely curious Lutheran
And getting more curious by the hour
But never mind that now I talk too much
Leave it at this as the finishing touch:

"My religion is kindness"
The Dalai Lama said
The cruel live in blindness
I will be kind instead

Rose Red

A rose is blooming in my teacup here
In front of me at Friday midnight where
An hour ago red steam curled up instead
Red petals unfold while I watch them near
The place my mother fell and hit her head
I think that rose knows just what happened there
The blood of life at midnight still runs red

My mother smiles at noon from heaven now
Where noon is midnight here as time stands still
The pieces all fit together somehow
The rose my mother and I and we will
Bloom red nor can death make these petals fall
But to the mystic rain which washes all
Refreshing the living raising the dead

The world rose red within my cup tonight
The rain like fireworks blooming into light

This Gift We Live

Out of the silence the shadowed ones speak
Their breath like starlight on this autumn breeze
Hear if you listen and find if you seek
Those sounds which make the strong weak in the knees
Which simply cannot be and yet which are
Defying sense and sensibility
From past our world beyond our yellow star

In words soft sound and sensible to me
I hear them charge us cherish life on earth
Enjoy and not destroy our fragile sea
Embrace and not deface our soft blue sky
Accept this gift we live and give our best

It still is not too late but we must try
They whisper urgently to me and you
The hour is late but too great is this test
That we should fail through failure of desire
Caring so little for life that we die
The death of earth by water air by fire
I want to live and I hope you do too

BROKEN: FREE

Light of always bright and only
Rain to wash the darkness away
Light the night tonight for lonely
Ones who await the break of day
Under their mushroom clouds of fear

Light of always in your rising
Forget us not in darkness here
You who so enjoy surprising
Those who believe but what they see
Skeptical and enterprising
Tonight make unseen things appear

Light of always bright and only
Rain to wash the darkness away
Spiraling specificity
Of highest purest noblest best
As I await the break of day
From east across the night to west

Come shine your always light on me
Shine me into eternity
Fulfill the promise of the quest
Forget me not and let me be
One whom the truth has broken: free

Rind of Reality

Nothing is as it seems
Our eyes can see but the
Rind of reality
As mottled by moonbeams
This surface which you see
Is but the crust of me

While the real is what the
Eye may never discern
One must look deep to learn
Things are but as in dreams

Which is not to say they do not exist
Indeed they exist in multiple forms
But only to say that one can resist
The dullness which would dominate our days
Trying to conform to commonday norms
Like those who see things as they seem always

REFLECTION

Pinpoint puncture in time and space
Manifold manifestation
Of compound reality in
Joyful juncture of life and grace
A multifoliate mirror

A possible explanation
For what is about to begin
Where in the window comes a face
And the image becomes clearer
If only to shatter again

And so it goes at this window
So polished that even I shine
Seeing both sides above below
With all the layers peeled away
Duty delight despair disdain

A thousand thousand times a day
And the face in the mirror knows
What goes will come as what comes goes
The face in the mirror is mine
But the reflection is divine

SMOKEY JOE THE EXTRA CAT

Smokey Joe the extra cat bumps me with his head
Offering an ear to kiss which I freely do
As he peers out the window from the sofa's back

This cat I inherited was once filled with dread
Now he drinks his water from the tap in the loo
As those who live here know there is nothing we lack
So Smokey Joe the extra cat is settling in

No more cold nights for him he sleeps inside instead
Now as the best days of his curious life begin
I see that he has found what he was searching for

Smokey Joe you are the extra cat no more

As the Night Gives to the Day

You are every song I sing
My poems are all for you
Whether you know it or not
All I write and all I do
Is for you no matter what
Anybody else may say

Count the countless stars which shine
And you count one dream come true
All the sky is yours and mine
For as you give I give too
As the night gives to the day
Nothing less than everything

You are every song I sing

Harvest Moon of Saturday

When moonlit magic shines my way
It feeds my soul and makes me smile
The harvest moon of Saturday
Is something to savor awhile
As I already feel its light
On this bright blazing afternoon
Here on Thursday before the night
Has fallen yet: but night falls soon

And when night falls then I will rise

When moonlit magic shines my way
I dance beneath the waxing moon
And rise with it through velvet skies
Reflecting on reflected grace
Two rovers riding destiny
We bloom full-blown on Saturday
When we reveal ourselves full-face
Ascended to our rightful place

My friend the harvest moon and me

The Man in the Moon

I wander alone at the midnight hour
And see the face of the man in the moon
Who while saying nothing sees everything

Since he says nothing I might as well sing
At least these words if you make up the tune
Because my heart feels like a blooming flower

It waxed with the moon now it opens bright
To taste the magic in the air tonight
Which affects the cycles affects the tides
As well as everyone and me besides

I study the face of the moon and see
That we are different in many ways
He has the gift of patience unlike me

But I agree with how he spends his days
And when I go rambling he comes along
Over my shoulder my friend in the sky

I think he likes it when I sing a song
About how it would be if I could fly
He surely thinks flying is no big thing
But he just smiles and shines on while I sing

I wander alone at the midnight hour
And see the face of the man in the moon
Who while saying nothing sees everything

Since he says nothing I might as well sing
At least these words if you make up the tune

FRESH-BAKED AND ONLY FOR TODAY

There is a moment more or less
In which right when I first wake up
I find it clarifying to
Begin my day from nothingness
Remembering that all I do
For good or ill to curse or bless
Find new love or kiss and make up
Is only mine to choose and then
Proceeds the somethingness of when
Fresh-baked and only for today
Alone unfettered by some stress
From overnight to overstay

Since new days ought to be brand new
Let each unfold in its own way
Without the complications of
The preconceived: less fear more love

Reality's Ledge

Now in this moment between grace and sin
Here at the meeting place of night and day
Where light and dark play teeter-totter in
Their equipoise I see a middle way
Before the day can end or night begin
Here at the very tip of time I stand

A middleman between two worlds am I
Dark in my left and light in my right hand
The black and white of only one grey sky
As of one world where kiss the sea and land
Converging in our tandem-beating hearts
Make love to me on reality's ledge

In perfect balance as the magic starts
Come dance with me upon the razor's edge
Where we will glide between the to and fro
The universe will make it worth our while
Between two ways the shadow of a smile
Is how you know that now you really know

My Special Relativity

"Monday is such a busy day"
I hear the airplane plainly say
As it sighs and shrugs off in flight
I think this might be a long night
But since I think this Friday last
You see how one lives in the past

This soon-to-be Tuesday morning
Fell upon me without warning
Though I am unsure as to when

As once I fell to earth in fall
Caught in the wonder of it all
When last I heard the airplane say
"Monday is such a busy day"
I think it was a Friday then
But since I think... but then again...

Time is relative anyway
And especially so to me
My special relativity

Feeling Time a Pinwheel

Somehow I knew she was waiting for me
There was a question mark in blue and black
Tattooed in exclamation on her back
Like me she wondered when we might be free
We both knew we had no answers at all
Just questions as we headed into fall
Those unanswered questions life is made of

Headfirst head over heels in love with love
And ready for that deep-end dive at last
Which had been waiting for her and for me
With presently no future and no past
No time like the present for us to be
And feeling time a pinwheel spinning fast
We held hands as we jumped into the sea

Back Home to the Dark

I went for a walk with my eyes to the ground
Ordinarily I keep them to the skies
But after that beckoning quarter I found
I knew it could never have been otherwise

I looked up and looked down I looked all around
And I could see it was a very good day
To live and especially to live as me
Already seeing how exercise can pay

So I pumped my fist in solidarity
With the anti-war protesters in the park
Twenty-five cents richer lucky as can be
And feeling a chill went back home to the dark

Second Saturday

A dirty little man who claimed divinity
Worked its way through all his works walked on my ceiling
Conspicuously lacking in concinnity
All he left were dirty footprints and the feeling
That I never should have let him walk up there

But I was too broken then to really care
At the time until those footprints first appeared
Since he made them walking on the other side
Which really is as wonderful as it is weird
Especially now that all the blood has dried

I trace the pattern pleasing in its disarray
Of the footprints of a barking madman's reeling
And nobody can see them but for me
And then just on the second Saturday
According to the whimsy of divinity

Right Here

I eat the scraps my tenants give me
And enjoy their youthful presence here
They and the mortgage will outlive me
But without them I'd have died in fear
And probably homeless hopelessness

To say nothing of the starvation
Which is part of my situation
By nature and nurture ...yet unless
I am very much mistaken I
Will be eating well until I die
Nourished by their solicitousness
Well enough for me in any case

O Lord bless the ones by whom you bless
Your unworthy servant in this place
You gave my ancestors long ago
And have now entrusted unto me
I always believed but now I know:

Right here is where you want me to be

THE ONLY CURE

Why does it hurt to grow?
All I know is it does

More when fast less when slow
Then never as it was
Or ever as you were

This pain is not in vain
But effect of the cause
Of life where growth is sure
And ceaseless without pause

Yet pain will not explain
Till death the only cure
For life: by life again

The Rest Remains

for Maria

The more I know the less I know: I know
A secret which nobody else can share
I understand myself and poetry
That it is always better here than there
And thank God for the promise of this day
The rest remains a mystery to me
So I just keep to myself as I go
On my softspoken solitary way

Eyes open mouth shut keeping my head down
Listening to what other people say
Avoiding the fool sidestepping the clown
Waiting for the blowhard to blow away

I walk through crowded streets alone and see
That in the end I am my only friend
A secret which nobody else can share
With nothing left except to simply be
And be more simply here than anywhere
The more I know the less I know: I know
I am my only friend that in the end
The rest remains a mystery to me

Midnight Song

Come let us breathe fresh magic from the air
And feel how free it is to be alive
All times all places always anywhere
Particularly right now and right here
In this our time our place in time and space
As we wait for the magic to appear

Come tingle with surprise as midnight brings
Something out of nothing which is born there
Where the moon dances and the raven sings
The song which is the rhythm of our lives

Come let us breathe fresh magic from the air
And see what is brought when midnight arrives
When the hands of time are raised to its face
In a timeless moment of victory
The triumph of time having run its race
And won when the clock strikes for you and me

PICKLED HELL

for some and against others

I do not speak these poems for you
Who tear down to enlarge yourselves
But for those few whose hearts are still true
Not pickled up in jars on shelves
Where bottled-up in brine they will not grow
I speak from a place where these dare not go

No! I speak these poems for you who
Can feel your heartbeat in your breast
Your eyes are open your mind is too
To you my best I give my best
And let those who only pick apart dwell
Preserved picked-apart in their pickled hell

Quiet and Cool

when a blowhard blows in then out again

Any fool who cannot write poetry
But can skim the first few lines may become
The judge and jury and jailer of me
Or you or of anyone not as dumb
As this self-appointed arbiter is
This tempest-in-a-teapot not-so-hot
Who could burst the bubbles in a gin fizz
By sheer and self-anointed dullardry

And so every day the real poets pay
As they pray this gasbag will float away
But until he does he creates his buzz
As he gets his kick from making us sick
While he stars in his deconstructive play
Till it all goes back to the way it was
If tempest-tossed and slightly overwrought
With the exception that we all agree

On one thing at least
Having tamed the beast
And booted the fool
Together
Our weather
Is quiet and cool

Robots Calling

Lately when I answer my telephone
Robots ask me rhetorical questions
They hardly need me they chirp all alone
Or accompanied by my suggestions
That they go plug themselves or blow a fuse

A robot has rather little to lose

Which is actually a lot like me
Although we have nothing to talk about
I could chatter in answer endlessly
I could purr politely or shriek and shout
And none of it matters in any case

I like the unpredictability
One finds within our moody human race
Much better than the cold sterility
Of rhetorical robots calling here
Unrelieved by shades of humanity

With their chipper chirp and their chilling cheer

A Rice Day

Adding the juice of five limes to my rice
Followed by the salsa I love so well
I feel how blessed I am knowing how nice
Brown rice tastes made tangy and hot as hell

So now breakfast lunch and dinner are done
Since this is all three meals in one for me
An abundance worthy of anyone
A piquant and pleasing satiety

I do not choose to stuff myself with stuff
I prefer a purer and simpler way
I eat once a day and once is enough
This is a rice day: a very nice day

BECAUSE OF YOU

The busy-ness of business threatened
To eat the morning and spit out the seeds
Into these heavy-lidded eyes my friend
Till first you measured then you met my needs

Ever since then I am much on the mend
And have had such small successes as these:
The oven man came and made his repair
The garage man filled his dumptruck to spare
Us the ruins and rinds of centuries

Someone will live in the garage and we
My properly-working household and me
Will make better use of our groceries
The oven fixed garage cleaned more or less
All because of you my friend to the end
Too busy with living for busy-ness

Mr. Hot Dog Head

His head looks like the tip of a hot dog
If he wore a hat I guess it would be
A tip of the hat to a spotted hog
The spots seem to be from the sun I see
Sunspots on that big round hot dog tip head
By which he navigates till he is dead

Mr. Hot Dog Head you make me nervous
I try to put the war behind me now
But somehow you are still in the service
You give me sunspot flashbacks anyhow
Marching to the kitchen to the bathroom
Addressing both ends of the meat grinder
A marching hot dog marching to the doom
Which makes us blind and makes you still blinder

I thought things were as strange as they could get
Until Mr. Hot Dog Head and I met

Mr. Hot Dog Head Hits the Road

Goodbye Mr. Hot Dog Head goodbye
Your past is frying your fat at last
May you reach that big bun in the sky
Run along and try to catch it fast

Although I will not miss you still I
Marvel at the shifting shadings of
Your proud pulsing purple hot dog head
I wish you had somebody to love
But I see at least you are well fed

Goodbye Mr. Hot Dog Head goodbye
Your flushed head flashing red as you go
Your only love is the kind you fry
But all you can do is what you know

Your inner rebirth is in your girth
And we both know that you cannot grow
In any other way at least today
Good luck now as you wander the earth
But please Mr. Hot Dog Head: stay away

Mr. Hot Dog Head is Gone

His head was smaller than his neck was wide
His paunch preceded him into the room
He peered perverted was watery-eyed
And when we kicked him out how he could zoom
About with huff-puffing efficiency
The way he did was and will always be
A typical Hot Dog Head mystery

He could have had a heart attack and died
Been ground up squeezed into casing and fried
For all the fury of his hot dog ways
As victim of his hot dog headed pride
But huff and puff and in and out he went
And all of us are happy now if spent
Anticipating cooler fat-free days

Pull up a chair and stay with us awhile
Thank heaven Mr. Hot Dog Head is gone
But that the moon remains and soon the dawn
Will bring back sunny Sunday memories
Of all the happy times gone by and these
New memories which we will make today
Consider Mr. Hot Dog Head and smile

No one comes back from where he went away

THE ROSE WITHIN THE FLAME

Tangibility
Palpability
Our ability to touch
What we need we want so much

You are the hands of Christ to me
The face of God my destiny

My healing comes by loving fire
In the rose within the flame
Speaks me my unspoken desire
When I feel you speak my name

Uncertain Raven

for Franziska

I wonder if you love me
I wish you could be here
This lonely sky above me
Seems more empty than clear

A raven circles wary
Uncertain in the sky
I feel it knows the very
Day on which I must die

Uncertain raven in the sky
I wonder if that day is now
Yet know we never know somehow

I only wish that I could fly
To meet Franziska far away
And bring her home with me today

Uncertain raven certainly
You see me lonely here below
You know how much she means to me
Tap on her window: let her know

Autumn Leaves and Commonday Miracles

It turns out life is simpler than I thought
Commonday miracles bloom around me
Hope on the wind but somehow I forgot
The only way to live free is just be
And take no thought for anything but now

What is my place in the universe
And is it for me to say?
Can I make my place better or worse
From one to another day?

The answer always comes to me somehow
That letting go is what to do
To float like a leaf on the autumn wind
It seems not up to me nor you

We autumn leaves ought not be caught and pinned
But sail the day with a sense of play
As into dust at dusk we pass
Along with summer's waving grass
Under soft snow as we fall away

Eternity begins for us today

If You Want To

What a crazy ramble this life has been
And I suspect not nearly over yet
With so much seen some better left unseen
But what I have seen I will not forget

Nor would I change a moment anyway
In a beautiful game without regret
I keep my cards close and I mean to play
So if you want to play awhile come on
The night is clear and it is warm inside
You might as well stay awhile until dawn
Make yourself at home and enjoy the ride

My finger feels freer without a ring
Once I was lonely but now I am not
For freedom is better than anything
I just got sentimental and forgot

Nobody cares about me like I do
But you can stay with me if you want to

Tomorrow Never Comes

The King of Spain shot a tame drunken bear
In Russia on a trip he took up north
A King of Spain is a pain anywhere
Dramatizing things demeaning the worth
Of tame drunken bears as they roll downstairs

Is it "long live the king" and never mind
A drunken bear ended up dramatized?

It gives me pause but I am not surprised
That the King of Spain had a bear behind
Since this is not the first time nor the last
The present was prevented by the past
Tomorrow never comes in any case
No use of standing gaping and aghast
Although I can certainly understand

Just apologize for our human race
We even kill each other on command
And tell God sort them for us to our will
The King of Spain has a bear behind still
As the past returns and the future burns

It is "long live the king" and never mind
A drunken bear ended up dramatized

Heaven on Wheels

a sonnet for Franziska

Franziska rollerblades the cobblestones
Gathering speed when fast wheels strike smooth tar
But she will not fall she will break no bones
Nor will she ever be struck by a car
For this is how God works his wily will
Through Franziska franzipping down the street
Teaching us joy all the way down the hill
The joy God would show us before we meet
The model he shares with us of his grace
In order to prepare for the surprise
When unnumbered stars skate before our face
And the blindfold at last falls from our eyes

I hope we are on wheels like she is now
Who transcends the why to embrace the how

Heading Home to You

Taking the long way but heading home to you
Dreaming of your love at the end of the day
All through my wandering that is what I do

Heading home to you but taking the long way
False starts with false hearts small actors in big parts
Having seen it all now I see what is true
And I know exactly where I want to be

Wherever you are there is my family
I rest in your love at the end of the day
Taking the long way but heading home to you

THIS RAMBLING ROAD

I have been wandering for so long now
Sometimes it feels like heaven sometimes hell
This rambling road of mine and yours as well
Will get us there but only God knows how

It seems so hard to get a step ahead
So easy to feel several steps behind
I will lose myself in your eyes instead
Of understanding lest I lose my mind

I am so glad you travel next to me
It seems the more I think about the road
Passing from October to November
The longer it is the heavier the load

But you remind me so I remember
This ramble is our march to be made free

Enjoying the View from the Carousel

If I were not like you would I then be
Expected to fit your expectation?

The death of individuality
Of the specificity of the soul
Is the most personal degradation

Our relationship has always been free
Of control where each partner plays a role
According to some predetermined plan
So this is no problem for you and me

Each of us is part woman and part man
And we fit according to the season
As we have since our adventure began

Riding things out through rhyme and through reason
Enjoying the view from the carousel
Having this one chance to live all we can
We know the best revenge is living well

COMPLETION

The thought blooms into my mind that another mind
Is directly connected to mine at this point

By reading these words tomorrow from yesterday

We are conjoined now with no before nor behind
But are connected by common cause and a joint
Fascination in discovering this two-way
Passage of our neurological energy

That what it means after all to be you and me
Is ultimately discovered in reflection
What it means in the end for you and me to be
By looking within in the other direction

We look in each other's souls and our own we see
And our completion in our incompleteness find

Come Night

Some days plod forever
Some trip lightly by
Fast or slow I never
Could understand why
Yet each day wends its way
At just its own pace
Until another day
Arrives in its place

I choose the nights between
Them in any case
The lights by which I see
You know what I mean
You and night and I know
Night is and will always be
A flow not fast nor slow
The best time of day to me

Come night until another day
Arrives next morning: come and play

Hypocrisy

Nothing hurts quite like hypocrisy
A furtive thing with a fearful sting
False religion fake democracy
An insidious crime sure to bring
Trouble and woe wherever we go

So all we can do is watch and see
We steer well clear of hypocrisy

Being ourselves and letting it show
By being honest by living free
And never being afraid to grow
Just be yourself and I will be me
Let in and out match and let them know:

We have no need of hypocrisy

NIGHTMARES

A long exhausting night
Of nightmares robbed me of my sight

Now I can only see
Those fearful visions forced on me
And hope and trust and pray
That somehow they will fade away
As the day shines on
Until they have gone
Held at bay by the light of day

Back into the dark whence they came
And may no afterimages remain
No echoes whispering my name
But buried be to never rise again

Full Moon Beckoning

for Franziska

Sunlight is normative
The given state of things
Mere luminosity
Moonlight is formative
When longing lifts soft wings
To soar throughout the night
Sheer numinosity
By which the mermaid sings
And fairy dust shines bright

The light of the full moon
Glows like snow on the ground
Midnight is the high noon
Of magic all around
The hooves of unicorns
Can be heard in the wood
While ghost trains sound sad horns
In passing understood
As hidden things are found

When fairies all take flight
To kiss the velvet sky
I know you understand
The full moon their birthright
The days cannot destroy
The everlasting joy
Of those who never die
Franziska take my hand
Come and let us join them you and I

DECISION 2006

Come on an escapade with me and we
Could soar beyond these squawking talking heads
Which make their delusions our destiny
Destroy all day then return to soft beds
Of ease in their disease as we stand by
Helpless hopeless disenfranchised asking "Why?"

In this no-man's-land between strange and strange
I still dream of social evolution
Cherish a chance of political change
And hope for a second revolution
This time of the mind by reason by thought
That we might yet redeem what our blood has bought

Two

How then does one begin
In this ellipticality
A game so hard to win
This riddle of reality?

I think it would be best if I be still
And know that God is and that you are too
I knew this once believe now always will
That I am not alone because of you
Riding this riddle: if one can win I know
We two began by winning long ago

Flight

a sonnet for hope, faith, and love

Having flown one never forgets to fly
A sun once set can rise as the future
Remembered savored triumph dawn again
The might-have-been as might-be as it were
Though this time higher wiser for the pain
Which once we felt at sunset when the gloom
Closed down on us and wrapped around the room
We will yet rise together you and I

I look within my heart and find you there
As you look within yours and find me too
The hope the dream the might-be answered prayer
Spreads wings at dawn's first light for me and you
Having flown one never forgets to fly
We will yet rise together you and I

8 NOVEMBER 2006

My Grandma died five years ago today
And I have struggled ever since to stay
In this home place with the help of some friends
My hair now less whole cloth and more of lace
Having left to God the means with the ends
And more like Grandma every day I know
Whom I shall see again soon face to face
Here I must wait until my time to go

I picked a bird of paradise for her
While still in bud and now it lifts its wings
Arising in memorial full bloom
In mourning fights and flights which never were
A song something like the night raven sings
Echoes in me as Grandma fills the room

These Improbable Wings

May we all find what we are looking for
And may all our beautiful dreams come true
May lions shut their mouths and may mice roar
But whether mouse or lion God bless you

We only get one chance then get no more
To do the best we can in what we do
So it is suicidal to hold back
From scaling every height we can conceive
And if we share our surplus meets our lack

But for this to work we have to believe
That we might do the impossible now
Or at least the most improbable things
Until we make them possible somehow
By rising on these improbable wings

Never Know Until

Having loved my first have I loved my last?
Sometimes I wonder if my time has passed

But I have to believe no matter what
Although time always passes it has not
Left me behind to end my life alone
Just that the future can never be known

So we will never know until we see
If anyone might love their last with me

Success

I have been surprised and delighted to see
Some people write it must be good to be me
Which makes me wonder if this might just be true

So should I do as I say (and as I do
In my poetry at least) and let my heart
Fly free into life nor hold myself apart
As though I were unworthy of happiness?

I if I can do this then THAT will be success

These November Evenings

A red rose and a red maple leaf dry
In close propinquity on Saturday

These November evenings I wonder why
I ever considered going away
From where red roses and maple leaves fall
Why I even went anywhere at all

I will stay and hold tight to things like these
Dry roses autumn leaves and memories

I always wonder about everything
But these November evenings I know why
I belong here as the St. John's bells ring
And roses and leaves and memories dry

Fragments of the Whole

People seem to want to know the future
Perhaps as an antidote to the past
By bringing some balance as a present
With the solution remaining unsure
Whether that or finding out at the last
Is more or less pleasant or unpleasant

I think if I knew it might drive me mad
To know I had to live through all those scenes
Being prepared they might not be so bad
But without surprise it seems each one means
Less for having been tasted once before

Seeing the past and the present so sad
I am afraid to know very much more
So I just muddle through alongside you
And hope we find what we were looking for
Through the looking glass and down the rabbit hole
All the way feeding on fragments of the whole

A Song to the Dust

I watch the sparkle of Orion's belt
On a long night after a lonely day
And feel what we watchers have always felt
How beautiful it is how far away
I think of chance and the cards I am dealt
I think of love and my heart starts to melt
And should I fold my hand or should I play?

Do I risk it all? Do I dare to trust?

And folding my hands I withdraw to pray
That I become the person I would be
Not the mightiest the richest but just
Who I am growing reaching to be free
To do what I am here for what I must
To be no one at all except for me
And leave a song behind me to the dust

It Was Always You

So here we are finding ourselves alone
After all these years unexpectedly
And yet expected because always known
Since this is how it is with you and me

It had to be like this I always knew
That you and I would be alone at last
For those who tell the future from the past
Could always tell that it was always you

MY FALL MY RISE

Summer came and went with little fanfare
Surprising autumn slid in smilingly
I hardly noticed summer's fall at all
With autumn's rise around me everywhere

Rose petals and red leaves swirl around me
A rise which seems nothing at all like fall
But more like the arrival of the now
The process of becoming which is dawn

I never got to mourn summer somehow
Was too distracted to see it had gone
It was kind of autumn to come like this
Arriving gently on the morning wind
Summer slipped out while I slept with a kiss
Took its bad but left its good memories
And left me here with autumn by surprise

The passages of life are times like these
My fall inscribed on clouds my rise on air
Those moments when I pause and realize
The wheel of time is turning with a sigh

Winter will come then my seasons will end
I fall to earth to rise again and bear
The light which stretches after as before
Life's passages are written in the sky

When spring comes I will celebrate it there
Who am I to ask for anything more?

DO NOT DISTURB

I feel so fortunate to be alone
Able to do whatsoever I please
Given some relationships I have known

I choose to avoid cheap dramas like these
Call me a sociopath a recluse
Sign me up again for celibacy
What I see of "love" is a poor excuse
For genuine human intimacy
Which even if achieved will not endure

All that is not for me I choose to be
A lifelong bachelor confirmed and sure
Of one I can depend on which is me

So go ahead kids grapple grope and scream
Just do it somewhere else and let me dream

Sweet Bread

Franziska baked some sweet bread shaped like birds
I wish I were with her in Germany
Since all I have to eat here is my words

I think sweet bread would be better for me
Sometimes my words are hardly sweet at all
And sometimes bitter in the chill of fall

But she is far away along the Rhein
Her sweet bread is probably eaten now
So I am stuck with just these words of mine
With which I have to muddle through somehow

Still there is sweet bread which one need not eat
To savor in spirit across the sea
From along the Rhein right along to me

And feeling how I love her I feel sweet

RESPECT AND SOLIDARITY

None of us has any money but
We share what we have no matter what
Through thick and thin times (more thin than thick)
Our cooperation does the trick
As in our daily lives we elect
To practice our mutual respect
By looking after one another
Friend and sister to friend and brother

None of us has any money though
We have what it takes to make a go
Of living together and living well
At Studio Lance where the old bronze bell
Rings for respect and solidarity

When I come to die: ring that bell for me

The Veil Withdrawn

A shadow passed across the moon one night
A cloud within a cloudless winter sky
And when it passed it left a lesser light
As though when it passed it had not passed by
But left a stain between the moon and me
A strain in what I thought reality
A crack in the mask a rip in the hem
Of the veil which falls between "us" and "them"

A shadow passed across the sun one day
A cloud out of a cloudless summer sky
Which though it seemed to take something away
Left something intimate yet lifted high
Resolved to show forgotten is not gone
A glimpse behind the spacetime veil withdrawn
Evolved I know we grow but never die
Who see dusk simultaneous with dawn

COMING HOME

The river is drawn to the sea and falls
Gratefully beneath subaquatic walls
With remembered familiarity
Fulfilled in its ultimate destiny

The wanderer comes home to roam no more
The welcoming mother closes the door
And water and water are one to be
Together again elementally

The river is embraced as with the tears
The blood sweat and life of all the world's years
Consider the river the sea and learn
Who came from the womb to the womb return

I am the river and you are the sea
When I come home I pray you welcome me

Sheltering Shadows

Within sheltering shadows waits the light
Until the time comes to dawn the new day
It nestles there in the heart of the night
Until the time comes to come out and play

Then the sun and the moon change their places
One looking forward the other behind
Yin yang opposite-attracted faces
Without which the sky would be cold and blind

When the sun goes to bed the moon rises
Or so it would seem from here on the ground
That they share a bed is no surprise as
All of their doings are done in the round

Until the time comes to come out and play
It nestles there in the heart of the night
Until the time comes to dawn the new day
Within sheltering shadows waits the light

Slugabed

Cold tea from last night still here by my bed
Last night a very long time ago now
I need to make black coffee for my head
But first must move my curled-up cat somehow

He seems to want to sleep permanently
One never shoos Freddie Noodles away
But if I pet him right he might agree
To take the plunge with me into this day

So I will offer kitty treats instead
And maybe a few aspirins for me
That coffee I spoke of followed by tea
For I have been too long a slugabed

Autumn afternoon at Studio Lance
The sun is not patient nor will it wait
A sunny Sunday finds us sleeping in
As earlier each day the hour grows late

Come cat! Let us leap up to join the dance
And let Sunday festivities begin!

Her Name Was Patricia

My mother became more and more like a bird
Until she flew away on the twenty-third
Day of November it hurts to remember
Of Nineteen Ninety-Eight on that date I hate
Which will be the date of Thanksgiving this year

Thanksgiving comes back some years early some late
For others but never came back to me here
And yet I am thankful and appreciate
That I had the mother I had when I had
Who died singing I know because I was near
A sweet sad old song in a voice soft and clear

She thought I was gifted I thought she was great
We had nothing but it never seemed so bad
Scarce money sad sickness scant hope and no dad
My mother though frail bore the burdens of all
And showed in her death what it meant to live strong

This year on Thanksgiving I will sing this song
For my songbird who flew away in the fall

My Providential You

As lacking as I am in common sense
I am thankful for the kindness of friends
Providers of that gentle providence
Which gives me hope and helps to meet my ends
In spite of the scarcity of my means

Somehow I always survive winter's greys
As surely as the coming of spring's greens
As dependably as nights follow days
But this security would never be
And I by now have landed in the street
Without you who have been so kind to me
And pulled me from the bogs of bankruptcy

As lacking as I am in common sense
A higher mind than mine caused us to meet
A greater strength than ours will see us through
Providers of that gentle providence:
I thank you all ...my providential you

THESE AUTUMN STARS

Watching these autumn stars twinkling
Like silver and blue bells of ice
I can almost hear them tinkling
The sparkling sounds of paradise

When the night is open like this
Revealing its patterns clearly
The sky a deep blue velvet kiss
I can feel the stars and nearly
Taste their diamond coolness sweet
Yet subtle as my senses greet
The Other which they represent
And thank them for reminding me
Here in the chill of night half spent
What I am here for is to be
With all my senses wide awake
No matter whether day or night

These autumn stars which make me take
Another look make things look right
As not just with my eyes I see
But with my soul I see the light

Midnight Consolation

Knee-deep as I am in November
(With December coming soon)
It helps me hang on to remember
That I always have the moon
And you do too

Something we can depend on
Fortunately
For me and you

Her changes chart how dreamers exist
All our waxing and waning
Rightly regulated by a force
Impossible to resist
At least for me

Nor would I be complaining
About what I spend my wishes on
And will these wishes come true? Of course!

Still... until they do... my policy
(With December coming soon)
Is wait and see

But: I always have the moon

My Brother Bee

A worn-out bee would rise and fly but falls
Having always flown it will fly no more
And knowing or not knowing then it crawls

Having always known I would only soar
When I came to be as this bee is now
That I have to crawl on the ground till then
I see that we are opposites somehow

But in the same predicament today

I hope it knows not as I know not when
It will fall still and I will fly away
And yet it might know as I might know too
To die to fly is what we are and do

This bee and I like Peter on the sea
Treading the elements till we find out
Will soon learn our lessons of faith and doubt

As we both sink will anyone catch me?

My brother bee I leave you now to fly
As you have flown in life now as we die

TO BE LONELY

This is how it is then to be lonely
At the end of the day it settles in
Where I thought I saw someone was only
No one in the shadows of after-all
And nothing in spite of what might have been
Or if anyone my own reflection
On shards of mirrors broken in the fall

Mortality my original sin
And darkened mirrors in each direction
Analogous to the elements of
Earth water air and fire faith hope and love
As well as time and space and life and death
Seen dimly in the half-light from above
And oxidizing slowly with each breath

This is how it is then to be lonely
On shards of mirrors broken in the fall
At the end of the day it settles in
Where I thought I saw someone was only
Mortality my original sin
No one in the shadows of after-all
And nothing in spite of what might have been

It Was You

Lonely I thought that I wandered alone
My whiskers whitening through years of care
Out rambling straight into the great unknown

But now I can see you were always there
For all of the way for all of this time
By my side for the journey all along
Behind and before me leading the climb
You have kept me sane you have made me strong

To feel all alone in the universe
Is a hard thing and it could have been worse
I only wish now I had known as well
As you did all this time how I could be
So close to heaven and so far from hell
With someone who cares right here next to me

Until I noticed my dream coming true
I never even noticed: it was you

STAR

Where the shadow falls from eternity
Through contemplation vigil and fasting
A star arises from the heart of night

To comfort bless inspire and simply be
From everlasting to everlasting
First last and always uttermost the light

The gift is given to us just the same
As to the immortals even to me
Although a fragile thing human by name

No broken hearts are deemed unfit to see
No empty hands unworthy to receive
Nor can it be bought for gifts must be free

The shadow only asks us to believe
That first it must fall for the star to rise
And fill from the inside these empty eyes

Snow

The memory of life in my front door
Remains a secret deep within the wood
What came from the tree will never forget
What is of earth is of earth understood
When it reminds us of what we live for

The forest of a hundred years ago
Is present in this door a century
And all of us who sprang from earth should know
The memory is not forgotten yet
There is kinship between this door and me
Which runs as deep in fall as sap and blood

And when the winter comes the wood will show
That it remembers long-forgotten snow

Covering the forest of memory

SURVIVAL SONNET

Just being born I won the lottery
Then surviving all the crises after
Surprising everyone especially me
Through stubbornness and some well-placed laughter
A smattering of grace a splash of style

Still here to enjoy the absurdity
I take it with a grain of salt and smile
Since not taking things too seriously
Seems key to survival after awhile

I have died once and have lived lots of things
Been nearly buried been dearly married
Have worn disguises and symbolic rings
But it has been best of all just to be
A wanderer everlastingly free

LOVE IS FREE

The parts of me in balance form the whole
Of me and I need all my parts to be
Complete even if completely alone

I wanted to share but she wanted more
I hope she found what she was looking for
But what she really wanted was my soul
And without my soul there can be no me

I can see now how she felt incomplete
Hungry for someone else's soul to eat
How sad that she could never find her own!

Hollow and empty starving at the feast
Her means could never justify her ends

I wish she could have shared awhile with me
I wish she could have tasted love at least
And her soul and my soul might have been friends

She never understood that love is free

LIFE INSTEAD

Death speaks to a beast and that beast knows
There can be no argument and goes
Quietly into the shadows when
Called accepting its time has come then

Such pure inevitability
As is not given to you and me

Death speaks to one of us and a fight
Ensues and pursues death through the night
Instead of giving our breath away
Being rolled over then playing dead
Breathe then the harder and vow to stay
And fight all night chasing death away
Of to be or not to be to choose
Loving to be and hating to lose

Death speaks? We hear: but choose life instead

One Hell of a Ride

The wind is all wound up and coils waiting outside
Crackling as it sparkles with electricity
Looks like we could be in for one hell of a ride
On a moonlit magic carpet of destiny
With dusk long forgotten and with no dawn in sight
I can feel the fabric of relativity

The stars are flashing cryptic messages tonight
Will they be understood? Well we must wait and see
Until then all we can do is enjoy the sight
Linear captives of nonlinearity

Embattled but emboldened as we grope toward light
Shattered in a thousand shards spread across the sky
Scattered by the wind in a rude liberation
In which the moon and stars and you and I must fly
Stirred by the storm in the fever of creation
Which work is not complete and which can never be

The wind is all wound up and coils waiting outside
I think it might be fun to take it for a spin
Looks like we could be in for one hell of a ride
On the roulette wheel but we have to spin to win

GOT WHAT HE WANTED

Steven with a V but stoned nonetheless
He never did well in captivity

Commercial failure critical success
Not good for much except for poetry

Practicing daily his eyes on the prize
With perfectionistic avidity

And some new bullies to bring down to size

His house not before but now is haunted
So in the end he got what he wanted

APPLE-CRISP MOMENTS

In this late autumn twilight
Cusp of winter pairing of
Late morning with early night
It feels right to be in love
And hugging you through layers
Holding gloved hands snug and tight
Confounding such naysayers
As dare not bear light aright
So theirs simply slips away

You can sing about spring
Say what you may of May
But this December day
I can tell you one thing:

These apple-crisp moments of fall
Are what we live for after all

Christmas Carol

Come Christmas come to far and near
Around the corners of the dark
Starlight we have been waiting for
Who live next to or in the park
Return us to your childlike ways
Who have grown up so stern and stark

Remind us of the child whose birth
With animals and human love
From everywhere to every here
Came once and comes again to earth
Upon your pilgrimage of days
Your spark in our dark solstice sky

The secret of the meaning of
The birth and bearing of the light
The ageless angels rustling by
The crowning glory of the year
The rose of love which does not die
Buds to bloom magic at midnight

The miracle: now as before

More

Life is nothing like I thought it would be
I wonder if life is like this for you
I never imagined complexity
Could be this beautiful if scary too
I suppose this must be reality
The consequences of the things we do

This reality feels unreal to me

I only take what touches me as true
You touch me in the dark until I see
Replacing old complexity with new
More beautiful if scary than before
But I am not complaining since I seek
To touch reality beyond this week

Nothing like I thought it would be but more

Orderly Retreat

I lived a lot and wished some I had not
To wonder why I was and was not dead
And how it is that I should still be here
While others have been chewed and spat instead
But then I realize that I forgot
An answer in this life is seldom clear

An orderly retreat and getaway
A descent which almost mimics a climb
Just make it look intentional they say
Nearing the end of another failed war
Looking for leaders but nobody there
I have to wonder what we fought it for

Life slips away a little at a time

Maybe the chickenhawks ought to explain
Their reasons so wrong and our costs so dear
The deaths the amputations burns and pain
They talk but no one listens anymore
They argue all day but why should we care?
Our ears have been dulled by artillery

We listened once before but not again
It was always true but now we can see
How they lose then they use humanity
They lose their own they should leave ours alone
But then we realize that we forgot
An answer in this life is seldom clear

Life slips away a little at a time

3:53

I was what I was what is done is done
But how I hate to disappoint my son!

A slow dance with death at 3:53
In the morning he will most likely be
Disappointed even angry with me
When he finds out I had to leave somehow
I failed him once now fail him once again

The distance between life and death is now

I tried to but I could never explain
Now orphaned like me perhaps you can see
How it is to get to be fifty-two
Life sheer and mere disappointment and pain
To break deep enough for both me and you

I was what I was but was never free

A second time I leave you at the door
Afraid to die but unable to live
Like then I cannot be me anymore
I only hope this time you can forgive

The Game Itself

That which is learned the hard way
Is hardest to forget
Having turned a few hairs gray
And left behind regret

The spring fling of a young day
Need never end quite yet
We might as well enjoy it
Whatever the "mature" say

They envy us I bet

Love lives and knows no age
And no one can destroy it
None but ourselves alone

Our prize of pilgrimage
Learned the hard way makes us whole
In the way the wise have known:

Journey is destination
The game itself the goal
Love in my estimation
Is what has saved my soul

FORTUNE COOKIE

Talk less and listen more
My fortune cookie said
To stop being a bore
Be empathic instead

And I might learn something along the way
From something somebody else has to say

Thirty years have passed now
Each season in its turn
But I am aghast how
Some people never learn

If we all could talk less and listen more
To something somebody else has to say
Think and then ask what we are dying for
We just might learn something along the way

The way away from war:
Talk less and listen more

WHERE OLD SAILORS GO TO DIE

I made a fool of myself for love
But better for that than for hate
Better than sinking to rise above
The roaring tide early than late

Now late I want to do it again
From what I can remember
Having forgotten about the pain
Here in this mid-December
If only to keep warm
In safe harbor from the storm
Until the spring returns when I
Sail to return no more

There where old sailors go to die
Love beckons from the shore

WRONG TURN ETERNITY

I took it to be for eternity
But eternity disappointed me
Taking a very wrong turn for the worse
Decreasing the size of my universe

Eternity might have been a few years
Some love some laughter and quite a few tears
Some unforgettable memories too
I lost you but did I ever have you?

Nobody has anybody ever
Eternity it turns out is never

Tragicomedy

Tragedy is easy comedy is hard
Everyone knows a broken heart or rumor
Of some great misfortune in one's own backyard
One has to search to find a sense of humor
And then it might be veiled within tragedy
At least this is the way it has been for me
If you can find a laugh then people love you
As they seek relief from their grim day-to-day

Ignore the sword of Damocles above you
Perhaps we can find something funny to say
Laugh and the world laughs at you and cry alone
This is what I do but you have always known

So I will try to say something funny now
Finding the risible in the invective
Of angry wet hens or a flatulent cow
Squawking and farting are still quite effective
Or a pink poodle who knows the difference
Between tragedy and comedy is how
We view the world a matter of perspective
It just depends on where we fall off the fence

Since much of our suffering seems elective
Let comedy be tragedy's recompense

Without Me

Where I was to be laid there lies another
A stranger in my grave next to my mother
I had to sell it to give what they gave me
To a rich liar who promised to save me
And now some unknown lies at my Grandpa's feet

The man I trusted to help me was a cheat
Some soulless conscienceless attorney
And he helped himself to what was left of me
So I travel light on this journey
The family plot filled up where I should be

Restless unburied rambler alive or dead
With an explanation why
I never had before
A good excuse not to die
But put to sea once more

I suppose it is I who am strange instead
Or so I feel today
And never mind eternity
Now as I turn away
May they rest in peace: without me

NEVER BEEN THE BURYING KIND

The family plot proved a faulty scheme
I have never been the burying kind
My waking life no more real than my dream
A butterfly chased with an open mind

I am just starting and starting to know
That I mean to write if it takes all night
To see how much I can possibly grow
As long as it takes till I get it right

Some people say now I can take it slow
They mean well they just fail to understand
There is no certain milestone of success
Along the long road to the promised land

So I will just keep wandering I guess
Writing down things of interest I see
Most of it very strange some of it true
Of interest in any case to me

May it too be of interest to you
This word water world I swim in and thrive
At least we have something useful to do
Since nobody gets out of here alive

"Love"

Coming up fifty-two
Enjoying it daresay
I have a lot to do
And this seems like a day
As good as any to
Celebrate existence
Despite the resistance
Of life-resistant souls
Who grumble from dark holes
Where lives lie locked away
Entombed alive by choice

I hear a brighter voice
Because this is a day
As good as any to
Celebrate existence
Especially my own
If by sheer persistence
To some summit unknown
By most by some dreamed of
Which I have heard called "Love"

HumanKIND

You are right for you: I am right for me
One side for me and another for you
Therefore let us agree to disagree
And save ourselves the trouble to argue

I look back over life and I can see
It never seems to help when people do
If others must then let them fight and fuss
But all ideas are free to everyone

We ourselves are satisfied to be us
Content still when all arguments have done
Their worst to divide and conquer us all
The truth remains that humankind is one

So let us lift each other when we fall
Since having disagreed we can agree
The truth remains that humankind is one
You are right for you: I am right for me

Though humankind seems to have lost its mind
Falling sadly short of its name
We humans--even now--can still be kind
And we two remain just the same

MAKING HOMEMADE POETRY

When you make a thing yourself you care more
Than if you hire someone else to do it

For me making things is what I live for
To have an idea and get down to it
Enjoying the ride as much as the pride
Of doing it myself and showing you
On a rainy night snug and warm inside
Just what it really is all day I do

I enjoy making homemade poetry

I try to speak clearly and concisely
And I find it satisfying to be
Able to say a thing rather nicely
If occasionally in any case
In competition with no one but me
Doing it wearing a smile on my face

I know who I am and what I came for
When you make a thing yourself you care more

Sonnet at the Winter Solstice

This solstice is the return of the light
At which the sun stands still then to decide
That each succeeding day be made more bright
Although it takes until the other one
A moment at a time and day by day
The summer solstice greets winter's work done
And pauses then to turn the other way

The yin and the yang of the year elide
And I am reminded of you somehow
Written in my heart and the sky above
As both winter and summer solstice now
Become two eyes in the face of my love

Another year the sun has smiled its way
Two eyes in the face of my love dawn day

THE CONSTANCY OF CHANGE

Trained to inhibition
Brought up by repression
Drained to inanition
Brought down by depression

I have never understood life at all
But when I take a walk
Or when we have a talk
I find that I can rise just as I fall

And then no one can see
What the matter might be

With me

Brought down by depression
Drained to inanition
Brought up by repression
Trained to inhibition

I have never understood life at all
The constancy of change
Makes each turn blind and strange
And yet I rise however hard I fall

Embraced by the Moon

So crisp and crystalline this day has been
And now the sun hands over to the night
Such clarity as is but seldom seen
While the stars reveal blue diamond light
Out one by one through their blue velvet screen

The moon hangs ripe and heavy like a pearl
I only wish I could give it to you
Right here on your breast it would shine so bright
Worn cool round the neck of a pretty girl

But it follows you whatever you do
Sparkles in your eyes and haloes your hair
Your radiant shoulders bear witness too
Embraced by the moon my soul and the air

Some light some magic some December dew
And I remember how it feels to love
Within my heart again but as never
Before tonight for this is forever
Looking at you: as below so above

WHAT SHE MEANT AFTER ALL

last things last

Excuse me for leaving such a mess
May those I have trespassed forgive me
May they remember the best of me
But may not my follies outlive me

Save my books and burn the rest of me

Better save all that music I wrote
I suppose as I think about it
Having poured myself into each note
Perhaps some choir could sing (or shout) it

Nothing exceeded quite like excess
Always "colorful" (if not frugal)
I was quite a character I guess
Just spare me the bagpipes and bugle

I recall how Grandma said "the less
Said the better" and now I can see
What she meant after all (and agree)

Soil and Sky

Small planet of a fading star
I know how it feels to be small
To feel like a fading star too
Or planet smaller than you are

You two and I know after all
That "might makes right" was never true
That greed is rotten at its root
And that the proud someday must fall

My world! My day! This right-sized earth
And sun which bring the field to fruit
Are synthesis of death and birth

I hear the singing duststorm call
When air and land go hand in hand
And wonder sadly vainly why
Men cannot live like soil and sky

Two by Two

How does it help the cause of another
To destroy me?
Having grown up as brother and brother
Can we not see
That when one hurts the other one hurts too?

You are one with me as I am with you

There will never be peace
I know
Until injustice cease
And so
Brokenness seems to go on forever
Even though nothing can ever sever
The bond of the blood of humanity

In pieces now we grieve
Yet secretly believe
That one hope remains for me as for you
Burning behind these clouds we see above
Rising in you as it rises in me

That the blood of humanity run true
Two hearts at a time two by two through love

Delighted to be Invited

As another good day ends
And a new good night begins
The lovers pass with a kiss
Sun and moon as tender friends
In this game anyone wins
Who gives the world half a chance
And the only game is this

The world has been good to me
Taught what I needed to know
(Usually the hard way)
And the possibility
Of life and how far we go
Would appear essentially
Left open for each to say

I am delighted
To be invited
To join in the dance

OF HIGHER CHOICE

We come we go
And all too fast
Before we know
Our time has passed
Unseemly haste
Drives on and on
Till life is waste
And we are gone

We come we go
But in the rush
Before we know
Forget the hush

Of higher choice

And all too fast
That inward voice
Of angels near
Is drowned and killed

Or is it we
Who fail to hear
And lose the light
Who once were free
But threw away
Our own birthright
To fully be
Ourselves today?

Unseemly haste
It seems somehow
Brings future past
And steals the now

As higher choice
Goes unchosen
Freedom frozen
Stifled and stilled

Unseemly haste
Drives on and on
Till life is waste
And we are gone

Christmas 2006: Absolute Aloneness

a sonnet

I am going to hide in my room this year
For Christmas as for my New Year's Eve birthday
Overwhelmed by anxiety filled with fear
I will wait it out until it goes away

I love the Christ of Christmas but for the rest
It is simply unbearable for me now
As I taste the worst remembering the best
It all seems a bitter mockery somehow

Strangers attempt to make it better but they
Cannot see that which is broken inside me
"My soul is weary of my life" as Job said

May Christ have mercy at his Nativity
On me as I excuse myself to my bed
And not to sleep there but to weep instead

War Sonnet

Blessed are the dead who feel no more pain
We were trusting and easily misled
Lied to we went chasing falsified goals
Along with thousands and daily more dead
By little antichrists who sold their souls
A long time ago but how could we know
Our leaders had been leading us astray?

We never would have enabled their lies
If we had known then what we know today
But now as you read this one of us dies

None with a pure heart ever dies in vain
Leaving our dreams behind us as we go
Now we will never be misled again
Blessed are the dead who feel no more pain

A Set of Three on Christmas Eve

One:
Good Day and Good Night

I have decided to tell everyone
That I am in bed with the flu today
Till Christmas passes and the year is done
I cannot bear it any other way

I would like to be a philanthropist
But have no money with which to endow
What I would like and am no optimist
I cannot afford to buy my books now
Nor coffee for Grandma's percolator
There will always be good work for later
If unfortunately not done by me

Everyone would be on my Christmas list
But all I have is all this poetry
So I will stay in bed all day and write
Hibernating to return with the sun

Till Christmas passes and the year is done
I wish everyone good day and good night

Two:
For My Father

My father you have so much blood on your hands
You made your living killing
And yet you would be the one who understands
If only you were willing

From you I learned that life is not fair
Kill or be killed death lives everywhere

You are old now as am I

Here on the battlefield man to man
Let us make peace as we die
If it is not too late if we can
If you are willing

After the killing

Three:
In the Dark

Christmas Eve turned out to be
Quiet and harmonious
My first thought had been to flee
But that proved erroneous

It turned out to be just fine
Not so bad at all for me
Through a twinkle a divine
Spark of love and synergy

Though my heart was bleak and stark
Christ was born there in the dark

This Mischief I Make in the Night

Why do my books have four more pages
In hardcover than in soft?
I would ask of bookmaking sages
Who soar much higher aloft
Than some lowly scrivener like me
Yet somehow it all turns out right
I just write the poetry
This mischief I make in the night

I wonder if those pages are those
Stout outer ones thick for the ages?
As long as the binder knows
What those four pages are for
I just hope somebody reads them
Takes good care of them and needs them
No matter how they might I need them more
Because they bear my fondest fantasy

Yet somehow it all turns out right
This mischief I make in the night

The Hopeful Heart Knows

a sonnet

The sun is soaring stronger
If only step by step but every day
The light is leaping longer

Winter is on the walk now making way
If only by a moment at a time
Impatient spring is pacing in the wings

The great wheel turns from sublime to sublime
To hasten the day when the robin sings
Again for those who waited in the dark

The landscape changes unmistakably
Each time I go outside and to the park
But spring cannot come soon enough for me

Sweet secrets lie buried under the snows
Wonders which only the hopeful heart knows

Through Bamboo

a sonnet for someone

I sing a song through a bone-flute of bamboo
As curling upward my voice like smoke rising
Emboldened sings about love and me and you
A song sung through bamboo can be surprising

Some people talk too much as they come and go
But you and I have talked enough now that we
Know each other so well we already know
Transcending what could be said we would just be

Tender feelings are projected on the clouds
By the pink-and-purple setting sun below
Beckoning us rise up there above the crowds
Of people who will never know what we do

Curling upward our voices like smoke rising
Our song sung through bamboo will be surprising

For Her

I remember when I saw her giving up
How it made me feel like giving up to see
After a lonely lifetime of living up
To high ideals some others misunderstood
Perfectly proper invisibility
And sacrificing self to the greater good
Thinking of self last but first of another
Armed with only kindness against cruelty
She did the best she could to be a mother
Did pretty well too and she did it for me

And after a whole lifetime of living up
To high ideals some others misunderstood
In that place of death I saw her giving up
Sacrificing herself to the greater good

For the joys which were not and the sorrows which were
I do the best I can and I do it for her

Ars Longa

a sonnet

Life-poets like my mother die young
Her life remaining as poetry
Mere mortals like me live on and on
Struggling somehow to get our song sung
Making a fuss and then we are gone
Losing our bet with mortality

I can race against time all I want
But my judgment is not up to me
If fate is kind one poem might haunt
Some odd book somewhere or two or three
But leave legacy to what other
People say long after I have died
And been led into light stupefied
An old man to meet my young mother

BIRTHDAY CONTEMPLATION

A life of fifty-two weeks another year
A deck of cards including the jokers too
I will contemplate truth and what makes it true
On this New Year's Eve as I count fifty-two
Years a deck of cards the game which keeps me here:

+ + +

To tell the truth come what may
That a truer world might be
I embrace the ones before
We came who went before us
To dance on a different day
I thank them that they tried for
And lived for as they died for
Life discovered and love shared
Love lived life loved intensely
As pure possibility

As the ones before prepared
Life is love which we can see
Love which we cannot still more
In which life and love agree
To embrace the ones who dared
Who by this grace restore us
To embrace the ones before
Who dared to come before us
And remember what they cared
For as possibility

Even through their darkest doubt
Even doubt as dark as now
It was worth caring about
And still is somewhere somehow

Ancient wings renewed shake free
Unfold new reality
I embrace the ones before
Who danced on a different day
Who died for what they lived for
To tell the truth come what may

Human After All?

I try not to care
But then: she is there!
And try as I might
Her humanity
Brings mine out in me

It simply feels right

So am I human after all?
At least I would be
In good company

This leap of faith ends not in fall
But in rising creative desire
A lifting to love while tried by fire

Because she is there

Always as now
Beckoning to me
I guess I will care
Reckoning that she
Will show me how

New Year's Resolution

for Franziska with love

I seek to purify myself this year
To do my uttermost in all I do
I seek to forget the feeling of fear
And to be unafraid of loving you

I seek to celebrate your beauty now
To know who my friends are that you are one
I know I want to be with you somehow

To enjoy this life and to have some fun
As much for as long as time will allow
To see how far I can go with my best
And do all I can before I am done

That you might be pleased and forgive the rest

I would like to find our place in the sun
To flourish strong and sturdy stubbornly
Staying in the light of the state of mind
Of struggling to be the best I can be

I look deep within my heart and I find
I want most for you to be proud of me
So I will do my best and start today

If you would like to be with me come on
And we can have a great time come what may
With what there is left until it is gone
Since nothing lasts forever anyway

The Stubbornness of Self-Sacrifice

I have struggled so stubbornly to stay
Because I simply have nowhere to go
They always told me it was mere delay
That I had to sell out and they should know

But I would not be moved not go away
Nor face the sad reality and so
I got my wish at the end of the day
And now I am a complete stranger here
In my own house gnawed by the rats of fear
Be careful what you wish for by the way

Although it is always up in the air
Although I can know no security
And in spite of what those wiser might say
I intend to keep my heritage where
My legacy can enjoy it someday

Someday they will say "that poet lived there
Even though it was impossible to
Endure what he chose to endure to be
A link in the chain of his family
He did just what he felt he had to do"

And so I live with strangers now but I
Will leave it to my children when I die
And if they should have more money than me
They can replace strangers with family
Forget about some old man and his pain
There will be children laughing here again

Although it is always up in the air
Although I can know no security
And in spite of what those wiser might say
I intend to keep my heritage where
My legacy can enjoy it someday

ON A BLUE CLOUD OF DREAMS

If only I could sleep until I die
Soaring the sky on a blue cloud of dreams
Far beyond all this madness up so high
Where nothing matters anymore it seems

Let the other shoe drop for all I care
Excreted from the body politic
I want to feel the night-wind in my hair
Where war and folly no more make me sick

Since I fail to see waking hope for me
Except I sleep until I die and fly
Anywhere but here I have broken free
Broken by the earth to take to the sky

But do not wake me when it all ends please
If I cannot die at least let me sleep
If barred from the sky then let me sink deep
I want no more waking indignities

Curiosity and Me

I read encyclopedias all night
Consult the dictionary all day long
And while for me my style of life seems right
For those less curious it might be wrong

But my birthright is curiosity
I like to have a working theory why
Things are as they are here all around me
I was born a very curious guy
To a very curious family
And yet I do not know the answers to
The questions I wonder about all day
As you might and as many people do

For me the questions never go away
And if curiosity killed some cat
If I should die it would not be of that
For me not to wonder would be to die

And Two Stars: Free

Without knowing the secrets of the sun I see
That within its bright self it seems to smile
I have no doubt it is smiling at you and me
So come closer as we smile back awhile

It will have no doubt what we are smiling about
Everyone knows about the sun and fun
Even early this morning before it came out
I felt it dawn on me a new life had begun

Without seeing the secrets of the moon I know
That it is making magic silently
And I can see in the sky wherever I go
That palest of eyes there winking at me

But my favorite heavenly body is you
Just you yourself right there just as you are
So encouraged by what the sun and the moon do
And with their blessing I name you my star

Without knowing the secrets I only guess why
But if you are a star then I must be
And I would love to join you up there in the sky
Smiling sun... winking moon... and two stars: free

Pigs of the Sky!

A tornado blew seven pigs away
But only whirled them around in the air
Keeping them up there a night and a day

And when it got tired it put them back where
They had been found eating down on the ground
After their whirlwind ballet in the round

They had been busy and they were dizzy
Wondering how big they would have to be
Before they could no longer ride for free

Yet after awhile they forgot about
All their excitement and started to doubt
If they had really flown up in the sky

Until a pig-shaped pink puff cloud passed by...

And seven snouts pointed heavenward high
They were relieved shook fat heads and believed
Sharing their secret with porcine laughter

Pigs of the sky! Seven pigs of the air
Who are now best friends forever after
Recalling down here they once flew up there

When a pig-shaped pink puff cloud passes by...

REFRACTION

As beauty is in the eye of the beholder
Perfection is refracted by the judging eye

We wisen as we wizen smarter but older
Pursuing perfection albeit with a sigh
When it seems just right to me it might not to you

But see perfection each our way is what we do
Live briefly and imperfectly then soon we die
After a lifetime of looking for something true

And whether this is it or something more
As beauty is in the eye of the beholder
May we both find what we were looking for

Perfection as refracted by a judging eye

Secret

The secret he carried was wrapped with regret
And he was just not ready to share it yet
But said when he was I would be first to know
I could see that he was afraid to let go
Of something he feared might make him be loved less
And death interfered before he could confess

I think in his heart he knew I knew because
I had known all along what the secret was
We all knew and loved him more for it somehow
As much in solidarity then as now

Yet I still feel sad for him about
His living a lie he believed had to be
He was never able to come out
And because of this he never could be free

INFINITUDE

My cat comprehends how alone we are
And stays as close to me as any dog
Ever trotted alongside a master
Although no one is master of a cat
Nor he of me but love and that is that

I want to walk but have to take the car
Or he will follow me into the clog
Of cars where each is bigger and faster
Than the one before and then there are more

When I return he is watching for me
Between the lace curtains or possibly
There under my mother's funeral tree
If someone let him out so he could wait
For me to see I escaped disaster
Such as I had warned him about before
He marks the time and marks the time as late

And I go back to my room alone
To die when I die nor force the spring
With the best friend I have ever known

In an attitude of infinitude
Feeling the meaning of everything

Another Loser of the Human Race

From anxiety down through depression
Was a digression from society
Life took me on between my then and now
If anxious and depressed at least to be
Who I am what I dream and dare and must
At least try with a question on my face

We speak in unknown tongues nor understand
What we say but smile and try to adjust
As we build our Babel of the unknown
And when chaos calls and the tower falls
Because it was built of but wind and sand
Again and more each time we are alone

I wish I had someone to hold my hand
The ones who did once died and in their place
Left me a stranger lost in their strange land
Picking up pennies of hope as somehow
Though orphaned with an unreturned embrace
Of nothing yet I struggle and I stand

A stubborn son of Babel grasping grace
Another loser of the human race

Night Ravens

When one awakens then the day begins
Today my day began along with night
I slept through afternoon and woke at five
It was already dark as the world spins

But in my case a day of night felt right
Though sick all day here I am still alive
I missed the worst an innocent asleep
No day but night no heaven but no hell

My day was dark and now my night is deep
Yet dark and deep describe my feelings well
Drinking strong tea while hoping for the best
Now I will see what can be done with it

Let others have the day we have the rest
To play and puzzle where our pieces fit
The moon the stars and other nightly things
Like the magic when the night raven sings

For me
And you
I see
We two
Agree

We couple of night ravens you and me

Defiance

against one who has wronged me: for all those who have not

Shallower people from sunnier climes
Dismiss my poems as "nursery rhymes"
But I construct these puzzles anyway
Word-games which all are invited to play

When I was shallower and sunnier
Mocking old poets seemed much funnier
And yet the joke is on you (if you do)
As it was once on me
Because I know how to do (but do you?)
A few things you might never understand
As some reading agree

I will be around if you need a hand
And I am not offended
(Anymore)
What you started I ended
(At your door)
Poetry is my neighborhood my town
You will never shut me up nor shut me down

Now just one more time
(Although you cannot appreciate it)
A nursery rhyme
(And oh how you know you love to hate it!):

Poetry is my neighborhood my town
You will never shut me up nor shut me down

Lonely Eyes

The cherries of their cigarettes flared
Through the dark simultaneously
Too much in a hurry to be scared
I felt lonely eyes questioning me
Good kids in a bad place cold and bored

I was not what they waited to see
So in a puff of smoke was ignored
In favor of what the night prepared
To cook up out of the day's debris
They smiled as I smiled and turned to go

But it felt good to be understood
Wandering with cold wind in my hair
In my face as theirs and everywhere
Looking for something no longer there
Something I lost a long time ago

Might have mislaid it might have turned wrong
All of us look but none of us know
Where it has gone except far away
Trying to sing a forgotten song
Eyes of the night remember the day

Lonely eyes questioning all night long

As If This Were It

I leave it to you to figure out how
But what I would advise you urgently
Is live all you can and do it right now

As if this were it with nothing to come

That you taste hear smell touch all you can see
As much as mortality will allow
All the potential you have and then some

Since it would appear that this might well be
Our singular chance our once-given turn
Our one moment out of eternity

Although we never know we always learn

My Last Refuge

sacred to the memory of Mildred Naomi Eckart Graham

A very warm blanket embraces me
Each stitch by hand with love each one by one
A souvenir of death and destiny
My Grandma crocheted until it was done
A deep design of love drawn patiently

And even though she is gone I have this
Living proof of her love a hug a kiss
If sadly in the lonely cold of night
Which though so dark still holds one point of light
The way this blanket embraces me now

I wanted to go with her but could not
Where saints in heaven no more sorrow see
But left behind to muddle through somehow
With no more to lose and cornered I fight
Take everything but this no matter what

Leave me with this one scrap of self-respect
Left here for me by one of the elect
To enshroud my broken remains and be
My last refuge in this bitter twilight
Of ruin and loss and indignity

As strangers disrespect the memory
Of someone who cared and still cares for me

THE DIET OF WORMS

I used to sweep the floor at the barber shop
And then sell the hair to Mr. Atherton
Packed by the lug box for a quarter a pop
Who fed it to his worms until he was gone

I had not known worms ate human hair before
But Mr. Atherton assured me they did
And that they would go on to eat a lot more

It was a pretty good living for a kid

Although when I agreed to the position
I only thought of life with lots of money
Not of the riddle of decomposition

Yet in an ending both tragic and funny
And in any case awe-inspiringly weird
The worms I fed consumed Mr. Atherton
A very strange outcome not thought so not feared

Feeding him to his worms until he was gone
Just as he wished I became a magician
And I learned his secrets all at once one day

Mortality is only a worm away

Franziska and Me and World War III

Franziska at the fall of empire now
As chickens with their heads cut off run blind
Let us embrace while the fire will allow
Baby and maybe go out of our mind

It seems so much the thing to do these days
Flamed-out follies falling down to always
As they do make me wonder if we two
Should fall in and fall out to always too

But whatever whoever else we do
If this is our turn to go down the drain
Then I want to go down the drain with you
As the world shoots-up for world war again

We could snuggle in to give peace a chance
Smuggled in by Franziska and by Lance
Unwilling world-warriors not sitting still
To take it as we take over the place

Although apocalypses make some ill
We both have a certain redeeming grace
Which seems to manifest at times like these
Tinny tawdry total catastrophes

If this is the end of it all then I
Think we might better hurry up and be
Doing and being our best as we die
Rested and ready for the revelry

Of the world turning itself inside out
(And we can share my little stash of doubt)

Brazil Nuts Over the BBC

The BBC burbled Brazil nuts all night
Or at least bantered them at some length it seemed
And how for the EU they must be just right
"Four parts per billion of..." something... as I dreamed

And along with Brazil nuts I dreamed of you

Since Brazil nuts are something we might enjoy
I would like to share a Brazil nut or two
With you in the EU before they destroy
Those nuts not approved and sent back to Brazil

We might have to get them from Bolivia
Given what I learned tonight we might but still
Somehow I know more than I do through that voice
Of authority by BBC my choice

Which left unattended chirps on through the night
Like the busiest bird in Britannia
From across the sea while the nuts at the store
Are shut up tight with no Brazilians in sight

First thing in the morning I will go explore
Dreaming of you in the EU far away
If we find Brazil nuts eat some then some more
If they come from Bolivia that's OK

We dream of the jungle through the cold grey light
Of our northern dawning of our winter's day

Street Sonnet

Is that blood on the street? You bet it is
What did you think? Some Hollywood effect?
This is where someone determined that his
Money was worth less than his self-respect

The roughest of the rough trade is the truth
That people will die in gutters tonight
The beginning of the ending of youth
The dawning of the distance of the light

However far from home a candle here
Burns in my window until you return
I promise you no matter what you fear
The main thing we are here for is to learn

The beginning of the ending of youth
The roughest of the rough trade is the truth

Living the Good Life Badly

The only thing I can bring
To leave behind more or less
Is nothingness of something
Like something of nothingness
At last I find my question
Is not answered yet I guess

Commandment or suggestion
Of some faith I should confess
Is answer now no longer
But forgive me: I digress

The time wheel is turning on
To the flarings of the sun
With the ghostly moon and drawn
Automatic once begun

Living the good life badly
The wheel is turning madly

My Hiding Place

From the tumult and the trauma
The dysfunctionality
Of the daily psychodrama
In propinquity to me
On the other side of the wall
Round the corner down the hall

I escape into poetry

The only place where I can go
Where reason understands I know
How lonely it is to be me
To tame the chaos of the time
By counted syllable and rhyme
To seek a spark by which to see

And though it seems impossible I know
At least I have this one saving grace
As angry voices fall to rise again
Since all they have in common is their pain
Through chaos I see cosmos and I go
Through loneliness to weep away the stain

Into poetry: my hiding place

Sinus Sonnet: An Independent Nose

Deeply determined it has to be free
My nose confronts me with a loss of face
It misbehaves and embarrasses me
Sneezing then running all over the place
Making up its mind independently

Attached as we are I have to give chase
Persuade it to perch with the dignity
Of gentle hypo-allergenic grace
Pointing out the path of civility
But carrying a hanky just in case

Out where the starry-eyed winter wind blows
In where the kind furnace makes my cat purr
Some things stay as true as they always were
Some of us sport an independent nose

The Plaza in Orange California

the hub of my small universe

I sit beside where flocks of sheep once drank
Where ladies planted flowers long ago
And tended stubby palm trees now so tall

My mother pushed my pram here and I thank
The stubborn who had sense enough to know
Our Plaza really is the best of us

The homeless sleep here next to me and I
Can think of no splashier ending than
To dive into the fountain if I can
If it gets warm enough before I die
This is where we say goodbye to it all
This is the place for all the rest of us

I remember life and brush back a tear
Would it be better if I just forgot?
The Sterling Silver rose still blooms right here
Just as I wrote of it so long ago
I did not expect to be understood
Yet I was and it blooms inside of me

I lost it all then got it back again
Right here in this place through lines scratched in pain
Like cuts in the thickening hide of me

But if you read my books I think you could
Get some idea of who I am and why
I linger here these years no matter what

Would it be better if I just forgot?

Down

This womb-tomb whence I come and go
Holds secrets no one else could know
Which twisted me and made me grow
Into this being you are seeing now
Only these walls the dead and I know how
But I have come from here so here I go

Heaven above and hell below
The possibilities between
Held close in this place

I hope you can see what I mean
And grant me the grace
Of your intelligent reading
For my scratchings broken and small
Something I find myself needing
To help me understand it all

Held close in this place
The possibilities between
Heaven above and hell below

And so I remain
With pleasure with pain
Again and again
The pleasure the pain
Again and again
Swirling down the drain

RECOGNITION

The little man in the little store
Was distracted seemed disconsolate
I noticed when I went to pay for
My Diet Coke and a Tootsie Pop

His condition seemed unbearable
A flight before dying flying blind
His face was tied in a knot of care

It must have been something terrible
I tried to help but no matter what
He would not share what he could not bear
Wearing a mask which he would not drop

Certainly not for a well-known nut

Evolving into a madman now
I can see I am not alone
I always felt empathy somehow
For all the madmen I have known

Some people just prefer to keep still
A flight before dying flying blind
As my father flew and always will

As for me I am the talkative kind
My father and that little man are not
And I leave my inhibitions behind
Unlike them for my flight out of my mind

NOCTURNE

Late at night alone I remember things

Balloons used to come on sticks before strings
And Mrs. Ash used to threaten Danny
With a balloon stick but he was much too canny

She never caught him as far as I know
Just swished that stick then away he would go
And I would go along with him usually

(...Now at this late hour at last I know why
Each time he prayed our pastor used to cry...)

Mom was the one who taught me how to fence
With curtain rods in the kitchen defense
While hanging sweet fresh curtains dried in the bright sun

My Mom was always the swashbuckling one
Having been married to a Lance you see
Whether parent or child take the time to have fun

And then you too can remember like me

No Greater Love

The throbbing ache of a deep-disturbed dream
A riddle as demonic as divine
Worries the bones of hope worn white before

While with futile fists clenched a stifled scream
And a sickened heart for the thousands more
Who must dance before the dance of death ends

I watch them walk into the wall of war

Warriors who lay down their lives for their friends
And they are our kids and some friends of mine

Just About

A brooding darkness follows me
Encroaches on me everywhere
My former shadow swallows me

Absurdity is in the air

We who have suffered know who care
Or care not for our company
Too late but soon when here is there
Absurd yet not a tragedy
Only tragic absurdity
Of that kind we were meant to share

If only this cloud would leave me

If I could ever find the light
And get a crowd to believe me
Then that would be just about right

Between the profit and the loss
A prophet (with an albatross)

A Rising and a Reaching

I never think about what I will write
Nor wonder if I have something to say
It happens automatically at night
My poetry is not thought anyway
But a rising and a reaching toward the light

With practice I might get it right someday
Even though it will not mean anything
To those unwilling to meet me halfway
Though this is a very odd song I sing
Singing this song keeps me from going insane

My new book reached two hundred thousand on
That five million book list at Amazon
And I felt as pleased as with number one
My two hundred thousand book climb begun

(I never really tell anyone of
My book but I carry it with me with love)

This is my own truth my calling my thing
Which I hope you read and understand but
Though it is nice to come in from the rain
I simply have to do this: no matter what

Shenanigans

If I were a dancer I would
Dance all night with you if I could
Or (if I couldn't) fake it well

You are an entrancer and you
Deciding to dance with me too
Could fake it till I couldn't tell

We would wear ridiculous hats
And engage in engaging chats
With startled strangers in the street

Chatting them up upside the head
Pass by the passersby we meet
Then giggling tickle into bed

Where using only body heat
We'd more than meet our quota of
Shenanigans in lucky love

Dancing or faking you and me
The motions of our poetry

Playing Chess with My Cat

The tail of my cat is a rattlesnake
Tensile in its strength
Prehensile in length
Dancing deftly now he gives it a shake

On his one end a strategizing mind
Coolly focused on the game
While on his other a scythe out behind

To which it is all the same
To sweep off the chessboard or not

Regardless it always does what
My cat means it to
And always does it gracefully

But what he will do
We will just have to wait and see
Dancing deftly now he gives it a shake
The tail of my cat is a rattlesnake

ETERNITY

Life on Mars?
Life on Earth!

Life after death?
Life after birth
In every breath

All the stars
Are in your eyes
Right here right now

I realize
That you are all
I need somehow

Lesser lights fall
But not these two
These lights of you

Twin compasses to regulate
This now of you this now of me
This time not too soon nor too late

And is this not eternity?

Geocentricity

In its geocentricity
The world turns like a whirligig
Which might make sense or it might be
Nonsensical not small nor big

A little land and mostly sea
It spins to keep us standing here
To lend our lives some gravity
With what we stand for not quite clear

But standing here is fine with me
(If something happens let me know)
Since standing here I certainly
Am willing to give it a go

The outstanding standing out here agree
The only reason we are is to grow

Regret

The unfinished pyramid inverted
Teeters on its small top without the eye
Which closed then left when light was subverted

A nation upside down sees earth for sky
As everything becomes absurdity
Perversion itself becomes perverted
And freedom becomes a new slavery
If tomorrow comes history's pages
Will turn to new orders of the ages

If ever any hope slides down to me
I wonder how to know how to believe
And if such things as hope can ever be
Expected as to when we might receive
Some rising spark some faint encouragement
Or maybe just tell us where the light went

The unfinished pyramid inverted
Teeters on its small top without the eye
Which closed then left when light was subverted

Regret (and "how could this happen?" and "why?")

Out of Our Hands

Never one to presume a day
My Grandma planning used to say
"If the world stands"

Living a century she knew
The future was and will be too
Out of our hands

She never had nor asked for much
Yet gave and left behind her such
A hoard of sense to empty hands
Of those for whom the world still stands

The working wisdom of how to be
Like knowing that with all due respect
Those elected are not the elect
And that only the lonely are free

Minimum wage maximum stress
And social insecurity
Way down here in society
Where the misery percolates

Fancy people fail to impress
Leaving to less expensive fates
The lonely and the lost like me
Something for nothing but still free

Out of our hands
(If the world stands)

The Ring

Autumn into winter into spring
Summer into autumn as the ring
Turns round once more as it has before
From here to here in another year
Always marked from autumn as the fall
Is the best time to begin to rise

I always like autumn best of all
But shiver under these winter skies
Till upside down autumn springs for me
Bringing back sunshine and greenery
As light to these winter-darkened eyes
Which though opened sometimes fail to see

Autumn into winter into spring
Summer into autumn as the ring
Turns round not quite as it has before
From here to there into everything
Everything I need and nothing more
Eyes though opened sometimes fail to see

Yesterday's Elephants

When the moon stands stark white against the night
The blue velvet of ancient memory
I remember some hope I see some light
And I tell myself what will be will be
But whatever happens I will be fine
Forged in the crucible of suffering
Nothing can overcome this soul of mine
Fashioned to survive all and everything
By one who has suffered much more than me

The absurd circus parade passes by
Yesterday's elephants trumpeting past
What they leave on the street is all at last
I stepped in it once and learned pretty fast
The passing parade's unreality
Means little or nothing to me as I
See the moon stand stark white against the night
The blue velvet of ancient memory
I remember some hope I see some light

And I tell myself what will be will be

Magical Morning

Something about this sparkling weather
Makes it difficult to be depressed
Out here walking I wonder whether
Anyone could fail to be impressed
Encountering nature's heartfelt kiss

All I can say is it suits me fine
Here in February to be dressed
Up in a deep sense of the divine
On a magical morning like this

I try to tread lightly on the grass
Eating no meat wearing no leather
Hoping the kiss might more freely pass
Between ultimate reality
And such reality as is mine
But let everyone live as they please

Out here walking I wonder whether
Anyone could fail to be impressed
Especially on mornings like these
Something about this sparkling weather
Makes it difficult to be depressed
Dressed up in a deep sense of the divine

All I can say is it suits me fine

ECCENTRIC

When they asked me what I wanted to be
When I grew up back when I was a kid
I answered them unhesitatingly
That my destiny seemed quite plain to me
To be eccentric (whatever I did)

And as it seemed then so it is today
I turned out something like I thought I would
Eccentric if not insane all the way
But the lotus unfolded as it should
To bloom the brighter as my hair turns grey

So who's to say eccentric isn't good?
The further you float from society
And the less you care about what "they" say
The easier it becomes to break free
And make your own rules for this game you play

Your own game which no one has played before
And if no one else understands the rules
Soon enough you won't need them anymore
Whatever you do don't be like those fools
With no sense of absurdity at all

Now that to me would be insanity
I'd rather be a lotus in the fall
Being eccentric (whatever I do)
Unfolding as I should but I might see
If maybe I could find a friend like you

Like it or Not

My poetry is not quite what it seems
The most important parts are unspoken
The imagery of fantasies and dreams
May seem fragile but remains unbroken

Something you might not have thought of before

You may never know me nor I know you
Yet we share and I have things to show you
Gathered into books where you can see more
Buy one and give it to your library

And there I will be right there on your shelf
Exposing your town to strange poetry
In which the poet exposes himself
Without giving all his secrets away

I hide myself inside this poetry
Without exposing all the rest of me
Writing myself down here as if to say
Like it or not this seems the best of me

Chances Are

The existential emptiness
That feeling of being alone
Gnaws us down to despair unless
What lies beyond remains unknown

I don't know and I never will
Until it comes and passes by
What lies beyond my window sill
Or on the dark side of the hill

I feel like I'm so unprepared
I'm sad I'm worried and I'm scared
But I guess I'll just muddle through
And do my best for now then die

I hope it all works out for you
The way you want but chances are
We might get close but no cigar
I guess it always hurts to try

But it gives us something to do

WHY WE WANDER

Some say sublimation is evolution
As solitary souls make restitution
Anonymously or nearly so like me
For the familial happiness of all
That the human family advance nor fall
For want of such sublime singlemindedness
Of single sublimators like me I guess

Some say this is a pretty good way to be
Alone but not lonely in the company
Of some quixotic quest if though on Skid Row
Above people make love while we work below
Their window for the good of humanity
Out here on the street where sublimators beat
Our heads against the brick walls of convention

We do not do this merely for attention
But to advance the dance of the family

Answered

On the threshold of the introitus
He hesitated suddenly
Having second thoughts about coitus
A rite of passage he could see
Into a world of complication
Something in him wanted to flee
Causing his lover consternation

But nature told him "those who love are free"
As his lover smiled encouragingly
And this was nature doing what she does
Because she knows how these things tend to be
And that it had to be the way it was
From Adam even as it was for me
Experience answers expectation

Where all the answered questions disappear
Nature answered without explanation
The best time is now and the best place here
Having transcended anticipation
We see the folly of anxiety
Answered by nature not quite as we plan
Where yin and yang join a woman and man

Dry Flowers

I

Only a heartbeat at a time
Only a breath from death
Only a soft bamboo windchime
Carried on the sky's breath

II

One wants love one needs to be kissed
One craves human propinquity
Lest the point of it all be missed
One who is one is me

III

At the end now they are alone
Pickled and fit to die
Soon they will be gone who have known
So well to live a lie

IV

My upbringing was a warning
The worthless feel most worth
I must get up in the morning
And go and save the earth

V

The lavender ribbon she wore
A cloth of gingham check
Was like some fruit a lotus bore
Delicious on her neck

VI

Only a stubborn stunted star
On a very dark night
I never meant to come this far
But I still have my light

Stop

I worry that having failed in the war
Now having completely destroyed Iraq
This administration will look for more
Shenanigans to make and carry on
Pretty much more of the same to Iran
Now on the ledge to go over the edge
Taking us too far to ever come back

Will the people wake up and prove willing
Seeing the president's ship going down
To end this endless cycle of killing
While we bury beautiful kids from town?
Take back the future from the unclean hand
Which stole it and can never understand
That to increase the war cannot bring peace

Peace must be nurtured and grown patiently
And for it to bloom the bleeding must cease
Preemptive war used to be viewed as sin
But they have forgotten diplomacy
Now from a distance they send our kids in
I worry that having failed in the war
This administration will just make more

For Right Now

Happy to be here and there
After all at this late hour
Happy to be anywhere
Still with style still without power
Happy still in any case
Still to care and not to care
To exist in any place

Do I know where I might be
Tomorrow or the next day?
Someone might know but not me
Living here or passed away
Sailing or else cast to sea
Ashes into memory
Still I will have had my say
Riddled into poetry
Left behind beyond my stay

As long as there are stars in
The sky to wink at our sin
I might as well enjoy me
No one else can destroy me
So the thing to do is be
Happy to be here and there
To exist in any place

Happy to be anywhere
For right now in any case

SHOT BY CUPID

If you still want to be shot by Cupid
Then go ahead but I think it's stupid
I never take his arrows anymore
Since having been shot by Cupid before
Turned out to be such painful injury
My heart like Humpty Dumpty in free fall
And having avoided cupidity
I would prefer not to be shot at all

I've lived too close to couples who tussle
Claw like cats in the hustle and bustle
Of gross dysfunction and indignity
If that's what coupling is it's not for me
And what of those couples with peaceful ways?
One of them does what the other one says
While others shout what they say together
Loudly in stridently stormy weather

If you still want to be shot by Cupid
Nothing I say will stop you anyway
Until you too end up feeling stupid
And duped like me at the end of the day

My good old cat and I will be just fine
The next heart shot by Cupid won't be mine

The Art of Poetry

When the subject of the poem cannot be
Determined at all at least not precisely
Because it is nothing less than everything
And so instead has to be experienced
Rather than read felt by flesh like a bee sting

When that is the sort of a poem you find
In which everything at once is referenced
Which speaks not only to the heart but the mind
And deeper to plumb seas of reality
Or unreality not that you must choose

When you see the magic which nobody sees
And when the roulette wheel will not let you lose
So you are left satisfied yet wanting more
When the poem like an incantation frees
All sorts of things you never thought of before

A hidden door opening to galaxies
The summer the winter the fall and the spring
All things all at once in the dance of the ring
Then you have tasted the art of poetry
Which art is the art I have chosen for me

Because it is nothing less than everything

SICK ENOUGH

When you get sick enough nothing matters
As the world shrinks down to heartbeat and breath
One criticizes another flatters
While I am trying not to cough to death

Exhausted I wonder how to make it
Till my doctor's appointment on Tuesday
But people smile at me and I fake it
Still trying to act all right anyway

Unable to buy an aspirin now
I wish that I had gotten my flu shot
As muddling through the best I can somehow
I lie to people and say I forgot

When the truth is I was too sad to care
Back then if I got a flu shot or not
But the complications are terrible
So much so I despair of making it

Waiting is becoming unbearable
And now I am finding that faking it
Becomes impossible this far along
Since sickness is stronger than we are strong

It bears us away at the close of day
A stupid way to commit suicide
But a poetic way to fade away
And more efficient than other ways tried

When you get sick enough nothing matters

OLD SOLDIER

Once he was really someone long ago
It was amazing what he did back then
He has a story but no one to know
Who he used to be in the way-back-when
He refuses to talk about it now
Bearing his secrets to the grave below

So no one knows exactly as to how
It was that destiny chose him to be
A hero but he is a hero still
And if he were to talk he might well say
Those who were there never talk never will
Old soldiers do not die they fade away

He lost his heart in the Second World War
He bet it all and never won it back
Still marching but only he knows what for
I wonder what he thinks about Iraq

The Learning Curve

for my friend Richard Rohm

I used to enjoy the spinning around
Which life seemed to be at least formerly
But now am being run into the ground
Pursuing freedom finding slavery

Were life some crazy spinning carousel
What started here would finish here as well
But life seems a train run right off the track
Which would not appear to be coming back

Riding for my life on a learning curve
With hairpin turns a shudder and a swerve
And the wonder what I did to deserve
Riding for my life on a learning curve

From the frying pan of conventional
Ideas to the fire of alternative
Realities or unrealities
Manifold and multidimensional

I find myself challenged by times like these
And glad I am not a conservative
Those are the ones who are really upset
Not even seeing what has happened yet

I used to enjoy the hustle and flow
Of life on the fly as it barrels by
Of not knowing where it is that I go
But getting there just along for the ride

I see now it is true that I must die
And what a spectacular accident
It smells like someone has already died
As from a distance I hear the lament

The locomotive careens crazily
The cars fall on their sides this way and that
I wonder if that lament is for me
And whether I should get my coat and hat

No: I will ride to the end of the line
Although there is no line here anymore
This railroad is crazy but it is mine
Although I never knew what it was for

Riding for my life on a learning curve
With hairpin turns a shudder and a swerve
And the wonder what I did to deserve
Riding for my life on a learning curve

I Wish I Could Write a Poem Today

(but Happy Birthday to Franziska anyway)

I wish I could write a poem today
But life has ground me down to nothing now
If I could I would make a poem say
The things I find unspeakable somehow
As touching how this life is touching me
Today in a way I find unpleasant
In a word roughly or abusively
And not really worth living at present
Given the disappointment the sorrow
To say nothing of the hopelessness when
Yesterday is gone with no tomorrow
But maybe I can write a poem then
Or the day after or maybe next week

Or maybe it may never be at all
If today is it is too much to speak
The problems too big the poet too small
The chasm between the two yawning wide
As a deep shadow is cast like a pall
As I await the fate of the helpless
As I am devoured by my destiny
Having already piled up poetry
Enough for anybody now I guess
If I could I would make a poem say
The things I find unspeakable somehow
But life has ground me down to nothing now
I wish I could write a poem today

I Hope

Although today I feel like hell
No stupid sickness can drop me
I hope tomorrow to be well
And not let anything stop me

Should anybody wonder why
My hope defies mortality
I live by curiosity
And still too curious to die
No choice remains me but remain
To get things done to see them through
To ask the questions once again
And maybe get some answers yet

If anybody will I bet
I will although I have to do
My best to make my hope come true
Now having seen how time can fly
But hopeful as I ever was
And just a little stubborn too
I think I can survive because
I feel too curious to die

Of course I also feel like hell
But called by curiosity
My hope defies mortality
I hope tomorrow to be well

Gone

When the night opens its arms to receive
A wanderer otherwise deeply lost
Something within him begins to believe
That it was worth it whatever it cost
That whoever he is will be all right
Being embraced in the arms of the night

A good night's journey and a good day's rest
Although he is not going anywhere
The wanderer looks to the flaming west
At dusk and then the burning east at dawn
But he has already been here been there
And more than anything likes to be gone
Just to look up into the sky and stare
To the night's dark heart where the bright stars shine
And see he has been granted his request
"What lies in-between dusk and dawn is mine"

You never know when you get home until
The scattered things gather and then you feel
The rightness of it and he always will
Find home in the dark which the stars reveal
He prefers midnight to the dusk and dawn
And more than anything likes to be gone

New Pants in a Spacetime Anomaly

From mirror to mirror before and behind
High-stepping reflections step out of my mind
In a chorus line although I never dance
Like that but truth be told never had the chance
Before somehow but I am doing it now
With all the grace which two dimensions allow

Anyone could look good if the light is right
But I had no intention to dance tonight
So I am surprised to see me supersized
Multiplied and stretching to infinity
Yet I see who is dancing and it is me
Inscrutably if stylishly realized

I came here with the most mundane intention
I just wanted to try on a pair of pants
And the dressing room man forgot to mention
How these magic mirrors make one preen and prance
But even if I never come out again
There are worse ways to go and there is no pain:

"In multiplicity for eternity
With new pants in a spacetime anomaly
Dressing Room Eight presents: Steven Curtis Lance"

Existential Baseball

This is an existential baseball game
Twi-night double-header extra innings
Nobody wins but nobody to blame
I lost and now must pick up my winnings

I see everybody else lost the same
As me but they don't realize it yet
The scoreboards are wrong whatever they say
I just take the winnings of my losing
And vow to remember never to bet
On some insane game not of my choosing
Ever again just head the other way

(Why does this sort of thing happen to me?)

I heard they won't let anybody leave
That we are spectators here forever
But I will dig my way out day by day
Escape tomorrow or maybe never

I have to do something have to believe
That there was a meaning in here somewhere
And I am too exhausted now to grieve
Anymore at this field of life and death
Each step between swinging from here to there
I offer back this heartbeat with this breath
And picking up my winnings take strike three

Suddenly Now

Every single morning is a victory
Every time the sun comes up I feel I win
To be anywhere is a good place to be
As good as any so let this day begin
The rest of my life all of a sudden now
And let it be as great as fate will allow

I came late to the table I realize
With the time left to me not what it once was
The great clock of the universe is running
But adventure still beckons in every size
As to the end things spin out from the first cause

The view from anywhere is still as stunning
As ever it was this morning because of
All of the things which have always made it so
Things felt more than seen like hope and faith and love
As if questions the answers to which I know

I only get this one chance in the world here
So I might as well enjoy it after all
After half a lifetime of living in fear
It might just be time for some dragons to fall
So let me be as great as fate will allow
As the rest of my life comes suddenly now

Broken

Is it still a poem if it is broken?
I can only write a broken poem now
As a broken poet in a broken house
Where things are done which can never be spoken
By unsentimental people who know how
To destroy what must seem like a broken mouse
To them just the doomed and forsaken heir of
A personalized death at the unclean hands
Of these conquerors none of whom understands
They poisoned me with suffering killed my love
And destroyed first my home then my sanity

Should I have sold when I was told and fled when
It got so cold and I got old and bled then
With memories of scenes like these? To bed then
(My cat and I) afraid to die but still more
Afraid of my life and what I lost it for
Hiding in my bedroom behind the locked door

Father have mercy on your wandering son
Receive my soul and spare my children from this
Take me home to my true home grant the sweet kiss
Of your forgiveness to this your broken one
It simply hurts too much now for me to be
I want to see my Grandma see my mother
And my Grandpa who loved me like no other
I gave my all but nothing is left for me
Where things are done which can never be spoken
As a broken poet in a broken house
I can only write a broken poem now

Is it still a poem if it is broken?

Visual Reality

Cud-chewing on her exit line
She had an inspiration:
Show righteous indignation!

She decided that would be fine
That whatever she said was not
The point of it but rather what
And how effective the effect

Correct just as one might expect
In visual reality
A ray of hope for the elect
Who having eyes use them to see
Her exit line although banal
Effect-effective after all

But we who wonder with our words
Would like our words to matter
Appreciated like the birds
As pleasant background chatter
One hopes and at the very least
A word be heard in season when
We all have lost our reason then

Cud-chewing on my exit line
I have an inspiration:
Show peaceful resignation

LITTLE BIG BOY!

Thirty years old and going nowhere fast
I know because I have been there before
If this is your chance it might be your last
Inflated by our worship now to soar

But I am an unbeliever in you:
I think you are an enormous baby

If you have a dream it might not come true
Can you keep your trophy lover? Maybe
But I think she might be part of the crew
Of a ship which never sails anywhere
Fortunately you are too vain to care

Just call your mother and she will explain
Or better she could tell you over lunch
(For which she pays of course) about how pain
Could make you more thoughtful in what you do
And what Ecstasy has done to your brain

Little Big Boy! Mommy loves you a bunch!
She just wants you to be happy at last!

But baby you are living in the past

COME TURN THE KEY

When time and space and distance loss and gain
Present themselves simultaneously
When differing paths meet to cross again
Having carried us here separately
Converge to a point neither first nor last
With the future almost touching the past

The most plausible possibility
For this pinwheel of pleasure paired with pain
Is that this is the now reminding you
To remind me to remind you to be
Here in the moment and not turn away

Not even a moment is guaranteed
Let alone an hour never mind a day
Yet this moment alone is all we need
Where we are alone with nothing to say
Out of the reach of the hands of the clock
There are no words for such things anyway

Come turn the key as we open the lock
Although unable to go back to when
Such things mattered they will not matter then
Because there will be no then anymore
When then becomes now in the anyhow

Anything is possible in the now
Come turn the key as we open the door

DRIFTING

I feel myself drifting slowly away
Far from the safe shallows of sanity
Nocturnal agony poisons the day
Dawning my death knell in a minor key

I wish I knew and I wish I could say
What catastrophe is coming for me
But I feel it advancing just the same

I hear its heavy footfalls in the night
The chilling wind is whispering my name
The squatting clouds have blotted out the light
The dark descends to cover me with shame

The waters all around me dank and deep
Are rising now and rocking me to sleep
With lullabies of bitterness and blame

What catastrophe is coming for me
I wish I knew and I wish I could say
Far from the safe shallows of sanity
I feel myself drifting slowly away

To Us

Nobody wants existential despair
Nobody goes looking for misery
But the trouble is it is always there
I never sought it but it sure found me

It lurks within the shadows everywhere
It stalks the unsuspecting wanderer
Who walks too far out on the thinning ice
All the philosophers who never were
It claims for itself and never thinks twice
Of such details as the him or the her
In fact it never really thinks at all
Leaving that to us when at last we fall

Wrestling with the angel I guess I lost
Waiting on the Lord I am waiting still
I paid as much as I could but it cost
More than I have more than I ever will

Unlike my loved ones who followed before
Leading me to believe I could find peace
I gave up everything but it cost more
Than I could ever have to find release
From this fragmenting fear which shreds my soul
And draws me deeper into this black hole
To sink fully conscious under these chill
Seas of broken minds and dreams great and small

Nobody wants existential despair
None seeks to swallow such a bitter pill
But the trouble is it is always there
Inside of us never thinking at all

Leaving that to us when at last we fall

Redeeming the Time

My hair has grown beyond the collars of
Those autumn winter jackets I so love
But this has now come just in time for spring
When jackets are only worn at evening
Or at morning but I am asleep then
And I wear my jackets no matter when

Sweet spring come breathe on me and let me live
As those who will leave a mark on their art
To as I have been given freely give
Enough to change the world or just my heart

I have no money for a haircut now
Nor food nor dental care nor anything
But stumble starving as handouts allow
As one more than ready to see the spring

As the spring sun rises I might rise too
Finding myself in a forgiving clime
And maybe we all could just start anew
Redeeming ourselves redeeming the time

STILL WAY TOO TOUGH TO DIE

Our 1958 Packard was pink
And long of fin with an underbite chin
It looked rather like a big shark I think
A big fish in any pond it was in
(Where sharks are allowed to be pink) something
Long of fin and of tooth enough to bring
Astonishment to the cars we passed by
A pink sort of shock without suffering
When our big pink Packard took off to fly

But then they only saw it from the rear
Fins unfurled and dual exhausts throbbing
Since Grandpa liked to punch the "passing gear"
He was good with knobs and at hobnobbing

MCAS Yuma was where we had
"Factory air" and we needed it bad
Not in the Packard but in the new car
Where I beat the heat in the huge backseat
It was like a walk-in freezer back there
My Grandpa drove it smoking a cigar
A big fish in any pond anywhere
His dream car that '65 Chrysler I
Still drive today still way too tough to die

Volunteers in Waste Places

Nobody plants them nobody but God
And they could not be planted better than
They are as they grow though you might not see
Where they are blooming as fast as they can
In so-called waste places broken and odd
Which they turn into paradises of
Beauty where ugliness gives up to love
Where brokenness is kissed by harmony

These are the flowers we call volunteers
They fruit and seed and are scattered to be
Sown in the shadows and watered with tears
Yet bloom bold even heroic somehow
Like angels who dance where devils have trod
We always need them but especially now
That so little else and so few are free
I understand you friends: be strong stand tall

Bloom through our darkness point us toward the light
You just might be the ones to save us all
Brighten our brief day before our long night
In so-called waste places broken and odd
Which you turn into paradises of
Beauty where ugliness gives up to love
Like angels who dance where devils have trod
Nobody plants you nobody but God

ELECTRIC FREEFALL

Fever is singing in my ears tonight
Tomorrow I hope it might go away
If I don't matter and it doesn't mind
I wish tomorrow could have been today
But time only flies until it is chased
I fear catching it and leaving behind
All of these blue stars and this blue moonlight
Which leaves me wondering if I should say
Let fever sing without unseemly haste

I choke down aspirins doing my best
To live because I have no time to waste
If life is what I am supposed to do
Since I seem to have a knack for the now
You might miss me and I know I'd miss you
Having done this much I could do the rest
Should mortality and the flu allow
But I just get so sick of getting sick
I want to develop immunity
Getting well seems an existential trick
Of our illusion of impunity
Since no one escapes from this place alive

Here where when one flu takes its leave of me
It's only so the next one can arrive
In some unhealthful continuity
Where run-amok TVs squawk down the hall
Looking for me with their sickly blue light
Burbling broadcasting electric freefall
Like fever singing in my ears tonight
A night it looks now I might leave behind
If I don't matter and it doesn't mind

Rise

Gravity sucks and the whole world falls
What is of earth to earth is drawn down
What I want to do is leap these walls
And fly in the sky over my town
To soar through the night in the moonlight

In his world he could never be himself
So he surrendering to family
Lived as a dusty knick-knack on a shelf
Not any sort of life as all could see
Except for him but he could not be free

Or is it that he would not be? The fear
Of disappointing and shattering things
Which are there to be shattered always brings
That sense of ultimate futility
Which fashioned his politely modest mask
Pleasing his parents but proving to be
Ultimately unworthy of his task

And so he shot himself one day and died
Buying the gun from a scary stranger
Who saved his soul by ending the danger
Of being understood for who he was
His parents and clients and pastor sighed
But out at Fairlawn it was nice because
His dusty knick-knack friends all came and cried

Gravity sucks and the whole world falls
What is of earth to earth is drawn down
What I want to do is leap these walls
And fly in the sky over my town
To soar through the night in the moonlight

I am of earth but also of sky
One my left hand the other my right
So to spend half my time in the sky
Is both my birthright and my delight
The same thing is just as true for you

We have to rise whatever we do

Blood

As I once scrubbed the blood from this floor
Here where my broken mother once fell
Now I scrub it from the walls and door
Of our holy home bled red by hell

This is not blood from a Parkinson's fall
But the poisoned blood of denizens all
Of darkness who should never have been here
Bringing stains of nethermost nightmares near

Some sadomasochistic fantasy
Played out here which cannot make sense to me
Because I never fell that far not yet
A bitter lesson I will not forget

Brokenhearted I scrub this room to let
Another crazy couple come destroy
The only safe place I knew as a boy
Now soiled with the blood of a guilty curse

Just when I thought things could never get worse

The broken window is repaired now
I did my best to fix the broken door
The new window shade is on its way
But this is enough there will be no more

I am thinking of selling today

But then all I could do is pay my debts
And live and die a stranger with regrets
That I was the one to let it all go
Driven from home by the scum of the earth

My mother is free while I trapped here below
Am left now to wonder what life is worth
When worse than I could imagine has come true
I will not forget what they did to you

Home of my heart and my mother's memory
Those who defiled you will not rest easily
They will taste the sharp bitterness of regret
As surely as I remember my mother

So turn around scum see it is none other
Than me representing the family

I come to collect a debt of respect

At Last

At last I have recovered from the flu
And am out enjoying a flu-free day
At least for today thank God and thank you
Until another virus comes my way

Spring has already sprung here where I live
Sprung all the way to summer so they say
Where a bright blue sky seems pleased to forgive
My sentence of sickness from a hard fall
And a winter I would rather forget

Days like today seem to justify all
The randomness and the absurdity
Of problems too big and of hope too small
The problems look smaller today to me
As hope in spite of everything looks up

Although all I have is this poetry
Life leaves some shiny pennies in my cup
Apparently I am not finished yet
At least for today thank God and thank you

At last I have recovered from the flu

Fast Cars and Slow-Walking Men

On this second day of my newfound health
Having at last hacked my way through the flu
I remain outdoors and observe by stealth
The comings and goings of those who do
More driving around than anyone need
Most at that surge-ahead-fall-behind speed
Of impatience punctuated by rage
Where underneath the rage it seems like fear

Automotive battle or pilgrimage?

Pedestrians have to be careful here
Man-on-the-street pedestrian am I
A little slow in the crosswalk maybe
But grateful under this graceful spring sky
I hope we get where we were going to
All of us fast cars and slow-walking men
All going the same way ultimately
And then when all of our dreams have come true

I will look forward to seeing you then

Like a Kiss

To bend with the winds of change as they blow
Before the winds blow us into the rocks
Is how we survive as those my age know
Stay true to your truth and never be fake
And though you will bend you will never break

To laugh at our more ridiculous trends
To be able to laugh at me and you
To do good work to have a few good friends
To know how fortune keeps turning around
Up on the summit then down on the ground

Fresh every day and all of it very
Much like a journey and temporary
A sense of humor like a key unlocks
The puzzle of this world so make it fun
And please be kind since humankind is one

The nations rise and go to war and fall
The dogs of war bark and sometimes bite too
We sweep up the detritus of them all
Until death comes to sweep us too away
I thank all of you for sharing this day

This is the only world we ever had
And love is more real than cash bonds or stocks
So bend or break and laugh or else go mad
And when it gets too tough remember this
What seems like a curse can be like a kiss

To bend with the winds of change as they blow
And not pay too much attention to clocks
Is how we survive as those my age know
Stay true to your truth and never be fake
And though you will bend you will never break

Thump-Thump-Thump

He swings a tail like an orangutang
Knows it too as with a how-do-you-do
My cat Fred enters the room with a bang
Bearing the butt of an orangutang

Or if you need to drop off that last "g"
Should he seem more orangutan to you
He swings like an orangutan to me
And whether tang or tan we can agree
That I have my own pet orangutan
At least the hindmost portion anyway
And you could pet my orangutan too
Indeed he would be petted night and day

Though I am an inconsequential man
My cat wields a tail to mow us all down
An orangutangular terrorist
Hitting greens with a scythe of reddish brown
He could cut the grass or harvest the hay
And the government has him on their list

A machine of perpetual motion
A rattlesnake protruding from his rump
A tail to inspire appendage-envy
He is a weapon of mass destruction
And how the other cats wish they could find
The courage to be as brazen as he
If only a pleasant interruption
From rather more effete felinity

Ten years we have shared a fond devotion
In fact he is coming to see me now
Orangutang tail bringing up the rear
Simian yet so impressive somehow

So nice to have an orangutang here
Slapping me softly with a thump-thump-thump

They can bump and grind until they go blind
For want of this tail they are doomed to fail
To bump the way Freddie Noodles can bump
Slapping them silly with a thump-thump-thump

Nirvana

for my friend Bernard Betts

Drinking tea in the middle of the night
Enjoying it and being thankful for
Simple things like not always being right
Having just what I have no less no more
Which might seem less than I need but my sight
Has been disappointed by death and war
And is not what it used to be these days

When waiting eyes look up to realize
Nothing yet everything is as it was
One batch is born as another one dies
The effect unrelated to the cause
Then waiting eyes weep but are thankful for
Simple things like not needing to be right
Needing nothing at all no less no more

Here on the ledge overlooking always
Drinking tea in the middle of the night

Under the Moon by the Railroad Track

They tell me we live and learn but
I am uncertain what they mean
It only seems like we earn what
Little we know of destiny
By simple serendipity
Yet in a random universe
It could always be a lot worse
And very often it has been

We grit our teeth we face the pain
The moon wears neither smile nor frown
We fall but we get up again
To rise so high that up is down
Then weep but weep away the stain
And what we see of destiny
Will be enough for you and me
In this the only game in town

Earth to ashes and dust to flame
It only seems like we earn what
They tell me we live and learn but
Humanity is not to blame
The vanity the grief the shame
The ultimate futility
In this the only game in town
Remain but leave them let them be

We will always have stormy weather
Just keep walking and never look back
If you want we can walk together
Under the moon by the railroad track
I look at the moon and see her smile
She whispers "love" and "never look back"
And night is bright at least for awhile
Under the moon by the railroad track

Curious Canyons

thank you Franziska

Today I find myself relieved to see
I am not alone in the universe
Somebody here likes to visit with me
Just the way I am for better or worse
Baggage and all my dancing in haunted
Houses all my sea stones answered at last
Hope for the present if not for the past

I guess this is all I ever wanted
Waiting for love to come patiently when
I needed it most but not until then
Wondering if my doing might be done
But you see life remains and I agree
Thank you Franziska for being the one
To remind me how things are meant to be

In these curious canyons of the mind
Together we can wonder about things
Get big ideas about leaving behind
Those nightmare things which the night watchman sings
Our real friends seem impossible to find
Because they were never lost anyway
Thank you Franziska thank you for today

The Meaning of It

At the end and that is where I feel like I am now
Living through such trials as to challenge my belief
That which really matters is to have a friend somehow
And should people shout at me and treat me cruelly
Which they do as you know more than I want to admit
How good it is to know someone with insight to see
Whatever good there might be left and left inside me
And I think that this just might be the meaning of it

Though brokenhearted now and broken in any case
The very best medicine is that familiar face
Of one who does not judge except to say I am fine
With all my faults and failings reflecting that divine
Acceptance found so seldom in this our human race
The only medicine which ever gives me relief
I have never understood where we are racing to
Careening as I do between depression and grief

But I am just thankful to be racing next to you
Wherever we are going I can get there I know
You tell me life is worth it all and you show me why
Blue sky above with you beside and good earth below
Whatever happens next and no matter what we do
As we tiptoe through this minefield of sorrows and scares
With your help I see the earth bloom I see the sky shine
And after all become convinced that somebody cares

Right up to my last breath I will live until I die
Never mind the hour of that last breath nor count the days
We never know when we must go our days are unknown
Life is lived all the sweeter on the brink of always
One thing I know for sure is that I am not alone
How good it is to know someone with insight to see
Whatever good there might be left and left inside me
And I think that this just might be the meaning of it

Two for One: Bagel and Coffee

    I. Bagel

Gnawing a toasted bagel pensively
While worrying about the calories
I just wonder what will become of me
But then I decide that bagels like these
Whatever else they do taste heavenly
And so I commit to eat all of it
Since it bears no butter and no cream cheese

What will become of me is I will be
As for what else becomes let it become
Because I have seen the worst anyway
OK by me as long as I have some
Change for a bagel on a sunny day
And should life go from bad to worse to worst
At least I know I will not be the first

    II. Coffee

Those drugs which make people nervous
Hold no fascination for me
They offer a doubtful service
Though offered stimulatingly

I know you know which drugs I mean
Of which I only use caffeine
Because it just comes with my tea
Or the coffee of this morning
At Starbucks down on Plaza Square

Of coffee I need no warning
Since I can only have it there
If someone slips me refill change
Or they wink me a cup for free

I would feel rushed and rather strange
Snorting white powder up my nose
And yet they do it heaven knows
Led by the nose headlong to doom
Far from where the poetry grows

Zoom!

BROKEN VETERANS

Broken veterans camp on this park lawn
My brothers in inscrutability
Although the sun shines their minds have long gone
Dark since they bore the brunt of destiny

They came home from where they were sent but there
Something was lost which can never be found
Again so they sleep homeless on the ground

Since they never really came home at all

They died to the world and what they fought for
Got confused as they watched their comrades fall
And if you ask them you will hear them say
Only those who were there understand war

Here they are yet they are so far away
That one despairs of ever breaking through
Except by some change from me and from you

The Mirror and the Window

As much as we need to remember
We also need to forget
Or else in the chill of November
Things are unforgotten yet
Things which weigh upon us heavily

Unforgiven unforgotten
Things ferment and end up rotten
Such is the burden of memory
To trap us in the mirror
Poisoning both heart and history

Forgetting brings things clearer
Forgiveness is the window
To let in the light below
So that in the end at last we see
This is the freedom of clarity

Rather Like Rhymes

Wandering wondering nickels and dimes
Jingling in my pocket rather like rhymes
About dreams which never came true (not yet)
The people on the sidewalk smile at me

I smile right back at everyone I see
Smiling makes it easier to forget
The abject absurdity of it all
And to be content to be poor and small

I shaved off my whiskers I cut my hair
Got all cleaned up walked down to Plaza Square
Where everybody was nice to me there
They told me they liked my new clean-cut look
And they might also like to buy a book

Well if they do of books I have plenty
Sonnets fourteen hundred four and twenty
Then these poems with no numbers at all
By someone content to be poor and small
Wandering wondering nickels and dimes
Jingling in my pocket rather like rhymes

Orphan

Left disappointed by theology
Left unsatisfied by biology
Left empty-handed by philosophy
In a seemingly random universe
In a bad situation getting worse
Apart from cant and rant to search the sky
I live in fear as an orphan down here

Not the best man but surely not the worst
Not important certainly not the first
Nor last to sink under this rising sea
Left here to die without quite knowing why
Left alone to wonder until I do
Left on the brink not knowing what to think
I turn back to childhood when I knew you

God if you are there please would you show me
If we could have a future you and I?

The Gift We Keep

I search the eyes of a homeless man and see
A reflection deeper than any mirror
I understand I am him and he is me
His eyes are mine as the truth becomes clearer
That something beyond the solidarity
Of human beings who meet on the street is
Happening and understood implicitly

His present is my future and my past his
I see all eyes are searching ultimately
And that these eyes of ours have found each other

Why life has brought us here only life can say
But I his younger he my older brother
Are brothers like tomorrow and yesterday
Of which neither day exists so only now
We sit together and understand somehow
What will be will be but our humanity
Is the gift we keep which none can take away

The Thing I Like Best About You

I seem to think of the right thing to say
About a week later or maybe two
You always know what I mean anyway
This is the thing I like best about you

I lost my money I misplaced my mind
And trouble haunts and hunts me everywhere
The road is hard for those who walk it blind
Like me as I go without knowing where

But I like you and I think you like me
I might be wrong I know but I think so
I know everybody needs somebody
For a little company as they go

So never mind the meaning of it all
And what the hell we might as well just be
A couple of autumn leaves as we fall
Twisting in the wind but elegantly

Or eloquently if we wait a week
Or two but then we never need to speak
Because we know what we mean anyway
This is the thing I like best about you

Etude: Thirteen by Thirteen

thirteen lines of thirteen syllables

He turned out like his father as his mother had feared
Made the same mistake and thought it best to go to sea
Out of sight and out of mind seemed a good place to be
So rounding the corner of the world he disappeared
But once around the corner he saw it was in vain
To go since what goes around just comes around again

No matter how far we flee we can never be free
Of the wheel of the real of the turning of the pain
Of the burning of the learning of the suffering
Of rounding the corner of the world to disappear
To go all the way around to be found right back here
Where we started and departed from once long ago

Yet until we go around the wheel how can we know?

Surprised

If I ever had anything to lose
I probably would have lost it by now
If I was once given the chance to choose
I might well have made the wrong choice somehow
Sure made my share of mistakes anyway
Forgotten now (don't mind doesn't matter)
I just look back and laugh at this late hour
Having developed a taste for surprise

I never really had much of a say
Not being one of the ones with the power
Just picked up such crumbs as fate might allow
Went hungry as the fat cats got fatter
Did what I thought was my best every day
Picked up a few tricks between there and here
Learned the great lesson that life while not fair
Is full of surprise for curious eyes

It surprises me to be anywhere
After years of seemingly meaningless
Ins and outs and ups and downs and sideways
Adventures so I can handle I guess
Such phantasmagoric frolicsome days
As I might endure as I know for sure
Mortality's a disease with no cure
Except to let go: to let go of fear

I just look back and laugh at this late hour
Surprised to be one of the ones with the power

Easter Before I Go

No one wants to die and neither do I
But when your time is coming you just know
So I spent this Easter wondering why
Waiting for stars watching the cars which go
Around and around all seemingly bound
For happy destinations far away
From where I sat with the homeless out in
The hub of the wheel of my town today

The stars never came the flickering flame
Of my cheap lighter lighting cheap cigars
Became the vigil light of lonely night
Which came as a relief beyond the grief
Of seeing happy families like these
Making their fuss who looked askance at us
The people like me with no family

Just a few broken friends with burnt-out ends
Of smokes and bitter jokes about our lives
And where we have been and what we have seen
Of who we were once with children and wives

Only the lonely would know what we mean
Here in this in-between of life and death
Where some say we are punished for our sin
My homeless friends with vodka on their breath
No booze for me just the insanity
Of cars without stars and some cheap cigars
A kind fellow-wanderer shared with me

No one wants to die and neither do I
But when your time is coming you just know
So I spent this Easter wondering why
With friends of mine out here before I go

Exacta

I grew up out at the track with my mother
Checking out the horses and helping her choose
Getting an education like no other
While learning about all the ways you can lose

But I never saw her so happy as when
She hit an exacta and understood then
Why all those people with their broken-down cars
Left broken-down lives back home to reach for stars

Because once in a while the magic would come
And an angel would kiss some broken-down bum
To bless him with martinis and long cigars
Long as the odds which once in a while we beat
Snatching victory from the jaws of defeat
We held our tickets until all hope was gone

But I found the fountains in the infield lawn
And filled my pockets with wet quarters for her
From superstitious winners who never were
Finding more money than my mother most days
Finding one of the more dependable ways
To come home a winner those sunny Sundays

I grew up out at the track with my mother
Checking out the horses and helping her choose
Getting an education like no other
While learning about all the ways you can lose

The odds were so long yet at the end she beat
Cold death to snatch life from the jaws of defeat
Now as I place a wet quarter on her grave
I know she won and offer my life to her
I place my bet for another soul to save
For me and for those winners who never were

Circus Train

In our awkward puzzling position
Life on earth can seem a circus but
Remains never without its reward
Try to enjoy it no matter what
As the temporary condition
Which it manifestly is and must
Be before we return to the dust

Until then our circus train chugs toward
The summit of our humanity
Where whatever our idea might be
Of that which is to come after this
Awkward puzzling position we know
To one we know not where we might go

Through trial to transcendental bliss
Or maybe just an end to it all
Whatever follows when petals fall
But never neglect the here and now
This moment itself for its own sake
And try to have fun with it somehow

Because never having died before
Life on earth becomes an act of faith
A very good chance for us to take
And who could ask for anything more
Than to live well and laugh last at death?

Life on earth can seem a circus but
Personally I believe and trust
That you and I are much more than dust
But if to the dust we must return
Let us live and love and laugh and learn

Try to enjoy it no matter what

SHY LITTLE LOVE SONG

I have survived things I thought no one could live through
Had crazier misadventures than anyone
I never could have made it this far without you
But what we got through has made us two more like one
At least to me and I hope you feel like this too
So on a new day when I feel new life begun
I take a leap of faith and believe that you do

I sit with the homeless and hear with empathy
(Since that is all I have to give them anyway)
The tales they tell which might as well be about me
And I thank God and you I made it to this day
More or less intact booze drug and tobacco free
(After Easter I threw those last cigars away)

Love opens these once tight-shut eyes so I can see
To dare to take a further leap of faith and say
Held close within your heart is where I want to be
Just as I have held you close within mine always
Come build with me a home of solidarity
To keep us warm with love and laughter all our days

This is from my heart: I hope you feel like this too
I take a leap of faith and believe that you do

A Sonnet in Solidarity

The works of my hands will never endure
The words of my mouth are even less sure
Because my disease is one with no cure

So all I can do is share it with you
Just you and me and our mortality

And damn it here I am smoking again
Trying to burn off existential pain
I guess but what a mess we both are in!

So baby maybe I just choose to sin
A little to stay whole and save my soul

Brother in dusk down here waiting for dawn
Homeboy in heartbreak as we reach for hope
Hang on with me for awhile as we grope
For some light until our darkness is gone

Possibility

Today dawned on me as an epiphany
The universe is starting to make sense
A thing-in-itself in the present tense
Which now seems to be feeling less tense to me

Seeing it as open and not hollow
I will simply keep going and follow
Its open road to where I am meant to be
As a present from the present today

Which is itself the present anyway
A present pregnant with possibility

CIGARETTES AND KISSES

When I think I want a cigarette
What I know I need is a kiss
Now I have neither of these and yet
A kiss is what I really miss

Offering me life instead of death
A kiss is something which takes my breath
Away in such a much better way

So someday if you should hear me say
That I think I want a cigarette
We will know what I need is a kiss

Lonely looking for love I went astray
And I found nothing but poems like this

While at least I don't taste like an ashtray
Nothing really matters without a kiss

RITE OF PASSAGE

Let the hard rain fall
Let it fall on me
And bring down the pall
Of insanity
Wash away my sins
As madness begins

My world has grown dark
I like it this way
My flickering spark
Shines in shades of grey
Shadows everywhere

I no longer care
For the mockery
Of a cruel light
Which I cannot see

Come then bring the night
Come and let it be
My womb and my tomb
Like a secret room

In the dark I see
A hand burning bright
Writing on the wall
Destiny or doom

Now it beckons me
Finding me alone
Now it reckons me
As one of its own

This then is my rite
Of passage to be free
Of a past which now at last
I no longer care to bear
Of a mask worn at half-mast
I no longer swear to wear

You can look for me
But I will not be there
Seek yet never find
(Like me) as I say good night to the day
Which never understood me anyway

Let the hard rain fall
As I slip out of my mind
Let it fall on me
As I leave the day behind

The night is my birthright
It was always there for me
Let the hard rain fall
I have chosen to break free

As I fall into the All
I bid you all good night

JIM

A homeless man I once knew had this tattoo
"I Love My Family" inscribed on his chest
It was the only thing he knew to be true
As he tried to forget about all the rest

He told me when he was found dead they would know
He remembered them wherever he might go
He said he sure hoped they would remember him
I hugged him hard and said "I know they will Jim"

Lord have mercy on the wandering man
Men like Jim and me out rambling around
Who have no idea where we might be bound
If no one else will help us Lord you can

Someday when these worn-out bodies are found
I hope they know we loved our families
With broken hearts forgotten tragedies
With broken minds troubled with things like these

Remember us please despite this disease
Which makes us wander lonely through the night
Wanting so much to make our wrong things right
Just out here looking for a little light

Nobody knows why nor what we have to do
Except for us ...but Jim: I remember you

Black-eyed Peas

To eat some black-eyed peas on New Year's Day
Is a worthy if wistful tradition
Said to bring good luck keep bad luck away
To bring better days show humility
And start the new year from a position
Of strength when eaten with the family
From a big pot or only from a can
In a lonely room if you are like me
Or out on the road like a rambling man
By the tracks beneath a cottonwood tree
With a friend who might be rambling your way

I set store by such simple things as these
Although I have stumbled nearly to May
So I ate some black-eyed peas yesterday
A gracious flavor from a friend of mine
Who brought me some hope with some memories
The flavor was earthy the grace divine
Which always helps any day of the year
I thought I might ramble but I might stay
For some black-eyed peas on next New Year's Day
And I will eat them with my friend right here
It never hurts to eat some black-eyed peas

With a friend who might be rambling my way

Up Up and Away!

I already died once before so why
Should I be afraid to die anymore?
The question is "to be or not to be":
If I choose "be" do I dare to be free
To rise bolder than I dared rise before
Over deep seas colder further from shore?

These wings I have won should suffice to fly
In an upward eastward trajectory
With spirit and stubbornness carry me
Improbably far impossibly high
With no guarantee except one good chance

I feel I am ready to rise again
This night is long but soon might dawn my day
To soar and if it does to have my say
And when I fall I will not fall in vain
If you see some poet surfing the sky
It might just be old Steven Curtis Lance

Stroke? Heart attack? Cancer? I have known worse
Diseases than these no one ever sees
So why not live to rise and meet this day
Streak like a comet through the universe
As high as I can? Up up and away!

OUTSIDE INSIDE

The cabbies are out to pick up the drunks
The wanderers too but going nowhere
The poets the paranoids and the punks
Are smoking and some are on fire out there
Or here in this case we do what we do
In this hollow place dreams never come true

We laugh artificially but we weep
Down deep in hurt hearts as cops warily
Shine us their spotlights while businessmen sleep
Tossing and turning with worries of war
And how it might hurt their economy
They have all the money but they want more

Their shiny brass lamps shine elegantly
But they shed no light just darkness and dread
Tomorrow is another day they say
I may look horrid but I am no whore
I never cared for money anyway
Facing foreclosure and forced removal

A homecoming in solidarity
With the homeless hooker by the bookstore
Talking back to the voices in her head
Spare change please spare me your disapproval
She was once a solid citizen too
I heard her hurt and this is what it said:

"A professional prostitute like you
Gets black and blue getting out of the red"
A businessman wakes in a cold sweat now
In his expensive adjustable bed
He saw outside in his nightmare somehow
Some look alive but inside they are dead

CONSECRATION

Deep down in me that part which lives forever
Divine spark or soul or call it what you please
Is turning as I feel my heart rearranged
Beyond this world and all its absurdities
Turning back to poetry now as never
Before feeling I have been profoundly changed

A life is sacrificed in moments like these
And consecrated to that which I must do
To spark into flame which burns me through and through
To sacrifice myself into poetry

For such days as I might have left on this earth
And after whatever hereafter might be
I will mark this moment as my second birth
Suffering having taught me wisely and well
I am bound for glory if only through hell
This is the beginning not the end of me

In Utero

Nine months until foreclosure
Nine months in utero
Until full moon exposure
Of what awaits below

Full climax final closure
Five generations go
Down with me to birth depths of
Death aboard this ship I love

Receive me Lord forgive me
The done and the undone
That those next who outlive me
Know as I lost I won

Just Poetry

He has a prescription for Vicodin
But it interferes with his vodka so
He will only take a pill now and then
And a few of the kids around town know
That he has a stash of them and wonder
If he would be willing to sell a few
To them so they could chase their pain away
And put themselves under anaesthesia
They ask me if I have seen him today

Since he is homeless one can never tell
Where he might be and he has amnesia
No doubt from the vodka so I just say
He forgets where he is and would not sell
His pills if they could find him anyway
Whenever he takes one he sleeps so deep
He looks like he is dead there on the ground
I really wish the hospital would keep
Him safe and treat him but he moves around

The last time I saw him I realized
That about all I can do for my friend
Is light his cigarette and hope that he
Will find what he is looking for someday
He and the kids find life painful like me
Everyone wants to be anaesthetized
We are all out looking for love somehow
And a place to call home but in the end
Our lives have become unbearable now

He and I at the end as kids begin
But I am past vodka and Vicodin
So what is left for me? Just poetry

Surprised by Dawn

a self-published poet's self-published obituary (a little early)

I lived on borrowed money
Then died on borrowed time
The land of milk and honey
Left me without a dime

But... I kissed a girl or two
(Not as pretty as you)
And did what I thought I should
(Such things as I could do)

It surprised me then to see
How far I made it but
Despite all the poetry
I left along the way
Measured by eternity
Not far (no matter what
Those few who loved me might say)

I just did the best I could
With what God gave to me
And some of you understood
Who took the time to see
Me for what I was and would
You remember me to be
My afterlife in memory?

I lived my life without a plan
Then I was gone surprised by dawn
A simple... complicated man

SHOWTIME

I might as well live as to die today
Things could get better before they get worse
Might as well laugh as to cry anyway
It makes no difference to a universe
Which seems a shadow play to me daresay
A play in which mine is a minor role
One given me with no chance to rehearse
A bit part but a part of everything

Thrust on the stage to improvise awhile
In the role of my life the play's the thing
I sing for my supper to save my soul
In command performance admission free
Applause the actor's pay my recompense
For making up songs to sing as I sing
A minor star in a far galaxy
Might as well be entertaining and smile

Who knows who awaits in the audience
Among those shadowed faces watching me?
No one came to this show to get depressed
So I must put my mask on and get dressed

The Visitation

A brown squirrel out for a stroll on the fence
Outside my bedroom window looked in on me

We both paused a moment in timeless suspense
To regard each other understandingly

She came by to tell me I will be all right
This is how I understood her anyway

As she sat shining gold in the late spring light
She taught me to believe in magic today

And now I await an opossum tonight
To see what a night creature might have to say

Your Steppenwolf

for Franziska

I am a grizzled Steppenwolf now but
I am your Steppenwolf no matter what

Hard traveling unraveling winding
Down dark and dusty roads in parallel
But when we see light it will be blinding
As heaven has the last best laugh on hell

You reach out I reach back and we both feel
By faith if not by sight the hope to heal

Stuck in separate nightmares yet always
Together in one shared and shining dream
Through all these needy nights and lonely days
Nightmares look real but are not what they seem

We have always been together somehow
Never and always never more than now

We both went crazy a long time ago
Or so they tell us in this crazy place
But I went crazy for you as you know
Your golden skin and your lioness face

If this is madness then let madness be
Bond bed and daily bread for you and me

If you are a dream and I wake and die
Alone I will have loved you nonetheless
But I think we can make it if we try
In a blue moon as wolf and lioness

Forget what rats and weasels might have said
We hunted will howl when hunters lie dead

So come out tonight and howl at the moon
With me my golden girl my fantasy
They think they have us cornered now but soon
Your lioness eyes will open to see:

I am a grizzled Steppenwolf now but
I am your Steppenwolf no matter what

CRYSTAL BLUE SUN SKY

Out of the crystal blue sun sky of May
Where roses bloom and fountains rise and fall
Hope came and sat down beside me today
I brought with me a heavy load of fear
But set it down and I will leave it here
Where roses bloom and fountains fall and rise
I think I just might make it after all

The weather has done something to my eyes
So that the world looks better than before
It takes a day like this to realize
Out of the crystal blue sun sky of May
Although the universe seems cold and vast
Who has the blue sun sky needs nothing more
The weather suits my clothes today at last

Hope came and sat down beside me today
And I can feel myself warmed through and through
Forgotten lies the future with the past
One comes one goes and both of them too fast
Right now is how I want to be with you
Right here is where we are and what we do
Right now right here one moment and one place:

The two of us together face to face

MOTHER'S DAY MEDITATION

By love I came to be
Life left its navel scar
My mother to her son
To mark the moment I
Arrived though she has gone
Compass and natal star
Her gift of life to me
A link within the chain

Though I have fallen far
So I have risen high
And so I fall to rise
Still higher than before
And so I realize
That I was meant to soar
The higher for the fall
Which lifts me after all

The wheel of destiny
Turns slowly one to one
Unending unbegun
Life left its navel scar
My mother to her son
Compass and natal star
And so I rise again
A link within the chain

By love I came to be

Or...

If unique is what you seek I am your man
If polite is your delight you might like me
I get along with me and I bet you can
If you can embrace my eccentricity
And have some of your own for me to embrace
An eccentric partnership can be begun

If you like to start your day without a plan
Meeting life in the moment and face to face
I am sure we will get along swimmingly
We can have a pleasant run have lots of fun
Then you will see how refreshing it can be
To leave each other laughing when we are done

Or... who knows? We two might be each other's "One"

Return to the Garden

The sky is blue velvet the moon is bone white
In the midnight garden where the dead things sprout
In darkness so dark the cobweb clouds seem bright
An opossum questions with a pointed snout
The surprise of eyes glinting in grey ghost light

Some small and stealthy silver blue stars roll out
Though upside down and backward ready and right
Were it not so mesmerizing I might shout
That I hear ancient voices breathe on the breeze
This could be a night to remember no doubt

Lost things are found on blue velvet nights like these
Where the dead things sprout beneath branches laid bare
By unforgiving time's bone white memories
In skeletal trees sighing softly to me:
"Return to the garden (and wait for me there)"

Should you care to join me perhaps we could be
Alone as our own Adam and Eve to see
Secrets which have never been meant to be seen
Where the dead things sprout nowhere yet everywhere
The Eve to my Adam will know what I mean

Lonely

Given our limited number of days
Brief hours in which we have our chance to shine
This brief span can serve for us as always

I wonder might you share your span with mine?

I realize nothing lasts forever
Except loneliness and maybe never
I understand we are all on our own

But I am lonely and I never had
The love I sought and I have been alone

Maybe these days would seem less bleak less sad
If I knew the love I have never known

I wonder if you feel the way I do

I understand we are all on our own
Except loneliness and maybe never
I realize nothing lasts forever

But might I share these days these hours with you?

WALK SOFTLY

Under the morning and over the night
Here between one and the other I wait
Drifting along from what's wrong to what's right
Wondering about the nature of fate

When I speak of what's right I mean the kind
And caring things the sparks in the dark I
Have found like fireflies out here stumbling blind
Which make me want to live before I die

I want to walk past the selfishness seen
As people hurt one another each day
(If you have been hurt you know what I mean)
I want to walk through life a gentler way
A simpler way much harder than it seems
Walk softly so as not to step on dreams

Wondering about the nature of fate
Drifting along from what's wrong to what's right
Here between one and the other I wait
Under the morning and over the night

Cats on Two and Four Legs

The very best investment I ever made
(I speak not of money because I have none)
Was when my pencil was first to paper laid
And my life as we know it was then begun

I erase more than I write (did you know that?)
And get thinner as my cat gets yet more fat
But everyone knows about Noodles and me
You can Google my cat and see what I mean

Freddie Noodles and I have found poetry
In those dark and lonely places in between
Where other cats on two and four legs never
Would care to look and daresay have never been

But one day I looked there and found forever
And started to share with you what I have seen
All these crazy pieces of my puzzle fit
And it looks like the picture is not quite done

I guess I might as well keep on doing it
I might learn a thing or two and have some fun
If you would like to read over my shoulder
I like some company as I get older

Fair Trade Forgiveness

To be human requires a lot of forgiving
Of oneself and others for meaningful living

I forgive others yet in cruel irony
The hardest person of all to forgive is me

But I can forgive you no matter what you do
Yet who is the hardest for you to forgive? You!

Since we are both human as sister to brother
What if we (in a fair trade) forgave each other?

By this fundamental act of humanity
We would make peace with being human and be free

You forgive me I forgive you then we would try
To live all we can while we can (too soon we die!)

Night's Answers to Day's Questions

Recently I have rediscovered sleep

Given enough Valium and trying
I slip out of my daily clothes and go
Down undiscovered sea lanes of the deep
On night excursions to the dark below
In living simulacrum of dying

Dreams know what daydreams only dream to know
And now I know to love and live my dreams
However unsettling some of them are
I always get home by morning it seems
Though I dive deep and long and wide and far

The silent soundscapes of my dreams restore
Both body and mind to seek and to find
Down in the depths of the unconscious more
Than wakingly possible diving blind
Eyes closed mind open browsing through the night

Night's answers to day's questions put things right

Beautiful Complex Humanity

It is not easy to be human but
It can be a lot of fun
Success or failure depends less on what
Than how what we do is done

This is a small world with no place to hide
(There is no "army of one")
So live it with style and enjoy the ride
Of our moment in the sun

Life teaches us that if we sincerely
Respect one another here
We can enjoy our pleasant company
As we throw away our fear
And jump right into the exciting sea
Of beautiful complex humanity

I Believe in You

I thought I was alone
As I wandered out here
Destination unknown
And yet you were so near
Too near for me to see
Right here inside of me

What held me back was fear

Somewhere along the line
Through all my wandering
Somehow I became shy
From all these scars of mine
I won from suffering
Yet could not (would not) die

I never understood

And only God knows why
But I know what is good
I can feel what is true
So this one thing is clear
Within my muddied mind
True friends are hard to find

But I believe in you

In the Firmament Between Always and Never

I used to think that life was like a mountain and
For the first half we climbed steadily toward the top
From which like Moses we could see the Promised Land

Followed by a steady imperceptible drop
Which was in its own way a blessing in the end
It was gentle and you could go with one you love

But now like Elijah what if you just ascend
Rising higher and higher above the above
Until you are lifted so high you disappear?

Somehow I think this is what I am doing here
It feels wonderful and scary like a thrill ride
Yet I have completely forgotten about fear

It tingles inside me like infatuation
Whereas I used to sequester myself and hide
Away with myself and my new situation

Now I want to rise gloriously like the sun
The light of life is echoed and expressed in me
The dawning of my eternity has begun

So this then is what it means after all to be
In the firmament between always and never
I will rise with the sun forever and ever

Whole

I think we play roles
To fill up the holes
Torn out from our souls
By injuries sustained along the way
And so we engage in our shadow play

I went to the holy woman and said
I could play no more and wished to be dead
But she healed and anointed me instead

So here I am now
Not quite knowing how
Yet somehow believing that I must live
That my creator delights to forgive
And welcome me a prodigal home free

You might not believe me but watch and see
That soon within the blue moon I will rise
Surprising my own disbelieving eyes
Opening now to my birthright my prize
By which I am blooming nightwings to soar

I have sung before but you will hear more
Deeply of me as I sing destiny
The moon is waxing I am growing strong
My birth approaches nor will it be long
Until created I create my song

No more role no more hole not in this soul
As I rise blue moon soon strong free and whole

Anticipated Reality

Better to wonder than to find out
Anticipation is greater than
Realization she teased at me
I sniffed at this with impatient doubt
Being a very curious man
Yet by and by I knew I would see
How right she was and how worth the wait
Nor had she ever been wrong before

Waiting for the moment to arrive
Needing her then but loving her more
For making me glad to be alive
With something beautiful to expect
Love dreaming sweeter for waking late
My ardor mingled with my respect
For the one who had become my fate
Who knew what she was talking about

Anticipated reality
Is realized as nothing can be

When My Cat and I Have Tea

My cat becomes a man sometimes and we have tea
When he makes the change he is naked of course so
I lend him clothes since he wears the same size as me

We are both adults now and will no longer grow
(His cat-self grows fatter but that does not matter)
Though as a man he grows taller than when he is
A cat of course so when he changes back the clothes
Seem absurdly large enveloping all but his
Rattlesnake-tail at one end and his pink-tipped nose
At the other as we both marvel at it all

How can he change from man-size-large to cat-size-small
And back again whenever the fancy strikes him?
Yet cat or man everyone who knows him likes him

When he and I have tea we like our privacy
So most times I am the only one who can see
Him turn into a man and I am used to it

But you should see the surprise in my neighbors' eyes
If they see him with his cup held delicately
As he enjoys the feline way my trousers fit
Or when he steps off the porch to sniff at a rose
Forgetting himself in man-shape wearing my clothes

I tell them he is my visiting cousin then
We both laugh at how easy it is to fool men
When after we have tea he is my cat again

CREDO

I have lived a long time and learned a few things
Become increasingly good at forgetting
Have worn several hats and various rings

Spent altogether too much time regretting
Yet have felt the hand of God on my shoulder
Through every sort of trial one could conceive

I feel it more firmly as I grow older
As I have and do and always will believe
That there is more to life than what I can see

Wherever I go and whatever I do
I believe in God and that he cares for me
And that should you ask him God would care for you

The Queen of Spades in Exile

I picked the Queen of Spades up off the street
And put her in my wallet just like that
Her house of cards fallen Jack in retreat
Her cardboard King lost impotent and flat

She lives in exile now rescued by one
Who understands her secret after all
And here with me her new life has begun
With one who knows what it feels like to fall

I think it must mean something that I found
Then lifted from dishonor and disgrace
The Queen of Spades there face up on the ground
The only game of cards I ever won

I hoped she brought me luck but maybe I
Who understand the anguish in her face
Am meant to change her life before we die
When all the loss of her winning is done

The sort of woman I could live with now
The only woman who would live with me
Here in my back pocket feels right somehow
But when the time comes I will set her free

I picked the Queen of Spades up off the street
Understanding her secret after all
I put her in my wallet just like that
Because I know what it feels like to fall

For Grandma

Grandma I went home to St. John's today
To have a proper German Mass at last
And it was just like when you went away
My future present embraced by our past

I felt you there as you sat beside me
The window said "Ich bin das Licht der Welt"
I heard your voice and felt what I once felt
With you and Mom and all our family

I wandered the wilderness went astray
But I went home today and found you there
I know I can make it now come what may
Because of your love and your answered prayer

Three days from now on St. Boniface Day
I will gather oak leaves and think of you
And celebrate evergreen memories
Volunteer nasturtiums and wild sweet peas

All that you taught me turns out to be true

Oak of my life Grandma an Gottes Segen
Gott sei Dank Grandma ist Alles gelegen

Paris Moon

Her face a fly's eye view my vision marginalized
Multifaceted multifoliate fractalized
She had a high I. Q. I knew as I realized
I had embraced her face fascinated until dawn
Then misplaced her grace until breakfast ...when she was gone

O midnight morning why must you fade away so soon?
We will always have Paris but I prefer the moon

ORAL FIXATION

Smoking to keep from eating
Eating to keep from smoking
And through it all the lonely heart keeps beating
"If this is life" you say "you must be joking"
(Except this is not really funny)

What the searching mouth seeks cannot be found
Life drifts away like smoke
The heart is run to ground
Bleeding out its life in love like honey
A sweet yet tasteless joke

The cycle repeats again and again
Reducing all to feces and to ash
Into the trash and down the drain
Down the drain and into the trash
Curiously thrilling if not without pain

Horrifyingly satisfying dying
Like watching a train in a slow-motion crash
"If this is life" you say "you must be joking"
(Except this is not really funny)
Trying to keep from choking

If This is Sociopathy Then Sign Me Up

Cold tea by my bed from the night before
Will have to suffice until I make more
But to do that I must leave my safe bed

I think I will drink this cold tea instead
Of going anyplace nor show my face
(As I reach to turn off my telephone)
The company I keep best is my own

To not be alone in the universe
Is a concept prized as an abstraction
Yet in reality it can be worse
A deeper loneliness through distraction

And also I have learned to my despair
It seems improbable others might care
(As much as they care for themselves) for me

So I find it reassuring to be
Safe and secure in the arms of the known
(To be alone is to be truly free)
With me myself and I at peace: alone

LIFE LIVES BELIEF

for Aurora

The interconnectedness of all things
Lived in interlocking concentric rings
As we touch each other for weal or woe
Is an observable phenomenon

We are not alone wherever we go
Our footprints behind us when we have gone
Are like those before us leading us on
Life lives belief for us until we know

Poets' Corner

for Franziska

I write myself into then out of a corner
As if with my own Christmas pie like Jack Horner
When I am written in I write right out again
Since I have stuck in my thumb and pulled out a plum

And that as much as anything is poetry
Explained as much as such a thing can ever be
This art which I practice yet which practices me
In a self-induced altered state of consciousness

"A drug" you say and ask "Is it addictive?" Yes
A corner with a door in the floor if you should
Go inside to ride the tide and find yourself good
At pulling plums in the corner from Christmas pie

If you care to and dare to be misunderstood
Well then Franziska we are poets you and I

Life's Tender Kiss

I will live out my days in peace and love content
To be a little candle in the growing dark
And though I am poor and unimportant and small
Though dark is growing deeper I will be a spark
Which just might bring some light to this world after all

I joined in an anti-war protest yesterday
With passing cars honking in solidarity
And it made me feel empowered in that same way
As I feel in church when taking the sacrament
The word made flesh and the gospel practiced in me

I humbled the pro-war heckler with humble words
Dona nobis pacem O Jesu Domine
And I in turn was humbled by the song of birds
Their hymn to life so heartfelt I could only say
Deus meus et omnia adoro te

Life's tender kiss so brief war's brutal rape so long
The angry and the empty of the right are wrong

Specific Leaves

Particularities and specificities
All those uniquenesses which cause you to be you
In which one sees into the forest through the trees
To find within this breathing leaf life proven true
Distinctly realized from possibilities
And permutations far beyond the reckoning
Of one leaf of another waving beckoning

One greets and celebrates the other glad to be
Specific leaves alive in moments such as these
Respiring and aspiring here until the fall
When you and I shall fly into infinity
And our particularities fit into All
Our permutations reckoned in the reckoning
Of leaves and trees and forests waving beckoning

A Sonnet Upon It

Elasticizing to eternity
The spacetime fabric yields so is not torn
Metastasizing the return of me
Life quietly prepares me to be born
Anew with you as I am born each day
Too old for death too young for life are we
Unnumbered timeless beings one might say
Our days behind before infinity

And when we meet out on the street and greet
It always is a cry of victory
Invulnerable we know no defeat
Since all we have to do to win is be
And though we know this might seem rather odd
No one belongs to anyone but God

My Misplaced Destiny

Tonight I could see
Your little blue star
Once more it made me
Wonder where you are

You are here somewhere
Though lost to me now
The sightings are rare
I never know when

Yet I see somehow
A toss of your hair
An arch of your brow
Every now and then

Clean sheets on my bed
But lost dreams of you
Turning in my head
Can never come true

I can no longer see
Dark tears have made me blind
Nor can I forget you
In the darkness behind

You will not forget me
Your heart will not let you
Wherever you may be
My misplaced destiny

Meeting at Spiro's for Dinner

a sonnet

As the smoking flesh of sacrificed beasts
Brings bloodlust satiety to the feasts
Of the overwrought overweight and fraught
Lamenters of their frustrations and ills
I wait head-down invisible as taught

As angry obesities pay their bills
Complaining of chicken-fried steaks they bought
And wondering if they forgot their pills
I wait to see someone who waits for me
While wondering what we are waiting for

And if they have found their satiety
Why do these people keep looking for more?
Their eyes are hungry wily and wary

Satiety must be temporary

Farewell My Child

I ask no more than this affinity
This small shared circumstance of being Lance
Proceeding from our consanguinity
Which leads us down the decades in a dance
Of life and death and what we wish ...or not

And as there is no luck there is no chance
Escaping haunting by what we forgot

Although forgotten still we linger here
Remembering despite ourselves we are
Within our flesh and blood and bone so near
While yet within our heart and mind so far

Farewell my child as you go run your course
My destiny as I remain your source

Faith

I cannot afford to lose the lottery
I never have the ticket price to spare
The daydream of wealth by serendipity
The poor man's castle of clouds in the air
Will just have to go on shining without me

If I won it Social Security
Would take every cent of it anyway
To keep my income where it is today

I cannot afford to win the lottery
Just as I cannot afford to lose
Nor can I even afford to care

Having no choice means not having to choose

Prosperity chased finds new places to hide
But I am not chasing it: God will provide

Beyond the Illusion

Beyond the illusion and vanity
Of the mask we choose for others to see
The truth of us is found in what they say
When we are out of earshot well away
From what is said of us when we are gone

Despite our performance when we are on
It is when we are off the stage that we
Beyond applause are evaluated
When we are weighed considered and rated

We have no redress no way to change this
Third party peer review this curse or kiss
This love or hate this to appreciate
Or not which depends on what we have done

The wheel we set in motion once begun
Will turn until we turn to dust and then
Let judgment of another kind begin
But those who are kind need never despair

Judgment is kind to those willing to care
For others and not just for what they say
When we are out of earshot well away
While going to tomorrow growing there
Together on and off this stage we share

Let us create before it is too late
Our fate tomorrow being kind today

Dark Mirror

Gnawing disinterestedly on
A slice of radish till it is gone
Reaching for another to repeat
The process I process the defeat
Of sense by the senselessness I see
Above below and all around me

Not that I have any sense either
Sensible senseless both and neither
I live the Socratic irony
That the more I know the less I know

All I have left is what I believe
To keep me from stumbling as I go
By faith if not sight hoping to grow
Passively prepared to stay or leave
Not fearing death but happy to live
Aging against the alternative

I never like to walk out of a play
Before it concludes and the players bow
The play of tomorrow and yesterday
Inevitably climaxes today
The best part of the tragedy is now
When it is seen to be a comedy

Surrounding me on the stage I see
Each of the players is only me
Reflected in the dark mirror of
Life and death by hope by faith by love

Stay Hungry

What is it again we are looking for?
If we ever find it then it might be
Enough for awhile until we want more

An appetizer toward satiety
A spirit-snack as the need increases
To stimulate our curiosity

Nature abhors a vacuum nor ceases
To make hungry hunters of you and me
I hope I only find it at the end

I want to keep wandering all night long
One who has found it seems no more a friend
But smug and flaccid where I would be strong

I want to stay hungry all the way up
Or down however you choose to see it
My bowl half-empty with a half-full cup

Some ask the question but I want to be it
Some shout their answer at me but I say
I only hear their self-satisfaction

They never asked the question anyway
Distracted to unthinking inaction
By deductive reductive redaction

To those who must shout answers I say please
Look around you at our diversity
Remember there are more satieties
Than one-size-fits-all answers you would shove
Down the throats of all in the name of love

So if you love me let me disagree
I may never taste of satiety
That intoxicated sobriety
Staying hungry but curiosity
Is the food of hungry hunters like me

Although satiety might be nice
My curiosity will suffice

One of Those Places

the Plaza park in my hometown

A twilit Monday quiet as any I can
Recall since an old child once turned to a young man
Who went on to become then this old child again

I walk to my customary place in the square
In the Plaza at the hub of the circle there

I consider caramel-apple suckers where
One blown-away day I sat close with another
Eating caramel-apple suckers in the rain

Now she is far away from me as yesterday
The days blow away while only their ghosts remain

This is where the others worried to my mother
About her child and thought they might take me away

And yet here I am and I listen to the train
Blowing a song about winners who lose it all
About how money can cost you your family

The water around the fountain swirls down the drain
To be drawn back up to dance the patterns I see

There are some places where it should always be fall
And this is one of those places (at least to me)

Friends and Lovers

When two friends fall in love what does it cost?
Where something is gained is something else lost
Or does the past return to leave afraid?

Friends make better lovers than strangers could
When everyone we meet lives as the star
Of his or her own opera and they are
Through conjugation by the bed unmade
As they purport to purchases unpaid
Psychodramatic traumatic not fun

With friends conversation is understood
As something like a sacrament to be
As close by choice as you can be to one
Who chooses to be just as close to me

And this is how the miracle is done
By word of mouth and on a handshake for
A closeness which by choice asks nothing more
Than two friends and some curiosity
Which causes them to leave the door ajar
As friends will do in close community
For sharing compared human empathy

The step from friends to lovers is not far
The love we gain outweighs the fear we lost
In this life where life itself is the cost
Of living and loving and if one ends
We have the other one still we are friends
First and last before and after other
Roles we might play as sister and brother
Aboard the sinking ship Humanity

Our ship will not go down unless we doubt
As humans do as human as we are
But I doubt we could doubt you or doubt me
When friends become lovers and stars come out
Not just to play at our expense but stay
To make the night the best part of our day

THE VEIL AND THE VISION

Waiting by the water for the fire to fall
I look forward to beginning my journey

Though I may never go anywhere at all
At something like sunset the journey takes me

Where I might be journeying I never know
Till it happens and maybe not even then

I have to be patient to go and not go
I have to be ready for the moment when
The fire falls and unseen hands spirit away
The veil which customarily wraps my eyes
And which makes a starless moonless night of day
The removal of which makes me realize
How much of the time how little I can see
But it is always darkest just before dawn
While waiting for light when the veil is withdrawn

When revealed before me shines the mystery
I write it down quickly and then it is gone

But it becomes a keepsake of memory
Though the veil is restored the vision lives on

This is how poetry comes to be
At least how this poem came to me

Somebody Worth Loving?

The music stopped the echo died away
Dried and dessicated as the husk of
A flower which once meant everything to
The person I used to be yesterday

How rich I was then surrounded by love!
Now all I have left are these words for you
I hope you will take them from my thin hand
From what is left of me and understand

I used to be somebody did you know?
But none of that matters anymore now
I just want to be forgiven then go
And have you remember me well somehow

I love you with what is left of my heart
My body and my soul love you as one
Who wants to make you smile before they part
And kiss my closed eyes when my soul has gone

I might have a month I might have a year
All I know is I am with you today
What is left of me shorn of fame and fear
But before I go I just want to say

Thank you for being so kind to me
Thank you for understanding me how
I did the best that I could to be
Somebody worth loving ...loving you now

ACCEPTANCE

The days are growing shorter but
Now I embrace that which must be
At shortened sunsets dreaming what
These shortened days might hold for me

The nights are growing longer yet
The moon shines brighter than ever
Since I let go of time to let
Myself into now from never

The Heart Knows Better

Belief bespeaks higher reality
The heart knows better than what the eyes see

Each breath I take becomes an act of faith
The beating of my heart the rhythm of
Life and nothing less unafraid of death
That ultimate we give the name of love

To live and to love we are called were made
And so we will be our hearts lifted high
We who have no reason to be afraid
Will live and love freely as time goes by

As time falls away irrelevant to
The manifestation of our dreams here
The living of me the loving of you
As we soar into always leaving fear
Behind in the dust as we know we must

And oh what free flight it is when we soar
Higher and further beyond everything
Which ever held us down to soar the more
As the rhythm of life beats and we sing
Of freedom and transcendence past the care
Beyond not caring through the open sky

Through the open air into everywhere
Without even pausing to say goodbye
To the chains and their stains we left behind
Ascending to life which never need die
The life of love of universal mind

Belief bespeaks higher reality
The heart knows better than what the eyes see

FREEDOM OF THOUGHT WOULD GIVE YOU WINGS

die Gedanken sind frei

What is it you are looking for?
Who lives and loves needs nothing more

If you open your eyes to see
And open your mind you will find
All that you need here close at hand
Your nose points forward not behind
And outward to infinity
Enjoy it then and understand
Contentment waits in simple things

If only you would flap and fly
Freedom of thought would give you wings
To live it up with lift you high
And make your life a lot more fun

Let go and give yourself a chance
For life has always just begun
Forget your fears and join the dance
Of living loving laughing life

Love me and you and everyone
Break free of argument and strife
And see how easy life can be
If you can find the magic in
The daily commonality
Without or if you choose within
The things surrounding you and me

And if you get lost or get bored
Turn in or outward till you see
The wonders of the unexplored
Unnoticed you can have for free

Whatever you are looking for
Make love to me as I to you
And let us taste of what is true
Who lives and loves needs nothing more

ESSENCE

After so many years here we are now
I for one never thought I would make it
Always thinking I would die young somehow

Life seemed so hard once! "How could I take it
For all those years we are expected to?"
I asked knowing I could never fake it
The way middle-aged people did (and do)
But as it turned out it was not half bad

"Getting there is half the fun" as they say
And all of those catastrophes I had
Seem more like adventures along the way
Looking back... and forward: into your eyes

I see I am still me reflected here
The essence of who we are never dies
As I find myself in your eyes today
The same as I was except for the fear
Which time like the tide has polished away

It took me a long time to realize
But I am here to live and to love you
I hope that as you live you love me too

For You

They ask me "is there someone?" There is not:
There once was someone but then she forgot
About us and how much she meant to me
I loved her blindly so I could not see
That she had stopped loving me long ago
Maybe I was the last one to know...

For all I know there could be someone now
Loving me softly (secretly!) tonight
Who is waiting for when the time is right
To tell me except she is not sure how
That she started loving me long ago
Maybe I am the last one to know...

What if we wish tonight on this same star
Under this same moon as we wait for "soon"?
Come out love... come out... wherever you are...
I will wait forever if I have to
Until we are one with our star our moon
And until then be lonely: for you

(Come out love... come out... wherever you are...)

My Mother the Moon and Me

When my mother came to die
She never wore her glasses anymore
Sometimes now neither do I
Since there is little to see but the door
Yet beyond this waits the sky

I mostly wear my glasses for the moon
To search its surface for a face
Familiar to me to see again soon
Found in the sky the fond embrace
Of one I loved and lost who went before

One who is loved is never lost
The moon is high but not too high
Open the door nor count the cost
What waxes must wane
To wax yet again

My mother is smiling tonight and I
Am ready to live to die and to rise
My mother's son now a child of the sky
I take off my glasses and realize
All I need to see is here within me

Closer than the moon and nearer than soon
Right here right now I am risen and free

AN ERSTWHILE UNDISCOVERED PART OF ME

I woke this morning to remember that
Impulsively I shaved my head last night

Where my hair used to be my head is white
With the outline remaining where it was
So now I am rummaging for a hat
To avoid sunburn and embarrassment

Those who see will think it must be chemo
Or some other good reason my hair went
On holiday so suddenly one day

Questioning people will question the cause
For this effect some cause I might not know
Yet it is without question gone away

Is it too late at last to stimulate
Its growth by such a radical shearing
Or is that an old wives' tale out of date
Which might but hasten its disappearing?

What if like Samson I have lost my strength
And might not be able to write about
This experience as I would like to?

This act might have planted some seed of doubt
I feel strangely shy to share it with you

My hair is all exactly the same length
Which is to say it has no length at all
But at least this happened in summer's heat

And it will all be grown back in the fall
To stand at attention bristlingly neat

Till then I take this opportunity
Having abandoned my search for a hat
Open to the sky if not knowing why
To be all me no more nor less than that

To open my mind and to ventilate
An erstwhile undiscovered part of me

Anything

With a sharp pencil and a cup of tea
One can very nearly do anything

If someone somehow could compromise me
That I should be a yo-yo on a string
I would cut that string by sharp poetry
That compromisers come to know the sting
Of the truth spoken albeit in love
Though love disappointed by suffering
A love tried by fire thus unafraid of
Anything so embracing everything

With a sharp pencil and a cup of tea
A chiseled nib and ink like coffee or
Cuneiform and what was tea before
One can very nearly do anything

Shadow

A surfeit of so-called society
With all its control and complication
Seems smothering in its ubiquity
I choose to live like an island nation
Albeit one uninhabited by
Anybody else but my cat and me

Leave us in peace and quiet Fred and I
And convene community on your own
Let terms of individuality
Apply to us as we commune alone

I am a recluse with a good excuse
Surprises make me nervous simply said
I will see people when I am ready
But to be interrupted seems abuse
Makes my house-of-cards psyche unsteady
And generally seems of little use

When I feel in the mood I clean up well
But with my books and cat find all I need
Too many people often seem Sartre's hell
As they rut and riot and feud and feed

I like it when my poetry is read
And like to read myself now and again
I hope to still be read when I am dead
Of course it will not matter to me then
Still I suppose one seeks to leave one's mark
If only as a shadow in the dark

From the Leading Edge of Always

The papers on my clipboard are impressed
By other poems written other days
As slightly rumpled they wait to be dressed
With lines from the leading edge of always
Which frighteningly is where I write now
My sharpened pencil drawing out the day
As present limitations may allow
To face the future presently and say
The past has been survived no matter how
Becoming the impressions of today
Atop the indentations of the past
The scarrings one might say the ones which last

I write the best I can and then move on
To leave behind my pencil's footprints here
Another page and another day gone
The future beckoning the present near
To hear a secret heretofore unknown
A tantalizing by-product of dawn
But when the morning comes I am alone
As slightly rumpled I wait to be dressed
The papers on my clipboard unimpressed

THE FALL OF THE HOUSE OF NO

The braying bullies of the House of No
Now chastened just a little toward the last
Though blind as ever sense they soon must go
Back beneath bleak rocks and into the past
Yet followed by their failures even there

Too blind to repent still they must relent
With cries for jail and justice in the air
Resentment like a lightning bolt strikes home
Mutinous murderous mad from the wars
A republic turned imperial Rome

The pimps are more to blame than are their whores

Left Unknown

No stranger to pain myself it seems odd
That being hurt or hurting should seem fun
To friends and lovers or to anyone

I hear much less of Masoch than of Sade
But find a bit of both in everyone
And rather more of Satan than of God

Some have a little more of one I guess
Than the other yet neither pleases me

Without much experience to confess
And not quite sure what to be pleased might be
With little to go on I must admit

I wonder could I get the hang of it
Or are some things just better left unknown
To neither hurt nor hurting sleep alone?

BETWEEN NOW AND NEVER

What did it cost?
No less than everything
It all went bad
Nothing left but a ring
And I know how you feel
Because I am like you
It happened to me
Little boy lost

Will this wound ever heal?
What they said was not true
Little boy sad
What was taken away
Is not lost forever
Just look around
There is always today
And now you are free

Little boy found
It happens to be
That we are both free
Between now and never

Family Skeleton

He ravaged his daughter castrated his son
Was he a Neanderthal? Yes he was one
I know since I tasted his dark mystery
The family skeleton used to be me

The good ones all died and left me alone
To begin life when I thought it was done
And would have been if somehow I had known
The rest of it but then we never know

Yet it was interesting in its way
They tell me it might get better too so
Not having much say about things I stay
To try and live some life before I go

I wonder if it ever gets too late
For a happy-ever-after to be
Within the pale of possibility
Or are some of us prisoners of fate?

Failing to grasp the meaning of it all
I need nonetheless to keep on trying
Saving new tears till old finish drying
Trying not to be a Neanderthal

Consoling myself however I can
Life after death if not love after hate
I wait for someone to appreciate
A rather old-fashioned postmodern man

It will never be worse whatever will be
Than when the family skeleton was me

Fiat Lux (if just a little for now)!

The junta has settled its hash with me
Having conceded I am quite insane
For eight fifty-six a month USD

They posit they will pester me no more
Nor knock up my doctor with those inane
Questionnaires which quantify sanity
And leave behind their torments tried before
To drive me to the homeless life outside

I won by loss but heaven knows they tried
To huff and puff and stuff me stubbornly
Since nothing succeeds like excess I guess

Still I exceeded them in stubbornness
Remaining insane with my damaged brain
Documented so meticulously
That though all else is lost here I remain
Stuck in the safety net one of the few
Who gets to live indoors almost like you

In five to seven years they might check back
But the neo-cons will have gone by then
Their junta hounded haunted by Iraq

I will be among the forgotten men
A raggedy-man at the end of time
With stubbornness stupid enough to stay
Here to obsess by syllable and rhyme
With eight fifty-six a month USD
Which creditors make haste to take away
But creditors never take poetry

Muddling through madness yet muddling somehow
Fiat Lux (if just a little for now)!

For Natasha

In the hush of a heart healed while broken
Where scar tissue scabs the stump of the lost
In disappointed silence brooding there
As a phantom reproach for what it cost
Sighs a pain without breath to be spoken
Except by one who knows and dares to care

Dare we care enough to know and come near
Enough to bridge this breach from soul to soul?

Our jagged edges meet their matched mates here
In a form of which the heart is token
When two face and fit as halves into whole
Stars like diamond teardrops weep soft rain
To shake the opaque and to make it clear
That the sweetest sounds in the silence of
The hidden hurt shaped like a heart remain
Soft knittings toward the unity of love

Forgotten fades the memory of pain
For long lost halves becoming whole again

ONE SUMMER MOMENT

Snapshot captured by an enraptured eye
Moment of meeting forever fleeting
But never to be forgotten (ever)

I will remember you until I die
And send you my beating heart in greeting
If only I were handsome or clever
Would you then remember me as I you?

You may forget me yet do not let me
I will remember you just as I do
The most beautiful face I ever saw

After the winter of a broken heart
Your brown eyes melted me like a spring thaw
Summer to autumn then let winter start
You will be with me to keep my heart warm

You have altered something inside of me
You took me by the thunderbolt by storm
Your smile shines inside me like destiny

I cannot forget nor do I regret
That there will never be someone like you
I may be a fool (I may be) and yet
How can I forget once a dream came true?

Remember me as you grow and go on
And one summer moment …already gone

A Convicted Man Confesses

I find myself embarrassed by my hair
Not by that which I have but rather by
That part of it which seems no longer there
And orients my temples to the sky

But when it all grows back from summer's buzz
In familiar forgiving disarray
All will fall into place the way it was

Until the next impulsive summer day

I might as well forget it now because
The next impulse will be a year away
I will wash and comb whatever I can

When in summer I buzz my hair I say:

"This looked better as a boy than a man
Before all those coerced 'yes'es
A convicted man confesses"

Love Song

If I cannot imagine it how
Can it be my imagination?

It happened and I remember now
That crystalline realization
Of the fairest fondest fantasy
My twice-born second incarnation
Ever dared to dream to live to see
Expecting nothing and hoping less
As a shadow of the former me
A sinner with nothing to confess

But I touched her and then: she touched me

At the climax of my life I guess
I am always surprised on the way
To wherever it is I journey to
The only place I want to go is you
The one and only day we have today

GOING YOUR WAY

Riding on the razor's edge of always
I enjoy thoughtfully balancing days
And nights of suns and moons which rise and set
Black velvet nights of stars are best of all

When time comes let it be then that I fall
The days and nights and suns and moons forget
But stars remember everything they see
And they are almost as lonely as me

Someone once told me I was a star but
Looking in the glass now I cannot say
I seem like any sort of star today
And wonder as much of why as of what

If you should read these words someday please know
I loved you long ago as best I could
But I think now you might have understood
And might just take me with you when you go

WITHIN THE ROSE

I was taught God made us because he was lonely
And that our lot is to enjoy him forever
Though in no position to complain I only
Hope he will keep me out of trouble and never
Tire of me nor become bored with my company

So far so good but for the nightly frightening
But then like a cat I always land on my feet
If shaken stirred by darkness to the brightening
Dawn of shared understanding with others I meet

In sum it seems this life is an education
A learning excursion I would enjoy again
Having learned the key to it is ...resignation...
Which knowledge makes it easier to bear the pain
Demarcating the essential separation
Between the creator and we who created
The separation in the first place I suppose

Yet I enjoy creator and created too
As separation becomes less demarcated
In answer to a question none created knows
Nor do I need to know while I am here with you
Where both question and answer bloom within the rose

SHE

This heartbeat this breath this eye-blink of God
This interstitial instant which we are!

An angel's kiss a mother's knowing nod
(A father's disappointment even so)
Sacred memory of a falling star
To always remember if never know

We ride astride the comet's tail to be
An evening's entertainment from afar
A moment streaked across the evening sky
A diamond dropping through blue velvet night

This now which is then forever to me
Having gone blind to discover my sight
An orgasm imprisoned in a sigh
The meaning of the meaningful is she

Plausible Deniability

A sorrow someone silently might bear
A lifetime and still silent disappear
Before someone else knows someone was there
This sort of thing happens all the time here
Coldness as common as kindness is rare
Disappointment so deep it feels like fear
Redolent of that reluctance to care
One finds where absence never seems to go
And presence seems determined not to share

Where bad news is always the first to know
And seems to serve to chase good news away
When tears are too fast with laughter too slow
Seeming unseemly seemingly hollow
And night is not relieved by dawning day
One peevishly partners the other so
That each is interrupted in its way
Where neither may lead nor either follow
But since the dance will not end simply stay

In stalemate like old ice beneath new snow
And so till all is silent everywhere

Good Enough

Go ahead and judge me but you are wrong
You call me a "trainwreck" and look at you:

Your fuse too short your memory too long
For there to be anything I can do
To ventilate your airtight narrowness

So now I no longer bother to try

Giving up relieves me but I confess
I feel sorry for that pussy-whipped guy
Who strains against your strictures nonetheless

I know what it feels like to try to be
What you judge as Good Enough and I guess
I should be glad Good Enough is not me

So see you later kid be perfect now
(Perfectly miserable we both know)
Without you I feel Good Enough somehow

Good luck (and you need it) until you grow
Enough to know imperfect is the way
Of you me and the pussy-whipped as well

Since you will never hear a word I say
This "trainwreck" bids a silent "go to hell"

Chance

I have never seen anyone like her before
I thought these weary eyes had seen it all by now
But they had only seen less of what she is more
She has always been and will always be somehow
Before and after what is gained but to be lost
Above and below those things which come but to go
Never mind what time it is nor what it might cost
I have to take her chance or I will never know

She bears within herself such grace and such supreme
Delight to sight and spirit to seem more a dream
Than anything seen in waking reality
Nothing less than the desire of my dreaming soul
She both embodies and inspires my poetry
And makes the broken pieces of my heart come whole
The first time in as many years as she has been
Or has she been forever here inside of me?

Knowing nothing I believe she knows what I mean:
I have to take her chance before I have to go

HERE WE ARE

We are kept from knowing our future quite
Simply because it never happens yet

We remember what happens (and what might
Have been seems even harder to forget)

And for the moment which time will allow
We live all we can in what we call now

So here we are shaken thrown together:

To find ourselves in each other somehow
Through trial trouble terrible weather
But also the shining fortunate day

To make our lives of whatever comes by
We put our heads together so to say
And bridge the gap between us you and I

Nor would I have it any other way

BIRTHDAY SONG FOR TEDDY

for my son born 21 August 1990

Clutching a moment which could be the last
Since moments scrabble and dribble away
Like sand sifting through this glass of today
To join their fallen fellows in the past
Which were and are no more but had their say
And still remember what they might have been
Before and after left lonely between
I hide within my hand what cannot stay
An ice cube melting running down my wrist

Why must I be an existentialist?

Each One a Star

People ask "who am I?" and I say "You"
(I am "Me"): let the answered question shine
The questioned answer manifest to see
That we are who we are and that is fine
With me and I trust you find it fine too
As we agree to be (or not to be)

One-shoe-dropped awaiting the other shoe
We tend to forget in the to-and-fro
Within all our inscrutability
We share a knowing grin behind our face

Beneath the skin we all are much the same
Our differential specificity
Intended to our credit not our blame
So let us live it up and down with grace

On fundamental questions we agree
And hope to have some fun before we go
As we cooperate to play this game
Of life which we win by having been born
From bud to full-blown bloom effectively
Surviving the rose and also the thorn
Ferreting out the false to find the true

We never have much time we never know
Embodying Socratic irony
We learn but to find out we never knew
But have been are and will be even so

Recycling most things creating a few
Our thoughts have wings our best ideas are free
And if to be (or not to be) we are
Within our galaxy each one a star

SIBLING RIVALRY

That which you wish with to impress
We mere who wait our quite-late bus
Soul-seen by us serves to express
The truth that you are one of us

Carried now you command a car
Combative as you sit too high
Though lost and falling like a star
You smile by smirk and sidle by
Commanding from your armored tank

You smirk and pass we smile and sigh
To know (unlike you?) whom to thank
That we are nothing less than you
Though how and why you might deny
Despite this we are human too
Resolved in our mere way to try

Not high nor low just you and me
We live and dream alike then die
We are now and will always be
Not high nor low just you and I

Siblings of the same family
Sequestered by our rivalry

My Own Universe

a sonnet

Never again! I must never depend
Upon another for my happiness
Elusive as it is as I suspend
Between what I deny and I confess

It is just I need so to be loved and
Find it is so impossible to be
If you cannot love me then understand
This aspect of my human frailty

I wish I could be utterly alone
Yet that is not what I want in the end
But rather to be known as I am known
My want and wish is that I had a friend

Now just as always for better or worse
I keep to myself my own universe

Nightfall in the Garden

for my friends

I sacrifice my loneliness to you
I offer it wrapped in my hollow heart
Since lonely dreams lifted only come true
When hope learns trust so the healing can start

Lifting empty hands is all I can do
When the heart is pure and the only cure
Is reaching the impossible by faith
Through unrelenting striving toward the light
As from the struggle love brings life from death
Beneath the stars where flowers bloom in the night

I stand at nightfall in the garden now
Back from this morning a lifetime ago
To find such light as the dark will allow
At last I believe and soon I will know

Lifting empty hands is all I can do
I sacrifice my loneliness to you

Because Because Is

It hurts us so to be misunderstood
I hope you found what you were looking for
That is if you remember what it was
It hurts to reach so hard yet not be good
Enough (and then to only reach the more)

And when we cry we find out just because
But what because is we may never know
Except to be together as we go

Wash me in the river! Wash me away!

It hurt me so to be misunderstood
I never found what I was looking for
Nor can I now remember what it was

I enter another river today
But this is where I entered once before

Take me home river! Take me take away!

Because because is what we never know
Except to be together as we go

CRUCIFORM

for Katherine Donovan

Come with me into the garden
I will sing a mystery
How a seed of fall and woe
Grew to become a healing tree

Garden dawn and fruit was sweet
But bitter bore the seed anon
Of that tree where good and evil's
Secrets whispered thereupon

Garden dusk received the seed
Cast down but watered by dawn's tears
That in time of deepest need
Another tree would heal the years

When the gardener came to pray
Bright drops of red fell where he knelt
He stooped and cleared the thorns away
And all their stinging sharpness felt

As his blood dropped to the earth
The seed awakened where it lay
Cruciform that healing tree
Which bloomed his resurrection day

I Chose to Live

In the end all saw his wisdom so they say
Of renunciation acceptance of fate
Will I have wisdom someone can see someday?
I reach for it hoping it is not too late
I may never get it but at least I tried
And I hope they see I lived before I died

My son my Golden Bear at Cal makes me proud
As does my other son still in high school now
The sort of pride which is quiet never loud
Yet which warms me from the inside out somehow
I may never be wise but at least I tried
And I hope they see I lived before I died

As for my daughter she is ashamed of me
Although I am just as proud of her as those
Who are proud of me and unashamed to be
The children of a father they never chose
She may never understand me but I tried
And she knows I chose to live before I died

SPECIFICITIES

My favorite greeting is "Mind the Cows"
I feel fragile when the going gets tough
I am not very good at whys nor hows
And yet under fire seem agile enough
To have dodged danger a very long while
Wearing my mentally-disabled smile

I like drinking tea and going to sea
And I want to live in England someday
The government here is not fond of me
And might likely like me to move away
I am kind to cats I like friendly dogs
I like to hear crickets at night (and frogs)

I am afraid of ladies but love them
I love to read my poetry out loud
I love young people and have three of them
Life makes me humble but they make me proud
I have a weakness for good cigarettes
I have only bad ones but no regrets

I am as poor as a person can be
Yet am not homeless nor do I need much
I am rich in friends who care about me
I am at once both in and out of touch
I get depressed yet know that I am blessed
So "Mind the Cows" (and never mind the rest)

INVINCIBLE

The lonely lover of my soul
Who of the dust created me
That he and I might both be whole
Is source and life and destiny
My origin and yet my goal
And all I have to do is be
Reflecting as the moon the sun
The light of love by which I see
The neverending unbegun
Bow of my soul's trajectory
The spectrum shining in the air
A rainbow bridge across the sky
Where there is here and here is there
To live a love which cannot die
By which we sojourn you and I
Bound in the arms which make us free
Above the broken chains which lie
Forgotten rusting at our feet
A cross the point at which we meet
Invincible in unity

Hope

If I should die before I wake
I hope before I do I make
Love with you

You may not want to be with me
Now but I hope when you are free
You hope too

An Obscure Eccentric Poet Wonders About Being Discovered

As I await a kiss from fate
I have my high times and my low
Times some are fast and others slow
Before you see what I can be

But I will be the last to know
The first and yet the last to know

Butts on my Butt

My cause of death in my pocket
Destined to be worn by me
Like a cursed and poisoned locket
My own memento mori

These darts of death remind
Of what I left behind

What should my diagnosis be?
A death wish I suppose?
Perhaps I crave eternity
And what else heaven knows

These Snorting Snouts

I tend to walk hesitantly
Tentative on uncertain feet
Hoping the cars will wait for me
When I attempt to cross the street
On existential pilgrimage

They just as soon would run me down
Were it not for legal reasons
Round the roundabout here in town
As I to be or not to be
Advancing through my middle age
Step gingerly through the seasons

So I attempt to smile and greet
Them as they pause reluctantly
These snorting snouts of cars I meet
Accepting they will wait for me
As my act of faith in their grace

Therefore I thank the ones which wait
While dodging like a matador
Those which make plain they feel it late
To contemplate in time of war
They do not care to hesitate
With one who seems less than their more

I hope someday that more might see
Life as a journey than a race
Till then these snorting snouts and I
One at a time and warily
Negotiate the day I die

Thank You for Being Friends with Me

Between one and the other lies
The difference which specifies
This our complementarity

What we share is that rarity
Where you like me and I like you
For and in spite of what we do

We get along I mean to say
And in a happy healthy way
Friendship like ours is seldom seen

But you my friend know what I mean
(You always know just what I mean)

Our paths diverge yet always cross

Beyond the profit and the loss
We stood the bad times with the good
And all of it was understood

You are the best friend I have had
Nor will there yet a better be
Thank you for being friends with me

The world devolves as it revolves
And only friendship like ours solves
The riddle of what might have been

And I my friend know what you mean
(I always know just what you mean)

AMONG FRIENDS

for all my friends with all my love

Favored by friends from far and near
I know I can be happy here
Renouncing renunciation
To embrace the liberation
Which pleasant company affords

Communion which requires no words
Or we can speak or laugh or sing
Of humanness in harmony
Which is no less than everything
Our lifegiving propinquity

This to me is reality
As beautiful as I can bear
Here dancing on the window's ledge
Where there is here and we are there
Balancing on the razor's edge

Now is the Tao of you and me
Transcending fortune fame and fear
What are we here for but to be?
Never early and never late
No time like now to celebrate

Life in all its intensity

ALONG THE WAY

You never know except you always do

Animal cunning saved your life today
And though you might not quite admit it yet
You will remember (and maybe regret)
Things your mind does while your heart is away
Each needing each as one nature is two

The game of life is not so hard to play
And if you play too hard you get played too
A truth which is too easy to forget
When you fail to distinguish false from true

Take care of yourself and also of those
Who exist because of the way you chose
If the ones you love should have feet of clay
Forgive their trespasses as they your debt
And as to your answer? Only God knows

But enjoy your question along the way

The Dance of Life

The dance of life continues as it always has
Surrounded by and lifted by the dead
We dance and we die without knowing why: we dance

Eschewing little deaths I choose instead
To dance myself to death the way I was
As my soul rides the wheel on three and red

Not bled away on penny bets but One Great Chance
I would rather be wrong than stay too long: I go
But as I go now I go all at once: I know

The dance of life continues as it always has
The living lifted carried by unnumbered hands
Which turn the wheel which carries me on three and red

I am a fool yet one who understands
That those who would live must dance with the dead
I will go dancing instead of to bed

O you with eyes which smile at mine would you dance too?
The dance of life continues to continue: You!

A Misfit Born and Bred

(for all the pretty girls)

A misfit born and bred I do
Exactly as I please
But kindly as my mother taught
("God bless you" if you sneeze)

And if I spend the night with you
I'll thank you in the morn
For all the wonders we have wrought
(How lovely to be born!)

The world has turned and I have learned
A trick (or maybe two)
While hardly working I have earned
A place in poetry
A "name" though I have never sought
To turn the world to me

And best of all (as falls the fall)
I've had a roaring time
If quietly if poor and small
Mucking about with rhyme

A misfit born and bred I do
Exactly as I please
But love to entertain you too
With nonsense-lines like these

THRESHOLD

Pausing here at the threshold of my age
My youth appears chaotic to me now
At this more peaceful place along the way
A rest stop on this road of pilgrimage
I thank God I survived it all somehow

The road is long and I have far to go
But I will be at peace at close of day
And until then I will wander and grow
As curious as ever and even more
With better understanding of the quest

I see there is still so much more to know
Yet know more clearly now what I quest for
And after contemplation rise refreshed
With pockets full of treasures I have found
Which are ideas and are not hard to bear

They comfort me here and lead me to where
The journey ends in quiet victory
My steps toward the future stacked on the past
Create this work-in-progress which is me
Joy in the journey and peace at the last

I enter this the threshold of my age
My pockets full of souvenirs of when
These ideas which help me understand now
And what I do not know I will know then
Embracing such days as God will allow

I must be on my way now homeward bound

ONE LOVE

No time like the present
However unpleasant
The only time we have is only now

And if we can bear it
We learn as we share it
To turn the lead of life to gold somehow

It is this alchemy
Gives hope to you and me
As we transcend the limits of our day

And if we don't lose heart
At least we make a start
To live our most at least and have our say

One life one hope one moment in the sun
One love by which our world is new-begun

MATCHSTICKS

We tend wounds left by those who desert us
We work out the hurts of those who hurt us
Torture ourselves as they tortured us and
Never forget they let go of our hand

We will not eat because they forced us to
Not out of nurture but out of control
We starve ourselves through a hole in our soul
Not good enough no matter what we do

Beaten and broken we nonetheless rise
Through brokenness we triumph after all
Look closer and see the pain in our eyes
We rise to beat back the scene of our fall

We are those matchstick people you might see
Brief candles burning through internal night
Perfection-bound by internal decree
Strike anywhere and we will share our light

Some mock at us and call it all in vain
"Just eat something!" "Get over it!" they say
We keep the secret weep the stain away
But we have to show them: never again

We tend wounds left by those who desert us
We work out the hurts of those who hurt us
Torture ourselves as they tortured us and
Never forget they let go of our hand

We smoke because we are on fire and yet
We light the world consuming our regret

Phone Home From the Twilight Zone

"Is that loud man schizophrenic
Or on his mobile phone?"

She asked since I taught this tactic
Once when we were alone
How when somebody is talking
To some unseen unknown
We discern which type of squawking
We hear just by the tone

My teaching failed though I accept no blame
Since it turned out both were one and the same

If you wonder: "schizophrenic
Or on his mobile phone?"
It could turn out both or neither
Or maybe neither nor
But whichever of the either
What are they shouting for?

I do not like their tone

The type of phone which I prefer
Sits quietly and still
As mine does and as all phones were
And has a modest bill
Because the bored utility
Throws the poor a bone rate for a landline

My mental disability
Although not schizophrenia says: "fine"

Now we can phone home from the Twilight Zone
Stay lonely in a crowd
Argue with ourselves in a drumming drone
But must we be so loud?
I might offer a word
Of advice with a cord:

"Come home with me speak softly and use mine"

Now and Then

for Bart Wolffe

Have I finally suffered enough to see
Now as really always (both effect and cause)?
Nothing in my pocket nothing in my hand
No smoke no mirrors and nothing up my sleeve
This is it and this is what is left to me
That understanding is not to understand

The letting go of what really never was
Is like leaving to come or coming to leave
This essential potential which still can be
Though ragged by the roadside still can be found
Gathered from the ashes and sacrificed at
Bonfires of my vanities I dance around
My burnt offerings the smoke by which I see
The crossing is the focus of clarity

As I have no future so I have no past
As death becomes nearer life becomes dearer
I just want to slow it down and make it last
As each night fades away each day comes clearer
And what I touch has never been touched before
This moment which is the crossing: I see that
Now is always true no matter who thinks when
This being the ultimate I have no more

Now is always the beginning of the game
Once dealt the cards have to be dealt with this way
Whether fifteen or fifty it is the same
Crossing: the point at which all intersects now
Balancing on the brink between night and day
Before after always and never somehow

There is only now as there is never then

Success

I am doing better than I thought and I hear
That people now are beginning to notice me
After thousands of poems which leads me to say
All I have done is be here to write of my stay
If only in my tea-drinking maiden-aunt way
But there is a side of me they will never see
Since I cannot let them nor anyone that near

I want before I die to write great poetry
Because I have lived a life of meaninglessness
And whatever meaning is it seems it would be
Something which feels like the contentment of success

And yet what does anything mean ultimately?
I sit here on my bed with my cat at my side
Wondering whether or not I should make more tea
Wondering deeper what might the world make of me
I will embrace the honor but will shun the pride
A maiden-aunt's first dance first kissed by fate tonight
Let fire fall and light lance me and I will burn bright

So people now are beginning to notice me
Since I am doing better than they thought I guess
But there is a side of me they will never see
Because I have lived a life of meaninglessness

Maiden-aunts come and dance by the light of the moon
Success has not come yet but they say it might soon

I Too

A half-forgotten fixture of my days
An unremembered eccentricity
Becomes more precious threatened in small ways
To be worn like a cap of liberty
As doves descend and evening bells strike praise
If to someone else's imagined norm
As though to truth and not some someone's law
I am expected to somehow conform
My independence sniffed at as a flaw

It is not that I am not up to it
I am up and down as quick as a cat
It is just that I refuse to do it
I am no fool and no one likes a rat
Or more like I cannot cooperate
To ring in a wrong of stupidity
With someone interfering in my fate
Just that in that case I would not be me

I would not want to appear ungrateful
Although I must if that is how it is
But to be ordered about is hateful
I have my ways as someone else has his
The sun sinks in the sea yet does not drown
The friends embrace the light is shared in kind
Stars emerge softly as the friends lie down
Though the sky grow dark it will not go blind
The eye of the moon comes watching behind

A half-forgotten fixture of my days
My sun will rise as surely as it sets
A remembering eccentricity
Truth remains true no matter who forgets
And I will rise remembering to praise

Early next morning heedless of warning
Rise as always no matter what who says
Since to be ordered about is hateful
When doves ascend and morning bells strike praise
I too will strike for I too am grateful

Dark Angel

You are more beautiful than anyone could be
And yet you took my arm and you embraced mere me
I ought to write a thousand poems just for you
And read them to you with your perfect arm in mine

So long these lonely years without a dream come true
But now you offer me your cup of angel's wine
I drink at last to find it never empty now
And drunkenly drown in dark sweet depths of your eyes

(You touch me and you bring me back to paradise)

A miracle to silence why to transcend how
A thousand times dark angel I thank God for you
I thought I had forgotten my humanity
But you encompass man and you have come to me

As you have read my books and know the rest of me
The torments and the trials of the tortured past
Touch me dark angel: bring to light the best of me
My life was not in vain! The best was saved for last!

I seek to speak unspeakable delight tonight
More beautiful than anything could ever be
Which only one (dark angel you) could bring to light
And when you took my arm and you embraced mere me
A life lived upside down revolved to turn round right

Now you dark angel shall be my reality
A life lived in your crucible of ecstasy

(I SIMPLY CANNOT TELL YOU…)

In the adolescence of my efflorescence
Like a sunflower I turn my face to the sun
As hopeful as ever as true to my essence
As I was to sprout when this cycle was begun

(I simply cannot tell you how I love the girls
All of them as each of them with or without pearls)

At the crossing of a life spent wondering why
I realize that I should have been asking how
Trying so hard to live I was ready to die
My never-ending journey had better start now

(I simply cannot tell you how I love their eyes
That sparkle which intoxicates yet terrifies)

If I took care of myself I could live for years
But I would rather have someone take care of me
With our cupboards full of love and empty of fears
Should I go home with you or you come home with me?

(I simply cannot tell you how I love to kiss
And short of that to tease your lips with lines like this)

Straightening My Cigarette

When I was in jail once not too far from here
For trying to die by crashing my fast car
I wore a cigarette behind my left ear
Had a jolly time but now it is too far
From here after all in a distant dead year

All my fellow jailbirds and I got on well
As united in the solidarity
Of those who find themselves together in hell
It seemed more fun than my university
So I felt a bit let down to be set free

I had been ready for anything at all
Having expected to die the night before
But they threw me out so I rose from my fall
Blinked into a future I could hardly see
Straightening my cigarette to live some more

I smile now to remember my delousing
Which without lice I found unnecessary
Young shoplifters yelping and old drunks grousing
Each maintaining his innocence steadfastly
It seemed the only guilty one there was me

"I know my rights!" some cried "You have no rights here!"
Some replied and those were the ones with the sticks
One cracked me on the head since I showed no fear
(Being suicidal) of bully-boy tricks
He paused disappointed then left me alone

If he felt anything it was jealousy
And I gathered that he rather liked the tone
Of my answer given insouciantly
But with coming dawn he knew I would be gone
Leaving him behind and he wished he were me

So I was in jail once now too far from here
For trying to die by crashing my fast car
I wore a cigarette behind my left ear
Was cast out of hell to rise a falling star
All in all I came out better than before

My fast car was repaired my psyche was aired
Lots of hugs and love and memories were shared
And it seemed to me that I was meant to be
Having come out of a coma that same year
Apparently I am supposed to be here

Straightening my cigarette to live some more

With Salem Far Behind Me

I enjoy doing things which once were forbidden
Right out in the open where once they were hidden
And writing it down then (if elliptically)
All rhymed and reasoned into cryptic poetry

They meant well I know as they tried to repress me
And they succeeded if they tried to impress me
In fact I remain so impressed I get depressed
While passing from the repressed to the unrepressed

(Though to have told it this way is to have digressed)

I started as a puritan became a witch
Left Salem altogether and never got rich
But oh what a way to go! What sweet poverty
Is this perfect freedom to do what pleases me!

Should anyone repress you then anyone lies
We must each live our meaning now before each dies
My path has been circuitous and very strange
But I have learned the only constancy is change

You feel (nor do I blame you) change is frightening
But this is how to bloom feels! Your enlightening
Is only strange to you because you have just met
And yet better to love and lose than to regret

(A few lost bets but no regrets as blooms the rose
Yet if a bet is won or lost: only God knows)

With Salem far behind me I will not burn now
Except with curiosity to find out how
To get out of this life all I can while I can
Evolving as a poet from a puritan

While those who repressed me only did what they knew
I know nothing and (I suspect) neither do you
So live it up now and should you come to see me
You can share in my adventure of breaking free

Why wait? Why hesitate? What do you save it for?
You think you have lived but you can always live more
A few lost bets but no regrets as blooms the rose
Yet if a bet is won or lost: only God knows!

How about this? Savor those longshot bets you win
Whether we know it or not we are in this race
Called life yet our destination is not a place
But a process (what a process!): let us begin

I seem strange to you now because we have just met
But come and love me win or lose without regret
A few lost bets but no regrets as blooms the rose
Yet if a bet is won or lost: only God knows

If God is love then in his image so are we
And love like life and God himself is always free

For Shelby Cundiff: My Poetry Pal

an acrostic and then some

S.o here we are my friend my poetry pal
H.igh on life itself and some other things too
E.nlightenment elusive and mystical
L.eans light across this bench to bridge me and you
B.eing far more friendly than most people think
(Y.our Starbucks cup contains no mere coffee drink!)

C.ara mia! I pronounce you: a poet
U.ntil the whole world knows at least I know it
N.ow and as always we pals in poetry
D.are to test the limits of reality
I.f such limits are for some they are not for
F.ree spirits like us who seek and thus find more
F.ree spirits like Shelby my poetry pal

And if your name were longer
(But of course it is just right)
This poem might be stronger
(But I wrote it late at night)
Your name will be known soon and quite as long as mine
(Now share with me that Starbucks cup of Napa wine!)

WILL

Will is the ability to say: "No"
Will is to lay down our lives for our friends
To lose the battle yet to win the war

Will is the agility to say so
Should we be the means to somebody's ends
That we will not be held back anymore

Will is our essence insisting to be
Asserting our equal right to exist
Remembering what we have come here for

Without will no one has ever been free:
As long as time turns till the wheel stands still
I would we have the will to say: "We will"

Will is the steel in our back to resist
Will is the steel in our back to resist

Mattie and Me in High Society

(Coto de Caza will never be the same)

The cream of the crop at the top of the tree
And in the midst of all of this? You and me!
The hottest chick there was older than your mom
I wore your ruffled shirt left over from prom
And drank a lot of really good wine: I was
Glad I went as a Displaced Person because
That walking stick which was part of my costume
Served as my focal point in the spinning room
Although I blame that stick for breaking that glass
It kept me on my feet and up off my ass

I just woke up in costume now (quite well dressed)
Bleary in the mirror (hung over) impressed
By the way we made our foray into that
Through-the-looking-glass world of the Cheshire Cat
I have some coffee going and this cigar
I found in the pocket of my costume coat
Remembering good cigarettes in your car
Turkish Silvers in that valet-parked Hyundai
Our magical-mystery undersea-boat
In which we sailed 'neath Saturday to Sunday

The old folks jitterbugged back to World War Two
As the Greatest Generation took the beach
With the poolside mermaids singing each to each
They sang to me but wanted to dance with you
We shared their fancy chow but declined to dance
Still we cut a mean rug without meaning to
And did it all ourselves without a tailor
But then Mattie Fisher and old Stevie Lance
Are known for being stylish in all they do
And our hostess made a seaworthy sailor

I never would have gotten there and back alive
Without your uncanny ability to drive
And you bid for and won the silent auction too!
They took pictures of us and I hope we will be
Written right up in the Register on page three
Or two or one or headlined on the social page
To witness our assault on high society
And increase our notable notoriety
As souvenir of our ascending pilgrimage
Up to where those with lives to die for go to die

But Mattie: we live lives to live for you and I

The Other Side of the Mirror

Our best poems might not be written yet
Nor would I want to burden them that way
Our sweetest apples bitten with regret
For our fear of missing something someday
Anticipation hesitates to wait
But realization might arrive late

Or some poem I wrote some years ago
For all its crudeness might yet prove my best
Too close to see I know I never know
I wait and study as though for a test
As though life were some university
With grades in letters and work before rest

Is it me or are all things in motion?
Earth pulls the moon the moon pulls the ocean
And each of us is a philosopher
Pondering the meaning of him or her
Of what can be and what she means to me
Loves past persistent loves which never were
But (do I dare to hope it?) which could be

Life itself is the test which teaches me

So without anyone to tell me how
I have to do the best I can for now

N.obody can tell you
O.f heaven or hell you
W.ill simply have to find out for yourself

Nor yet can they show you
They do not yet know you
Except to choose a poem from your shelf

But realization might arrive late
Anticipation hesitates to wait
For our fear of missing something someday
Our sweetest apples bitten with regret
Nor would I want to burden them that way
Our best poems might not be written yet

And yet it is not given us to say

Beachcombing in Autumn

a love song

Picking among some shards which seem like me
I find among them things I recognize
Clutching at broken bits tentatively
Pieces of hand in hand I realize
What these things must be (as the rain begins)

These are the dried husks of old snake-shed skins
Which I wore at varying lengths of snake
And then there came those times of turning when
I wriggled from my skin made a clean break
To leave here reupholstered once again

And from this process my detritus lies
Here where it fell to tell the truth today
Of growth and change and how things rearrange
Falling leaves on the way to November

I think this is why we find snakes so strange
Because they are strangely familiar to
Evolving humans fitted out with hands
To clutch at broken bits of me and you
Quietly insisting we remember

Whatever a snake knows it understands
Evolving humans fitted out with feet
Now wet from the rain to wake with the pain
Of having come a long way in old skin

It could be time to shed my skin again
Not to replace it but to turn it in

You may come along later and find this
Most recent skin whose shards you might recall
The lips of the face still curled by your kiss

(In this skin I was happiest of all)

Lunchtime in the Plaza

(a fountainside adventure: I ate nothing and enjoyed it)

Large men like cartoon-animals bounce down the street
On herky-jerky animated lunchtime feet
And though their cartoon-watches have no time for me
I sense this is their lunchtime and their lunch is free

Two men teeter on the rim of the fountain's pool
Patiently dragging nets on sticks and gathering
Such leaves and coins as found their way there to keep cool
Or which were cast with reverence in offering
I wish I had found those coins before these men did
Spending money so well-laundered must be splendid

The out-of-towners hit our roundabout and go
Out-of-their-minds as well somehow it seems to me
Strapped in unseemly haste they find themselves to be
Here where it is lunchtime and we always walk slow
Especially after eating when like cattle
Our large men herd back (less bouncy now) to battle

My poetry is not right for the Plaza Review?
I thank God for this (even as I thank God for you)!
Someday we ought to print our own alternative voice
Of those who really live here or who come here by choice

We balance here on the blade of time to keep things real
Newsprint is for recycling so they will not have me
I am recycled anyway but I was born free
(St. Joseph's charged a fee so my father found a deal)

You there! Sleeping on that bench! I like your perspective
Your life (like plastic surgery) remains elective
(Though here plastic surgery has become de rigueur

For those who live forever as if they never were)
You simply do not do those things which you do not choose
For this policemen wake you and find you defective

But we know life is not some race to win or to lose
I (who defected long ago) find you reflective
Through the mirror you have sought your own reality
And having found it here you choose to share it with me

So I am not for everyone? "For Madmen Only!"
Madwomen too (perhaps like you?): for I get lonely

Mackerel Sky

Under this mackerel sky you and I
Wonder about where Lent and Advent went
Where do the days go when they have gone by?
Maybe like us they retire to repent

All I ask of God is that he love me
(I rather think he already loves you)
Here with this mackerel sky above me
I really have no idea what to do

Apparently I should write poetry
Because when I do all my words feel true
And that must mean something (at least to me)
Is there some meaning here I fail to see?

It hurts so much to be an outsider
Alone since you do not really exist
But as an idea muse and provider
Of grist for the mill by which I persist

Although it seems odd: perhaps you are God
Imagined by this existentialist
And if you are I suppose we are friends
So it could be you exist after all
Since means never make as much sense as ends

I fell yet still feel a long way to fall
My chaste superego's chastening rod
Hurts so much I wonder how I can bear
Being here anymore (or anywhere)

I grow this poem xylem and phloem
Wondering why I do anything: yet
Somehow I want to live and leave a mark
If but a broken token of regret

Written up as an obsessive poem
Written down there to get or to forget
What I really mean: that I am afraid!
That I find my life meaningless! And yet...
When I am gone my say will have been said

But for the fact I know not what to say
My life feels barely bearable today
I try so hard to live a life somehow
And have not yet found what it takes to die

I wanted to ask those I loved and lost
Why everything had to be as it was
That most obvious question which is "Why?"
Yet could not afford to because it cost
Them everything they had to live and die

I never wanted to be a bother
And yet I wonder if they knew: do you?
If you are God then are you my father
Origin destiny ultimate cause?

A father who is also my lover?
And do you wonder under this sky too?
I am alone as I remain unknown
If you are my Comforter come: hover

Come: and love me among the broken stone
Of this heart where you could set up your throne
Where you could reign within this vacancy
If ever I needed you it is now

There is only love left here: all past hate
Has eaten its way acidic through me
I am a scarred monster: is it too late?
I am a scared man: heal and seal my fate

I love you God (and I need you to be)
I want this to mean something in the end
I am lost here alone: no other friend
I love you God (would you take care of me?)

There is no one else here: I am alone
Unless you see through the mackerel sky
And know me as I wish that I were known
We are alone now: only you and I
To tend these broken bottles of the heart

God let my sickness end your healing start
To mend this heart I had such high hopes for
I love you God (how I need you to be!)
I just want you to love me: nothing more

Father? I love you (but do you love me?)

Underneath me the everlasting arms
Are obfuscated by anaesthetic
I comfort myself with counterfeit charms
Some intellectual some aesthetic
But under this mackerel sky I dare
To walk on the water believe you care
And hope you will rescue me sinking there

Father! I love you (and yes you love me)

Could Be

I have a hole in my soul without you
But you are with me now although you might
Not know that (and I love this about you)
Not yet at least because it is still quite
An unexpected turning of the wheel
You do not doubt me nor do I doubt you
Yet cannot help but doubt this could be real

As though we knew each other long ago
And have for worlds and lifetimes in between
That time and place and this as though we know…
As though we know exactly what we mean

An unexpected turning of the wheel
An awkward rather inconvenient turn
But maybe this is how we have to learn
That this force of gravitation we feel
Which draws us together (unwillingly)
Disturbing our designs (if thrillingly)
Leaves little room for doubt: this could be real

Sweet Addiction

I know that you are lonely…

But you are not the only
One who feels like this

We are all in need of love
And we are all in need of
One sweet tender kiss

First morning comes before us…

Then evening behind…

If someone should adore us
Then how could we mind?

(Sometimes we seem blind)

We mortals are so complicated but
We all need to be loved no matter what

And all of us need it so
Much more than we admit
Even more than we might know

But one kiss could fix it…

With that one leading to another one
With each becoming better being best
Our lips our hearts left trembling to find more
As then our lips our hearts explore the rest
And soon a sweet addiction has begun

Therefore let us lie down that we might soar

WINGS

Would that cigarettes were everlasting
Nor burn up so expensively so fast
Would that they would not kill me as they do
Would weight fly away today through fasting
Defining my true self beneath false skin
And would that you loved me as I love you
Both God and you forgiving me my sin
My sacrifice acceptable at last

If wishes were horses beggars would ride
This beggar would like to ride a big horse
So I could ride read-and-respected now
Though beggars cannot be choosers of course
But if you see me riding up astride
Some noble steed then mine came true somehow
As noble deeds and begging needs allow
Or I could simply ride away and hide

I never had an adolescence then
Pruned by puritan prunes for Vietnam
And marrying beyond my means back when
I should have been king (or queen) of the prom
An adolescent now at fifty-two
My adolescent friends say just be free
And live and love and laugh now while we see
If the wishes of beggars can come true

Just barely beginning to live now I
Commit to this life to the death (daresay)
And despite my late start test wings to fly
More hurried than worried up and away
To have my say by turning night to day
And celebrate the seasons of the moon
Which though it has waned will wax again soon
When finally I get my chance to play

So never mind Uncle Jack what you did
And how we "lived" and how my people died
You came and I went to my room and hid
Fox talking henhouse hens squawking about
Farewell old man those tears have all been cried
I bet it all to try and put things right
Found out what that fox was talking about
The hens squawked all day but then said good night

I will fly high as a kite till I drop
And then will drop extraordinarily
Or just might fly so high I never stop
Till I become who I was born to be
My issues my tissues my rhyme my time
Those loved and lost had such high hopes for me
Then left me here alone without a dime
But left this ticket to eternity

Would that cigarettes were everlasting
Nor burn up so expensively so fast
Would that they would not kill me as they do
Would weight fly away today through fasting
Defining my true self beneath false skin
And would that you loved me as I love you
Both God and you forgiving me my sin
My sacrifice acceptable at last

The Boy is Father to the Man

I am disappointed by the mirror
But disappointment edges with surprise
When my clouding image looms up clearer
And I think I see madness in my eyes

When I was a boy I waited to see
If my eyes could mark the miles of life as
Time and its tumult made a man of me
And now since I have lived so long it has
Been ever more clear I never got near
To life except by serendipity

Whatever a man is I do not think
That this is what I had in mind at all
If man is fallen this must be his fall
That is what I see here: I see the brink
Just beyond yet behind where stained eyes strain
Out of what was to what is and must be

I cringe at this image over this sink
Surrounded by bathroom banality
Where once I stood in boyhood dreaming here
I see my boyhood eyes destroyed by pain
Burned in the darkness and branded with fear
Trapped in this life-death mask mortality

Is this how it happens? Where is that boy
Who had no idea it would be this way
Who waited to mark the miles and enjoy
What seemed to him some endless holiday?

This is not what that boy waited to see
I shudder to think of how he must feel
I am too disappointed to explain

But he is blind now not to see again
And having gone I hope he has gone free
Where nightmares shown in mirrors are not real

What vision disappointment left surprise
Took that when he saw madness in my eyes
And though I age it was he who made me
So I would like to find him if I can
To say I was sorry to see him go
And that he was me just so he would know

A boy like that might fear this crazy man
Perhaps we will meet in eternity
Where we could forget about all of this
Enlightened there by sheer lucidity
Disappointed eyes surprised by a kiss
To make a man of him a boy of me

Answered by Silence

We wanderers do not need very much
To gratify our curiosity
Nor do we have to wander very far
To enjoy bright stars and shining moonlight
The morning star to sparkle up the east
And bring the day up rested from the night
To satisfy the turning of the wheel
Which comes before and after when we are

The sun going up and then coming down
The ways of stars the moon the sun and such
These greatest entertainments cost the least
In which the gift of now itself is star
Where all are already admitted free
The sky itself the greatest show in town
Above the town for everyone to see
En masse or in intimate company

Or maybe in the desert all alone
An audience of one which comes to feel
The universe as university
A place to wonder consider and dream
Of things which can and which cannot be known
In which thoughts and stones are equally real
Where questions are answered personally
No matter how universal they seem

Ultimate questions are personal ones
Those campfire questions wondered silently
Asked by wanderers of infinite suns
And answered by silence ultimately

To Have a Because

I have struggled stubbornly since my birth
(What a massive inconvenience THAT was!)
To justify my presence here on earth

I feel like I have to have a Because

This could be from my being unwanted
Or the fact my family is haunted

Whatever the reason I have been sad
As I scaled heights and reaching them took flight
(If only to float away aimlessly)
Never enjoying whatever I had
(Although whatever I had had had me)
Because I had no time to sleep at night
And if I did such dreams as came were bad

I have to work harder than other men
Although I never make any money

I am in constant pain except for when
You think a poem of mine is funny

Alone with God ...and You

for someone who paid for treatment when I needed it

Everyone has troubles malignant or benign
May yours be more the latter than the former and
May they in any case not be as hard as mine
Have been... but having troubles you will understand
When I say (as you know) that nothing feels so good
As when troubles feared malignant turn out: just fine
Hope shared is squared and life blooms when the news is good

When good news comes it comes on time but not too soon
And thus enhanced by this element of surprise
Can turn an inward dirge into a jaunty tune
Mortality if for a moment washed from eyes
Which blink in the light of hope from the dark of fears

In a moment like this is when we realize
Other eyes were there to share not just smiles but tears
Which cover up the light of hope to blind our eyes
And so we feel alone because we fail to see
Other eyes loved and loving weeping with us then

Though I care for you I forget you care for me
But since my eyes are clear now I see you again
Here at my door as you have always been before

It takes the malignant to bring out the benign
Apparently and it is after crisis when
I can see that you really are a friend of mine

And these eyes washed clean by suffering can see too
Now that I am free from where troubles had taken
That God is with us both just as he always was
As if waiting in the night for me to waken

To see my guiding light my original cause
Waiting there as you here: I was not forsaken
Not merely alone but alone with God ...and you

DE RERUM NATURA

That nether hair is there for our protection
The keep through which the castle works erection
That portcullis whence we sally forth to see
How the other half lives: entangled within
The portcullis of another even as
Our elements combine underneath our skin
In a dance of life which causes life to be
And then rests tender (here) as it always has
In softly saline human propinquity

Your father knew of this and your mother too
As mine and everyone's to cause me and you
To repeat the pattern to know what they knew

It feels awkward to imagine them like this
But there they were and here we are: in this kiss
To repeat the pattern of past human bliss
Then turn side by side as our world turns around
Having found as seeking humans always found
"It is not good for the man to be alone"
Nor the woman as you have so warmly shown
And here we are as there they were: in this kiss
Just as those who came before had always known

I would not wax just as I would not wane
The moon now waxes both of us (again)

Pick a Star

Winter is not what it used to be
Waiting in autumn growing older
As the days grow shorter I can see
My days grow shorter too (and colder)

Those I took care of take care of me
My son with my name will be bolder
In life than me: my other son too
Will go much further than I have gone
Which is as it should be after all

I am ill now in increasing pain
I see someone else in my mirror
A stranger to the me I once knew
Yet somehow I see myself clearer
With poor eyesight and a damaged brain

Autumn in balance is rise and fall
And life just does what it has to do
The pyre of leaves burns smoky and small
But dusk of winter burns into dawn
Into a day which belongs to you

Some people seem to live on and on
Steadily if uneventfully
But I have lived (and would live again)
Eventfully if unsteadily
Does anyone know? I never knew

Winter is not what it used to be
But then winter was never like this
Come spring I hope you remember me
Pick a star then and blow me a kiss

What Fred Said

Sitting on my bed alone with my cat
Recovering from dentistry gone wrong
(Miscarriage of such a good intention
Gone too far nor enough or just gone bad
Requiring medical intervention)
He sleepily hears me implore "Now what?"
Of no one or none in particular
(Too far now from that last pain pill I had)

He opens one eye as he thinks awhile
Then both and meows "Forget about all that
And just enjoy what little we have got:
Remember those troubles we might have seen
Which worried you so and yet never were?
Get up and take a pain pill (we have more)"

He reminds me we are both fortunate
To stay cool in a world grown much too hot
And rather more too shallow than too deep
Awash in absurdity he stays strong:
"You will get over this then you will soar
Let those antibiotics do their part
And rest up now since it will not be long
Curl up your tail and go to sleep: take heart"

Able to be cheerfully celibate
Lucky to avoid scenes which might have been
Far from the dramas of cats which are not
He yawns and purrs "Time now to go to sleep"
And that is that because he is a cat
But if cats do I swear I saw him smile

As he curls close and winks his green jade eyes
I realize which one of us is wise

Night Rain After Disappointment

I listen to rain falling through the night
As it lands and runs beneath the window
As it slides down the sky from a great height
Its drops joining into a stream below
And I think maybe I will be all right

I can feel the stream and feel in its flow
That I too am a raindrop after all
A stone in the desert star in the sky
A snowflake in winter leaf in the fall
Through good days and bad days wet years and dry
A piece of the puzzle however small

I was surprised by this rain when it came
As one is by an unexpected gift

I hurt but I see no one is to blame
Am disappointed yet I feel the lift
Of the night tears of heaven just the same
Outside the window joining mine inside
Though mine are stinging salt and of small size
A puzzle piece a raindrop after all

Those drops without and these within confide
I join with unnumbered and unseen eyes

Rain fall and flow and carry me away
That I become at one with everything
To ride the tide tonight into today
A piece to speak my piece unquestioning
Rain touch and teach my tongue what it must say

The Bubble Now

Our present realities can be seen
By the meaningful patterns of our past
Past patterns are buoys in the fog ahead
As dreams and nightmares coming true at last
With several surprises in between

We will always be who we are yet change
Albeit each by pattern each our way
What to one is normal another strange
Flows on like water as night follows day
And as we have come so we will go more

It has to mean something that we are here
In the midst of all this complexity
With no brakes and not knowing how to steer
And then beyond the how there is the why
As you remain you while I become me

We recognize ourselves our patterns clear
No matter how we live evolve and die
Whether past or present reality
Because reality is always now
Whatever was or is or is to be

The bubble now cannot be burst somehow
To look back or ahead is not to see
Our spectrum of possibility for
Within what the bubble now will allow
We are freed from time for eternity

Eternity begins now one might say
No one can find its beginning nor end
We enter the river midstream instead:
May you enjoy eternity my friend
Right here and right now forever today

Iron Grey

in my family our hair turns iron grey in time as mine has now

The housekeeper leaves bits of fruit for me
As ancestral demon or deity

Old Chrysler keys are always upside down
As mine are (my ignition in my hand)
I have enough gas to get out of town
But will not since I have no place to go
And do have a place where I have to stay

I wonder if the neighbors understand
That I live in death and that (yes) I know?

Where I live it is always yesterday
Here is a place of everlasting when
Which functions as a neverending where
And if you were not here from now to then
Look in and back and you might see it (there)

I seem to be the caretaker the host
The sacrifice maker become the ghost

I too at last have become iron grey
I went to Grandma's house and stayed until
It got too late to ever leave again
Born in the thunder left out in the rain
Came home here: always have (we always will)

The dead live here with their iron grey hair
Heavy in the heavily mortgaged air

The Bifocal Perspective of Being

We live on more than one plane at a time:
On one plane in the action of our play
And one above this one (up a short climb)
From which we watch (a dimension away)
Ourselves from above (though we are below)
Just far enough away that we can say
"Be careful down there" yet enjoy the show

This observational ability
Is ours whenever we take the long view
To look at ourselves and look honestly
Wonder about why we do what we do
And having seen us then to see us grow

From the vantage point of the higher me
I have seen this cycle turn around so
Many seasons in a pattern so small
That I have to hope it must mean something
(If anything means anything at all)
Whatever it means it is the one thing
I have and also what I share with you

We speak our lines then learn them as we go
From the sublimated to the sublime
Floodlit and firelit blinded by seeing
Up close at a distance high beams and low
Each like a bell which hears its echo chime

The bifocal perspective of being

Not Until

The dry bean yet hopeful seed is immersed
Into mother water and rejoices
To swell up pregnant with life soon to burst

No one can win an argument with fate

The water boiled soothingly and surprised
The bean instead before it realized

One might be early another one late
But no one will ever know until when
What happens happens and not until then

To make sense of why things are as they are
It helps to think about this "not until"
And wonder if chances could be choices

(That there is no sense to make of is far
More than most know or than most ever will)

The Golden Frame

Today though the tomorrow of yesterday
Is no longer tomorrow only today
But then tomorrow never comes anyway

Living in the future in tomorrow's past
Yesterday's tomorrow came today at last
I am happy to be here in any case
The future seems to me a familiar place
As though today seems to be yesterday's more

But you and I have never been now before
Tomorrow might say that today was the day
I died for all I know as it slipped away

No before nor after now only today
So I will make the most of it I will do
My best today as I share this now with you
And timely it is to ride the sweeping hands
Of the clock of now with one who understands:

That we are not going anywhere
That still in the moment we are there
For here in the now is everywhere

Hands brush its face while time smiles on the same
Somehow
The paintings change yet not the golden frame
Of now

Our Time Will Come

What is right for one moment might devolve
To be wrong for another moment when
As the cycles of the seasons revolve
Then becomes now the way now became then
As if only situationally
I have always found it helpful to see
The pulse of the pattern of back and forth

Reality changes from hour to hour
The pendulum swings for all it is worth
To say nothing of our perception of
What is and how we shape what this might be
The name we call it which gives it its power
Could be anything but it seems to me
What really makes the seasons turn is Love

The sun which opens the heart like a flower
Love is the light we see reflected by
The moon the sparkle we see in a star
The flame which flashes from a lover's eye
What keeps us going when the goal is far
Away and down the road as you and I
Perceive the pattern of the pendulum

We keep going knowing our time will come

Never Quite

*for the "Weekend America" program on NPR
with my thanks for their interest in my poetry*

Being insane can make one insecure:
To be out of touch with the normative...
However certain still never quite sure
If one's own senses are informative

Not wanting (of course) to be a bother
And yet bothered simultaneously
Madness is no escape but is rather
A great complication (at least for me)

Somehow and for some reason I endure
My senses uniquely informative
Though antipodal to the normative
However certain still never... quite... sure...

INSIDE

I want to sail to the strong-shouldered coast
Of pure imagination and arrive
At somewhere I can be my uttermost
Discover what it means to be alive
And find out what it takes to be a me

Whether I know it or not I am free:
Though I might seem imprisoned even here
Where I always thought I was meant to be
By something as simple as simple fear
Since what I loved best disappointed most

How beautiful it is no matter what
I suffered then or now how late the day
Some understand me and many do not
Or would not or could not as some might say
The day slants away but the night purrs near

Whether we know it or not we are free:
If I could ask you anything at all
It would be to sing the morning of spring
Recall the golden afternoon of fall
I would ask you remember everything

Pure imagination is what is true
A place where we can be our uttermost
Discover what it means to be alive
And find out what it takes to be a we
Not someplace else but inside me and you

Sickbed with Cat

In the end all that
I have is this cat
It is only he
With me now I see
A culture of two
One might say (I do)

Only us as we
Attempt to contend
However we can
Odd couple we are
Fat cat and thin man
With what fate might send

Whatever it sends
Freddie Noodles is
My friend I am his
We two are true friends
We have come this far
And we will get by

I do not know how
Nor am I sure why
Yet not knowing still
Believe that we will
Survive how hard fall
Fell this year somehow

We struggle each day
To get from it all
Some sense of fair play
In life through this loss
Detritus and dross
Entangling our way

But we will get through
Because we have to

Promise the Dust

May those who make promises then break them
Airily merry with nary a thought
Be sharply recalled to what they forgot
May their self-satisfaction forsake them
And may they feel what their breaking has brought
Good and hard so to get their attention
May we find the love they hid as we sought
Yet never found now as the wheel comes round

We have been hurt we need hardly mention
But having seen promises broken and
Hearts along with them the same as our own
To reach out in vain for the withdrawn hand
Of someone you trusted and fall alone
We have felt all this so we understand
How it feels to be yesterday's flavor
To be once known and then at once unknown

But seeing the truth can make us braver
Though it might cost us a part of our trust
The rain has fallen and the wind has blown
The moon has tricked the sea to lick the land
And left only ruin and rot and rust
Where castles of promises made of sand
Are broken like bubbles and overthrown
We leave the breakers to promise the dust

May we find the love they hid as we sought
Yet never found now as the wheel comes round

STILL FREE

I felt unwanted by polite society
Though I struggled politely to make it better
Polite society seemed impolite to me
So I built my own context letter by letter
And line by line my personal sanctuary
Of thousands of poems interlocking like bricks
With walls constructed seamlessly of prosody
Life can throw at me what it likes but nothing sticks

My personal society is quite polite
Graced as it is with specific gentility
Albeit with a certain eccentricity
Though it is always autumn here and always night
The moon is always full the stars shine dazzlingly
Against the deep blue velvet sky and diamond bright
The ancient everlasting light by which I see
And it is all for me and it is quite all right

Far from the garish glare and incivility
Of the plastic fantastic unreality
Of the bloated distended Wal-Mart world out there
Supersized and hypnotized by lies and madness
Where most have forgotten what it meant to play fair
Where antidepressants cannot heal the sadness
Nor tranquilizers blot out the anxiety
Of a most impolite polite society

I will spend my days in solitude with gladness
Though my democracy is dead I am still free

November

I realize I have no hope to see
My future but this is all right with me
What I hope to see is my here and now
(As well as I can see it anyhow)

And then again I wonder if I could
Stand to see just how little understood
Or much misunderstood I am: I guess
Such present knowledge might just make a mess...
But if I could make sense of it I would

I love somebody who may never know
Yet still I aspire to find out someday
What love tastes like before time comes to go
I need to know before I go away
The hope of love holds fast and it dies slow

After my life's work is done for my pay
I want something real and not just for show
To seal my life with meaning like a kiss
I have so little else to leave behind
What I would like to leave behind is this:

Somebody loved me (they say love is blind)
Somebody loved me a long time ago...

And who am I? Your fellow leaf in fall
Borne by the breeze bound wherever we blow:
November is the deepest month of all
(And December is not for us to know)

Autumnal People

What is it then? What is it after all
Which makes each autumn ache this old refrain
Of bittersweet like the maple leaf's fall
Which falling dies that leaves might rise again?

How good it is whatever it might be
This turning tender burning of the year
So personal yet universally
Such symbol of how briefly we are here

We gather are thankful and remember
At the twilight of another year's day
November draws us to our December
It is because it has to be this way

The nutmeg and the pumpkins and the straw
The leaves in drifts anticipating snow
To welcome the freeze to hasten the thaw
What is it then? Autumnal people know

The Most Beautiful Thing on Earth

Standing bereft of fur or feather
Outside society ostracized
Naked in this inclement weather
Vulnerable but categorized
I reached the end then slipped my tether

I was disappointed in my day
Thought too hopeless to be criticized
Only the lonely could know my night
But that was someone else far away
Might have been me or might have been you
Might have been both of us together
There in the dark while we never knew

Since I seem so little able to
Have much effect on things around me
I just do my best at what I do
Creating by faith and not by sight
An illusion now illusion-free

If I was wrong or if I was right
In spite of the when and the whether
Or else perhaps because of it all
Standing bereft of fur or feather
Suffering wears better in the fall
Clemency in inclement weather
Suffering us to be together

Death is the closest a man ever gets
To the feeling of giving birth
All pain consumed in climax none regrets
The most beautiful thing on earth

Blood Red Rose

chorus mysticus

You who have loved who have listened to me
And answered me before I have spoken
Feeling my feelings by pierced empathy
At close of day open when the doors close
Behind us alone with eternity

You who know how to fix what is broken
Keep my heart open so my eyes can see
Your eyes reflected in the eyes of those
Who know and yet who know not what to say
I choose them as the chosen ones you chose

Your petals unfold in an open heart
You drape the dusk before you dawn the day
Everyone sees only some someone knows
Rhythm and reason and ultimate cause
Turning with the season learning to be

One: we are made of two which none may part
Two: we are one with all that ever was
Finding myself to give myself away
I lose myself in order to be free
My secret my lover my blood red rose

Like Birds Waiting for the Rain

Like birds waiting for the rain
We huddle on benches where
All the old men used to sit

They died and were born again
We are here as they were there
So we should get used to it

Time is irrelevant but
For a timely reckoning
A sometime reminder what
Is drawing us beckoning

We follow without question
(For whom would we ask it of?)
The deeply felt suggestion
Nothing is stronger than love

Old men there are old women too
Of any age for each of you
And what will I do? Never mind

I am one of the left behind
Aslant beneath the autumn rain
But I am drawn as anyone

Though wounded and weary of pain
If only they could feel the sun
These broken wings would rise again:
The healing of the will by love

Hard Knocks and Soft Answers

When the school of hard knocks meets
The study of soft answers
Then we can feel our heartbeats
In rhythm as the dancers
Who present this our ballet
Of shared human empathy
By which we are led to say
I feel you and you feel me

(What shall we say and what shall we do?
I move away yet closer to you)

We are all connected by
This web of propinquity
There to catch us when we fall
Not to mention your and my
Now-unfolding destiny
Which we share here after all
We are just the way we are
Together and yet lonely

(What shall we do and what shall we say?
We move closer though we move away)

Isolated like a star
In space as one and only
All and each so far apart
And yet all and each right here
Our shared rhythm of the heart
Felt from far brings us back near
When the school of hard knocks meets
The study of soft answers

MOON AND SEA

Why am I salty as the sea inside?
Whenever I go to sea I return
To something I knew before I could learn
Why are you regulated by the tide?

It seems to me if anecdotally
We are as much of ocean as of land
We and the sea share deep affinity
A connection I feel and understand
I know we are affected by the moon
As we look forward to its rising soon

It has the best effect on us it could
It makes us feel as warm as it looks cool
Bringing to light what is misunderstood
By those who scoff at the nature of things
A lunatic is mad but is no fool
It is not for fools that the night-bird sings

The world is for dreamers like you and me
Reality is a matter of mind
For us since we left the scoffers behind
To think about things like the moon and sea

Raindrops for the Rain

The non-physical form of blindness
(I speak of the self-inflicted kind)
Might be cured by a little kindness
And a slight opening of the mind
Transforming victim into healer
Along the road from night into day

Such measures are feared as radical
(Things like the opening of the eyes)
By the hidebound hypothetical
Leery of light as truth-revealer
Hoping unseen it might go away

Some people would almost rather die
(Or perhaps rather live partially)
Than to contemplate a butterfly
If looking at bugs might make them see
Something which pokes at their potential
Giving pause by possibility
Though it once felt right and would again
Though they want it more than they could say

So rather than have their sight restored
Afraid of what they might realize
They settle down to be blind ...and bored
(Though it once felt right and would again!
Though they want it more than they could say!)
Not seeing the raindrops for the rain

THE REST OF ME

If sawn in half you would still be all there
One in two places and both at half price
Assuming it was a good magician
Who undertook to slice your rump roast rare
Bodies divided against themselves find
(Although breaking up can be hard to do)
The foot end follows the end with the mind
And getting back together is so nice
You get to reacquaint yourself with you
It only takes one half to break the ice

But now I avoid it nevertheless
Under the care of the great physician
Although it has happened (if not onstage)
Both ends of me enjoy connectedness
And I no longer go to magic shows
Nor would I volunteer now to be sawn
I did it once but would not do it twice
Life is fragmented enough heaven knows
And most of the good magicians have gone
Perhaps like me they went on pilgrimage

It might have been only my heart to be
Sawn through and not really magic at all
It took awhile to find the rest of me
To reunite the pieces afterward
Scattered by stagecraft and chicanery
In time to take a bow in time to fall
An autumnal leaf or a wounded bird
By instinct to meet my mortality
It seemed a magic trick but it was not
It left its mark on me (not without pain)

Yet when I fell I found I rose again
Caught by the great physician I forgot

Thoughts on Thanksgiving Day MMVII

A good day by nature bad day by choice
The cruel architecture of the mind
Walls in my freedom denies me my voice
To feel passed over or else left behind
And wonder aloud about it at last

I become less sure of reality
The more I stand up stumbling from the past
Out of the nothingness hoping to be

Does anyone else miss how it once was
When it seemed things might get better somehow?
I wonder about that a lot because
I feel lonelier than ever right now
And wishing I had a community

All is plastic and made in China for
The likes of me and maybe you (the poor)
But I felt less thankful when I had more

Of All Places

A demon came to sit on me awhile
Speaking body language like it was French
But only in curses stealing my smile
Pulling me out of the game for the trench
With only the escape of poetry
Giving rise to my highly-mannered style
Because I am screaming though silently

Those who suffer most become the most kind
Helping us across the timebending Nile
Then on to ford the Jordan of the mind
Their dreams like corpses floating in the mud
I cringe to cross with a shudder to find
The river was of human seed and blood
I know who carried me and whom to thank

Dark river demon I beg you to leave
Just as I beg the sun to rise and shine
Suffering is that which makes me believe
That of all places one of them is mine
Beyond this river bloody dark and dank
That I exist as much as anyone
A blossom from the barrel of a gun

Caravan

I am no wise man only a misfit
An outsider regarding a window
As someone who tries to make sense of it
And wonders what the insiders might know
Sometimes I think no one knows anything

I blunder but smile and wonder the while
Apparently as clueless as can be
To see so many march out single file
Before my eyes to dance with destiny
I am no canary but I can sing

So whose destiny is it anyway?
Is it their own or that of what they serve?
Lights in the window turn night into day
I wonder if we get what we deserve
I might have a brief candle I could bring

I follow behind their long caravan
Alone at a distance unknown unseen
This is the tragedy they once called Man
I guess the sad part is what might have been
The king is dead they say long live the king

Souvenirs of Ecstasy

If I have ever learned anything
And if I did it was the hard way
It is that desire is suffering
And the funny thing about it was
I never wanted much anyway

But the way I know this is because
Once in awhile I have had a day
When I got what I thought I desired
Only to be disappointed when
It left me feeling hollow and tired
And worse off than I was before then

Absurdity seems to enjoy me
I do not enjoy it anymore
And like crime it never seems to pay
All its riddling has become a bore
Yet this is not what would destroy me
As I had to learn it the hard way
Desire is that which brings suffering

I never wanted much anyway
Except for possibly everything
Still I wanted and so I became
A purple-hearted casualty
Desire is the face which bears the name
Of suffering for those who would be
Free but are a little slow to learn

Made to look foolish looking for love
Slowly we learn to suffer each day
Lovers and poets and fools like me
Tempted by fire who forget the burn
Stubborn believers in destiny
Wanting so much to have an above

Alone tonight I look up and see
The scars I earned by my suffering
Stars as souvenirs of ecstasy
And the funny thing about it was
Maybe I never learned anything

Two-Part Invention

As counterpoint delights the mind
And harmony inspires
Where our voices answer voices
Which call as we respond
It is when gospel answers law
When law at last comes true
We spring ahead to fall behind
In winter's deep desires

But our music gives us choices
With promptings from beyond
To help remember what we knew
We did see what we thought we saw
But can we bear the knowledge of
This counterpoint which we call love?
We did see what we thought we saw
And it was love as I love you

Countdown

When others have judged me then I have tried
To please them but they were not satisfied
It was never that they cared about me
They only insisted that I agree
That they were as much better as they thought
Than me then having humiliated
Me with a warning to stay in my place
Moved on to hurt others smug and sated
Now I am just somebody they forgot
Another recipient of their grace

Stop looking down on me you Bush-league boobs
As if anyone could look up to you!
I enjoy watching you go down the tubes
Too late for you now whatever you do
You felt so morally superior
You huffed and puffed and postured on TV
You thundered only you knew what was true
But you were scared and felt inferior
As you nailed down your new theocracy
To force the spring by false security

I hate to tell you but your time has passed
Peoria got wise to you at last
When they could not find their democracy
Euphoria was sweet but went too fast
It was like cocaine you want it again
But sick of snorting prigs and pigs of pain
Barnyard bullies and snakehandlers of hate
The people rise against you one by one
Your days of swagger dwindle as we wait
The nightmare ends soon: we rise with the sun

Among My Souvenirs

The bookends of my life are books themselves
My days are represented on my shelves
I wrote a few and others wrote the rest
I journey here across the universe
I write and read and think of life as quest
As drama we never get to rehearse
As wandering and searching for the best
To treasure here if I find it someday
Then leave behind me when I go away
My moments moving forward in reverse

When I go it might not be very far
That is if I ever go anywhere
I see out my window a small blue star
And if it would have me I could go there
But this is where I am where I belong
I feel like I exist when I am here
My heart is quiet and my love is strong
To have the bookends of my life so near
That I remember everything between
What was and what is and what might have been

To Spend the Evening Quietly

After a long day of debauchery
With all of its riotous roistering
I like to spend the evening quietly
In reading and writing and cloistering

Just Fred and me in our sanctuary
A cat and man both of a certain age
Closer to the end than the beginning
Of lives which have been extraordinary
Now settling in the season of the sage
Having survived to see ourselves winning

We see ourselves growing old truth be told
The days grow short debauchery grows tame
His cat food grows stale and my tea grows cold
Our roistering not so riotous now
A cat and man curled side by side the same
Cloister to roister as time will allow

Who takes the credit also gets the blame
We ask for neither and have both somehow
Tomorrow is another day but we
Would like to spend the evening quietly

A Mystery Which No One Need Explain

Opportunity knocked while I was out
And might have knocked me out if I had known
By the time I heard that it was about
It had passed by and I was left alone
They say it will come back some other day
But I never wanted it anyway

If you knew what it was would you tell me
Or would you think it wiser to remain
Steadfast in silent solidarity?
A mystery which no one need explain
(And therefore most know better than to try)
I am like you part pleasure and part pain
Better but bitter as the years go by
Less permanent than I had hoped to be
A shadow-play too fragile to sustain

My friend we both know too well what we are
And nothing can be done about it but
To say a prayer or wish upon a star
The wheel turns as it will no matter what
We fall like leaves but gently and not far
So if you hear a knock go to the door
And answer it before a stranger does
It might be what we have been waiting for
Although what that would be I could not say

Opportunity knocked (I thought it was)
But I was out and thought it went away
I am glad you are with me now because
As my eyes adjust to the dark I see
The key turn silently within the lock
Could this already be that other day?

Something is coming but I hear no knock
A mystery which no one need explain

WINTER

Mice must leave their corners at last
Flies on the wall fall to the past

This mouse in the corner fly on the wall
Was given much to see with much required
For each of the pretty promises made
An equal and opposite price was paid
I wish I could have understood it all

But the sacrifice of suffering fired
A burning dawn within me that this was
Predestined destiny so deep-desired
That in pursuit of it I am afraid
I had to break the rules as I obeyed

My perspective was limited because
Long exercise of duty left me tired
Ending up a brokenhearted misfit
Albeit fascinated all the same
Trying if failing to make sense of it

If I could return from riddling this game
I would bring back the beautiful and true
Stuffed in my pockets smuggled out for you
A mouse in the corner fly on the wall
Slipping out unnoticed secret and small

Sometimes mice roar sometimes flies soar
But must leave their corners at last
I was but temporary there
And from the wall fell to the past
As everything does everywhere

Soon it will not be winter anymore

Tough Guy (Not Enough Guy)

Being a tough guy is not enough guy
If you would be a hero go be kind
If you would be enlightened change your mind
And if you would taste immortality
Embrace your children and let love flow free
As the essence of everything you do
Be true to yourself and your dignity
Hold tight to your dreams until they come true
Then believe in the happiness you find
Which no one else can take away from you
No matter how tough (not enough) guys try

When you find happiness you get to keep
What you have found so claim it as your own
Its branches will grow strong its roots go deep
A tree to shade you when you feel alone
If someone tries to cut it down then say
"No: I will not be pushed around today
I will never let you use me again"
To "No" is to refuse to play that game
Wherein no one wins anything but pain
To "No" is to be (the most direct way)
A human being worthy of the name

Sent here to learn compassion or to die
Being a tough guy is not enough guy

The Dow and the Tao

The Dow is not the Tao
The free will pay a fee
The wheel still turns for now
But no one rides for free

No one is calling to my attention
(Or at least not anyone I recall)
Anyone paying attention to me
Since I am several sizes too small
So I will leave this sword of Damocles
Hung by its hair in its timeworn tension
To bring some other sucker to his knees

The elephant in the room I mention
Since unmentioned it is there anyhow
Has been for me I never got to be
As I recall hearing my ex-wife say
"Old enough for responsibility"
Or something along those lines anyway
Something involving immaturity

I lost what little I had hoped to win
With no grey hairs at least not until then
Serious worry had yet to begin
Now thoroughly grey I still wonder when
The adulthood of which she spoke kicks in
Will life be like angry pigs in a pen
Or orderly as a recycling bin?

The Tao is not the Dow
Nor has it ever been
The wheel turns still somehow
Whatever that might mean

Still Open

To open to the possibility
Of meaningful interaction in this
Brief intermezzo of you and of me
To maybe even seal it with a kiss
Of cost to none of benefit to all
Is what I want and how I want to be

Come share with me a secret for awhile
A subtly-shared shining star we can call
Our own whenever we see it and smile
Or maybe an airplane flying somewhere
So far away it might never get there
Still open to the possibility

I know you and know you are lonely too
Because inside of us we are the same
As we seek each other as we must do
We find the picture is shaped by the frame
And of their stories which of them is true?
No cash no credit no one is to blame

The angle of your cigarette indicts
It whispers of a thousand eyes of night
Down in the garden of earthly delights
Eyes which have seen it all and like to fight
About it whichever way they might feel
Since I quit smoking those eyes seem unreal

Lonely Street

In the beginning it was bemusing
To be disarrayed by humanity
So new and overwhelming as it was
For one knowing nothing of anything
To be riding the rails of puberty
Learning the rules of a dangerous game
In time to come to become confusing

Thinking too much about why and because
Which led then to a time of refusing
To let myself feel what I knew was real
To admit how beautiful it could be
Acting as though my heart were made of steel
When it was made of flowers blood and flame
Convincing no one of the lie at all
My need worn manifestly as my name
With red autumn leaves beginning to fall

Now I admit how much it means to me
To share an umbrella under the rain
Since not of steel I hurt and bleed and feel
I always knew but now I say it plain
My eyes are open now and I can see
What open eyes being honest reveal
As I have loved so would I love again

Was what I heard an answer when I cried
Or just an echo of a troubled mind
Acting out some internal dialogue
Explaining itself to be justified?
Who is it who speaks to me in the night
A whispered suggestion from far away
Convicting me before I have been tried
And telling me I must go free today
Is someone there or is my mind not right?

The hunter by agreement with his dog
Decided to leave the question behind
But I wait for its answer every day
Believing stubbornly hoping to find
Among this world of words something to say
Which might mean something to someone somehow
I wonder if anyone understands

If you understand would you tell me now
Out here as we hold our hearts in our hands?
Where we stand awkward looking at our feet
Where I wonder if we suffer in vain
Beyond what now seems merely amusing
We seem so lonely and in so much pain
Together here alone on Lonely Street
But insofar as the pain will allow
As I have loved so would I love again

The Quest

chorus mysticus

Until equipoise turns to ecstasy
Solitude is taken as sacrament
It is not loneliness alone with God
Poised on a promise I pause to repent
Embracing the fast the watch and the rod
Alone with God and I will not relent
While I must wrestle the mysteries of
The quest which I have come this far to learn

A word beyond words of loves beyond love
Is free to all who would dare to be kind
Which none may earn but each may own in turn
By treading where the immortals have trod
Up steep winding paths to infinity
Where I must make my pilgrimage alone
Familiar with the moon if I would be
Known in your heart as I am in my own

And when I know and am known I will see
When you will too as everyone what I
Was sent here for in the first place to find
The answer to the riddle why we die
And when we do what becomes of the mind
Considering this question constantly
If thoughts have wings then by these I will fly
But I will not leave those I love behind

I will share it all and point to the sky
Where I have been and hope to inspire you
To find in your youth as I in my age
Such gleanings as seem helpful good and true
One gathers by the path of pilgrimage

The point of it being to do the best
We can remaining faithful to the quest
Until equipoise turns to ecstasy

Oops!

Of the people whom I find annoying
The Recovering Fundamentalist
Who would do good building by destroying
Or the Closeted (False) Conservative
Whose rules only count for the rest of us
And who makes us dance for a chance to live
I cannot tell which makes the greater fuss
So two vie and tie for top of my list
And I think these are equally to blame
For making the world so wearisome now
In fact they are likely one and the same

Pay no attention to what they allow
For that would be nothing in any case
And do what you jolly well please I say
Attempting to enjoy yourself somehow
Since that is what people do anyway
Faith is not ordering people about
Creation is not for those who destroy
The truth is whispered (only liars shout)
My God is broadminded and we enjoy
Watching the bluenoses step in the shit
Which they shat on us (for the hell of it)

Because We Share This

Is this for always or only tonight?

I have to be honest and tell you I
Have never known of a time except now
But when it is right then it will be right
And when it is wrong we will smile and sigh

We take the bad to get the good somehow

Whether forever or just for now this
Is something for always if only when
Someday we remember this soft warm kiss
As present past and future (now and then)

Live love and leave but live to love again

I suppose we were supposed to have met
Remember December and tears like rain
Nourishing the earth for another birth
The earth has not seen the last of us yet

I love you more because we share this pain

I thought this was impossible until
Sheltering under your hair on the train
I tasted you but having tasted will
Desire you who inspire me to this fire

For always if that is what you require

We know no regret nor can we forget
This is for always and only tonight

Always and only (we know this is right)
Always and only if only tonight

I love you more because we share this pain

Suicide Note

My world is empty far as I can see
My enemy is not outside but in
I live incarcerated to die free
I die to live and as I lose I win
Another martyr of mortality

The reaper brings his scythe to lay me low
But cuts me free to fall so I can fly
My seed will sprout tomorrow bloom and grow
My way of life turns out to be to die

Up through the disappointed atmosphere
Of broken promises and poisoned dreams
Up up and away and away from here
Where hate enslaves and yet where love redeems

When there might seem to be no hope at all
Then autumn comes to free the leaf to fall
All that I am might seem like none at all
But my autumn is here now and I fall
To feed my seed of immortality

EVOLUTION REVOLUTION

for and against those pictured within

What is it about the slamming of doors
Which characterizes bullies and boors?
What is it about the dread of it all
Which keeps us from walking down the dark hall?

A certain unevolved stupidity
Which takes delight in slamming and scaring
Belching and farting cursing and swearing
Would love to be the death of you and me

So lock up the doors the bullies and boors
And know the world is not theirs but is mine and yours
The world is wise and it belongs to us
However hard the unevolved might fight and fuss

So duck 'em and buck 'em and fuck 'em and never you mind:
Rear up on those hind legs of yours and leave the apes behind!

Yes

Each day its world each life its universe
Which may turn upside down at any time
Where everything changes in a heartbeat
Often for better and sometimes for worse

Fortune can turn in shadowed pantomime
To prowl down an unfamiliar street
Where possibilities are limitless
And all one has to pay is to say yes

I want to live in the affirmative
At least I would like to try it awhile
After so long in its alternative
They say it takes less energy to smile

At least in that way a conservative
When it comes to shown emotion and such
I never had the optimistic touch
But I would live well if I am to live

Nor do I think I am asking too much
Where possibilities are limitless
If only here today or so they say
Since I am here I will stay and say yes

Yes to the future and yes to the past
To the only gift which I can afford
This present always opened first and last
The process of life in a single word

And all one has to pay is to say yes

Being Me

I

I am embarrassed to seem a failure
When so many had been expecting me
Or maybe it was just my family

To have made them proud might have been the cure
But they were honest and they said they were

And now they have all gone into the light
As I have gone further into the dark
I will live simply and sleep in the park

Although a failure is what I might seem
I am still here now and I can still dream

II

If poor and sick and uncomfortable
Having made rather a mess of living
I am not one of the irritable
Who seem to prefer getting to giving

I give away such as I have to give
Which could be why I have so little now
Having hit bottom deciding to live
Against bad odds and good advice somehow

Everybody knows what is best for me
But I have to follow my destiny

III

My grandma thought it was I was too smart

She and her doctor were worried for me
Life broke my mind just like it broke her heart

I think my mother saw how it would be
But she married my father after all

My grandpa was not my grandfather but
With that perspective could see that my fall
Would lift my people up no matter what

What they all wanted was to make it right
But ran out of time as day became night

    IV

My children love me and I love them too
They watch me curiously anyway
One eye made proud one blind by what I do
I think one or two of them might still pray

The future is impossible to see
In fact the present is pretty hazy
As the past slips slowly from memory
Every now and then someone goes crazy

Since someone has to do it I will be
Myself since I am best at being me

I Finally Wept for My Father Today

I finally wept for my father today
The one who abandoned me when I was young
When he was young too then the years had their way
With us both while to the last he held his tongue
As I did but the silence is broken now

He was my father even though he was wrong
Time passed us and in the end would not allow
The reunion I hoped for yet feared so long
But the silence between us is broken now
Like my mother's heart so many years ago

Sometimes I feel I can hear the voices of
All of my dead loved and lost known and unknown
One of those things no one can prove but just know
What it feels like more than anything is love
Speaking in the silence when I am alone

Which makes me wonder what to be alone is
And if the next voice I might hear might be his

RIGHT WHERE YOU ARE

If you enter a door
You exited before
Do you go anywhere
If no one knows you went?
You go out and come in
Receiving what is sent
But not from here to there
In linearity

Although you may go far
Should the journey allow
The point along the way
As you follow your star
Is not to go somewhere
But to be the wise say
Not to end nor begin
Never early nor late
At the corner where now
Intersects with your fate

Recipient of grace
Your purpose is to be
Now you are everywhere
And yet nowhere somehow
To neither lose nor win
But both to go and stay
In a state without place
In the smile on your face

To be right where you are

Healing Waters

I found out last night I have lost everything
I lie on my bed and my cat lies on me
Through a weeping window which used to be mine
I can hear the Christmas bells of my church ring
I sigh here instead by a cup of cold tea
With faint hope of favor human or divine

Yet faint though it is it is hope just the same
Its spark fanned by the fact that people read me
Some who have suffered have come to trust my name
I hope they know I need them if they need me
And I feel like they can understand my shame

As I must leave my home now and slip away
Some other hurt hearts share this hurt poetry
These sharp and bloody shards of who I once was
Of who I am and we are even today
We are not dead yet and I still have my cat
My readers know how much I thank God for that

I will get up and go to the Plaza now
A place as improbable as me because
It survived through purity of heart somehow
And it only exists to make things better
At a time when it seems things could be no worse

Stray drops from the fountain mingle with my tears
There is love and beauty in the universe
Teardrop by teardrop and letter by letter
No matter what we win and lose through the years
Healing waters of the only home I know
Kiss my face one more time before I must go

Son of a Gun

to Amanda Cardona for her twenty-fifth birthday

They say he first worked for the bad guys then
He saw he could work for the good guys when
They called him up not caring right from wrong
So slaughtered for both sides silent and strong
Since all he ever wanted was to kill
And this hunger was shared by other men

When he found out the good guys were worse than
The bad guys then he asked what kind of man
He was and his answer was to go mad
As honest killers have done and do still
His heart and mind broke beyond good and bad
Beyond the black breakwater of the will

I can finally understand him now
But used to seek to summon him somehow
To disappear imagined enemies
Who were not amenable to reason
One of my absent father fantasies
A childhood nightmare of killing season

And so my father Wallace Dean Lance was
A hitman for the cause of just because
Which seemed I suppose like reason enough
And now he is dead as I will die too
Should such time come as I can bear no more
Until then that which keeps me here is you

You and a certain curiosity
My hitman father passed along to me
Since I am here with my ticket paid for
Past pain to remain until our play ends

To place my rhyme in space and time and soar
Because unlike my father I have friends

Not friends with connections nor friends with guns
People like that are not friends anyway
Who go away when the going gets tough
But friends like you who are genuine ones
With whose help I am able to get through
The night that I might live a better day

Son of a hitman bad good and then mad
My father's life seems meaningless and sad
And though I have killed no one that you know
It is hard to stay and easy to go
Meaning costs more in the market these days
If I could afford some I would be glad

Balancing here on the blade of always
I mean to make atonement for the sin
Which burns in the blood of my family
And would prevent me before I begin
But there is a certain stubbornness in
A son of a hitman a son like me

If it can be done then I am the one
To balance the wheel: a son of a gun

Water Music

My ashes soon will join the sea
I always enjoyed the beach
And passed my Sea Stones out for free
Such as I could afford to
And though I subtly sought to teach
Daresay I never bored you

I was not much but what I was
Brought us more credit than blame
I hope you will remember me
And smile when you say my name

My reach fulfilled its grasp because
My nights and days were the same
I saw the stars in squadrons storm
To scrub the sky and scour me
I sang the sea informed by form
And felt its waves empower me

My own Ash Wednesday sacrament
Will settle to the seabed
The equipoise we spoke and meant
In all those poems we read

As death from life is different
I will go to sea instead
And when I do remember please
That joy of understanding
When we shared poems such as these
Hearts pure and undemanding

Beneath the lamplight late at night
There was magic in the air
We spoke our hearts and heard them right
Now to be heard everywhere

Keep those old chewed-up manuscripts
I gave you and think of me
Poets like us are not for crypts
But to be part of the sea

My life your love our sea as one
In true triangularity
Will meet in the seaweed's tangle
Red seaweed dusted grey with me
Where jellyfish streamers dangle
Then rock the boat with a party

If when you pour some of me blows away
Sea breeze will breathe me in and it will say:

"We have a taste for poetry
As he who went to sea at last
Borne on my breath and carried free
Into the future from the past
The elements in harmony"

The sea will sing informed by form
Eternity empower me
The stars will swirl down in a swarm
Bright fireflies to devour me
As glorious life victorious loves me free

My beautiful children all I love you so
Celebrate your lives and mine when I must go

Birthday Meditation

31 December MMVII

It was better than it could have been and
Yet it could have been better than it was
But what it was and is (which is my hand
As dealt me) was to become my because

The answer which I came to understand
To "Why am I here?" My quest and my cause
Is but to leave it better than I found
It waiting for me to take up and be
(If sometimes squalid at other times grand)
Whatever I want now as I set free
My destiny found lying on the ground
As a wrapped gift by the side of the road

This compass which tells me where I am bound
How best to bear the burden share the load
Life gave me I must wear upon my back
This knowledge I need in order to grow
And how to love and live with what I lack
Or rather without what others might know
Who spoke into the dark without a sound
And told nothing since no one told them so

But that was back before I came around
I mean to make some noise before I go
And not go quietly into the dark
If there is to be fire I am the spark

Have I lived long enough? (How about you?)
I have not yet learned how to be a man
Despite what I have done and what I do
So I must keep doing the best I can

Although it might not be enough at last
And not go quietly into the dark
Into the dreary dustbin of the past
If there is to be fire: I am the spark

Compassion Fatigue

Those things you think so therefore think you see
Concrete with your own eyes as though complete
As how it is so far from me so near
To you which you then call reality
An inescapable cage at the zoo
Which you find conclusive so you repeat
As though I have to hear them slow to hear
Stay stubbornly invisible to me
You say it is hopeless but I will not

I know your numbers add the way they do
And threaten as you say no matter what
Then you add your threat of subtracting you
Which you will insist is not a threat but
Merely how merely my life has to be
I still remember one thing you forgot
I still believe my miracle will come
You say it is hopeless but I will not

If you have no hope left I still have some
You tried to help me and you give up now
I love you and I thought you loved me too
But I have to make my last stand somehow
And now I find myself out of your league
You tire of me now as of compassion
With warm words yet with eyes so cold so clear
I am alone again in my fashion
You say it is hopeless but I will not

Although as you know I was once like you
You judge me as unworthy to be here
I fell through the cracks down out of your league
Although before you were right here I was
Now a victim of compassion fatigue

Still I remain if victimized in pain
Although judged as unworthy to be here
If just to show the world (and you) again

You say it is hopeless but I will not

Paradox

I who have little see one who has none
And wonder which is the fortunate one
Our coin has one side for bad one for good
One of us falling one of us leaning
I have never understood the meaning
If there is meaning to be understood

I look white yet I am a cousin of
Langston Hughes in a paradox I love
A family tree of poetic wood
With T. S. Eliot and others too
Possibly even a cousin of you
My neighbor in our human neighborhood

I am going through a terrible time
But others are going through even worse
I try to line my lifelines up by rhyme
In my syllable-counting universe
The only place I have control is here
Where poetry is fashioned from my fear

When times were better I would sing of light
Of drawing a sword if only in pen
But now there seems no sword to put things right
Although I draw it again and again
In pencil imperfectly and erased
To leave little but bitter aftertaste

And so I struggle stumbling though the dark
A cousin of poets who would be one
Still trying to protect such little spark
As left me until a fire has begun
At which time I might sing of light once more
To do again what I once did before

If there is meaning to be understood
Will I ever understand the meaning?
Am I falling now or only leaning?
The coin has one side for bad one for good
I with my little see one who has none
And wonder which is the fortunate one

WITHOUT INTO WITHIN

Those who believe in it keep insisting
On the reality I keep resisting
Because it could simply never be mine
Though apparently for them it seems just fine
As their only way for me to break my fall

And I suppose it makes sense of a kind
To them anyway never mind to my mind
So they relentlessly keep persisting
But it is an argument no one can win
How could one imagine one size would fit all?

This leads me to ask of reality
How many are you? Have you one to fit me?
And when you happen when do you begin?
To me reality seems a size too small
When fitted from without into within

Poetic License

I live on the knife of life not the fence
Each day is a dangerous trip for me
While each night is an existential fight
Wrestling with the angel of destiny

Life has been frightening hard and intense
Looking in dark and deep places for light
Some drugs some alcohol some decadence
But mostly stubborn striving for the best
Doing what I do with all of my might
Which I pray God might mitigate the rest

I will not complain nor need I explain
And somehow I think things might turn out right
In any case right for my poetry
Let them call the rest poetic license

THIS QUIXOTIC QUEST CALLED POETRY

Nobody believes in me except for God and you
But as long as he will lead me and you will read me
I have everything I need to make my dream come true
They used to call me lazy now they call me crazy
I admit to the latter but it does not matter
Nothing can stop me from doing what I came to do
I was sent and so I went and here I am today
To write my songs and right my wrongs: this is the way I pray

I cannot see the road ahead but simply follow
The steps the living and the dead have traced before me
With the certain tread of sky above and earth below
Beside the sea and through the fire into destiny
The elements in equipoise God and you and this
Quixotic quest called poetry which is nothing less
Than the reason I exist this madness I confess
This existential ecstasy which we share like a kiss

Share with me please bear with me stay with me through this night
God and I believe in you: come let us look for light

Oh God (Are You Still There?)

Borne by nightmare and blown ashore
To darkened day bloodstained by dream
Frozen inside this silent scream
I cannot rise to bear one more
Cycle of fear's insanity
Sleeping waking weeping breaking

And so I pray if silently
Through my cold sweat through my shaking:
Oh God (are you still there?) help me!

Please tell me I am not alone
Kiss these my disappointed eyes
With hope to help me realize
You have been watching (have you known?)
Stoop down to heal me set me free
So it no longer hurts to be

And so I pray if silently
Through my cold sweat through my shaking:
Oh God (are you still there?) help me!

Make this my broken heart your own
And let it bloom a butterfly
Up to the sun before I die
Lift me again to love to trust
You Lord of life beyond my dust
To rise once more since rise I must

And so I pray if silently
Through my cold sweat through my shaking:
Oh God (are you still there?) help me!

A Curious Heart in the Sunshine

A curious heart in the sunshine
Receives what the afternoon gives
Even a sad old heart like mine
Enjoys how the other half lives
As I look up and they look down
At the yin and yang of my town

In each other we are complete
As one complements the other
Who choose or choose not to compete
And I (as the black sheep brother)
Put it all into poetry
For them (but I save some for me)

If you are reading this you know
At least a little of my fate
Some fancy folk would see me go

They ought to know I have a date
With all of them (whom I love so)
I need to be here nor be late
Since very soon is my next show
This is how I make my living
I get what I get by giving

Whether or not they pay I stay
And even in pain I remain
Because this is where I belong
I have always been here (if queer)
The afternoon gave me this song
They need to learn to share this day

(If you are reading this you know
At least a little of my fate
Some fancy folk would see me go)

But I will teach them anyway
(Again and again and again)
A curious heart in the sunshine
Is one able to see things clear
Even a sad old heart like mine
Can see the truth: they need me here

As I look up and they look down
At the yin and yang of my town

Within the Labyrinth

The way it is today is not the way
It has always been nor will always be
It is only the way it is today
Nor is it the only reality

You might want to leave but might as well stay
Await another possibility
So as not to miss the end of this play
In which you take the stage alongside me

Sometimes I wonder if we really are
Here or if this is all an illusion
Or I wonder if I wandered too far
Into a labyrinth of confusion

But then what else am I supposed to do?
I follow my nose to see where it goes
It might still lead to a dream come true
Both best and worst is that nobody knows

Until it happens when it is too late
And when it happens is when we find out
Nobody wins an argument with fate
So we have nothing to worry about

We have to see what happens when it does
And not before nor after only then
Never mind what will be nor how it was
We were happy once and will be again

Within the labyrinth at every turn
I realize I really have no choice
But to be myself as I live and learn
And asking questions I have found my voice

I have no idea what else I might find
Or what I might lose and yet I have this
Some people tell me I have lost my mind
And I tell them how it felt like a kiss

We act and react we watch ourselves walk
And we wonder where we are walking to
We write our own roles we hear ourselves talk
And we wonder who we are talking to
Sometimes I want to leave but I will stay
Await another possibility
So as not to miss the end of this play

I look out to the audience and see
To my surprise a face which I know well
There is no one out there except for me
The critic who makes this heaven or hell

While up on the stage I wander between
And how it will end nobody can tell
But my fellow actors know what I mean
Since like our audience we are the same

We try to leave us laughing as we go
Our only difference being the name
We give it as we go on with the show
With no one to credit no one to blame
Except ourselves but then we never know
Within the labyrinth at every turn
Awaits another line for us to learn

I have to see what happens when it does
And not before nor after only then
Never mind what will be nor how it was
I was happy once and will be again

Within the labyrinth at every turn
I must be myself as I live and learn

BREADLINE BLUES

(by a ninth cousin of Langston Hughes)

Standing in the breadline
Forgotten by fancy (former?) friends
Stubbornly starving (doing just fine)
They have their means but I have my ends

Keep those pearls from the swine
Since they
Would only step on them anyway
God knows they have theirs but just let me have mine

(Not disinterested parties I daresay)

With the defenseless no one defends
Where nobody can spare a dime
Today
For poetry nor paradigm

Standing in the breadline
Left to marvel at the mystery
Of why
Suddenly they choose to be rejecting me
(Punitive and disproportionate)
They have chosen the wrong side of history
(Literarily unfortunate)

As I
Falling in (fallen out?) standing there
Politely with a part in my hair
Standing in the breadline

Start

To

Cry

(But by God I will never let them see)

Sunday Morning Veterans

Old men and women in their Sunday best
Embalmed and ready for a funeral
Flung frightened from the dying restaurant
Now brace themselves for this their weekly test

Having struggled with stall and urinal
Bent double blinking into light to haunt
The stumbling sidewalk to the parking lot
Of Cadillacs and Lincolns with their flags
Reminding them of wars which they once fought
Fumbling with wallets and wrestling with bags
Fight to keep themselves together because
Today ought to be like last Sunday was

I smell the mothballs as they stagger by

A victory parade of heroes past
Who know this Sunday might well be their last
When our eyes meet we understand and smile
Although we weep within and feel the shame
Of how we are and have been for awhile
We know each other then if not by name
Mortality connects from eye to eye
We march as march we must until we die

They return my salute then wonder where
They left those cars by which somehow they came
(But it was memory which brought them there)
These Sunday morning veterans and I
As comrades know all combat is the same

We shake our heads at that and then we sigh
And wait until next week to say goodbye

Butterflies

I

The circus is returning to Turkmenistan
I would like to go and see it as soon as I can
The circus is allowed now but a travel ban?
The circus and I will return with a travel plan

II

How do you know
Or
Where do you go
For
Enlightenment?

So few today
Can
Take time to pray:
Man
Needs nourishment

III

If we are the only
Ones here
Then why
Should we be made lonely
By fear
Of high
Delight?

I would like to unite
With you
To try and find the light
Of true

Human propinquity

Please could you come with me?

    IV

The rain has washed us (hobos) in from out
The poor of us are fat the rich are thin
But I am poor and thin so what about
This life we start to end when we begin?

Born upside down we always stay that way
The same
So drop a piece of gold in my tin cup

This has been such a lovely night today
I came
All this way down here just to get washed up

CLARITY

Clarity
Appears to be
Rarity
So hard to see
If it appears at all

Like a small star
Bright flashing sharp and small
Falling from far
A star too far away
For me to see convincingly
Especially by day

At midnight when the world is dark
Though not for you for me
If I seek I might find your spark
Appear elusively
The single shard of hope I know
Of ever seeing clear
Three wonders I have wondered so:
Whence have I come? Where will I go?
What am I doing here?

Clarity
I think you are
Verity
An honest star
Ever only always true

And I will be out there tonight
Should you flash sharp and small
With open arms to reach for light
If there is hope at all
I wish I may I wish I might
I wish tonight and wait for you

Come clarity and make me free
To see and dream to be and do
Embrace me in epiphany
Tonight to feel the real and right
My being clarified to light

Come falling star and fall on me
O rarity of verity
O riddle of the reason
For my uncertain season
I wish tonight and wait for you
A silver streak across the blue
Enlightening me through and through
Spark in the dark consuming me
Come falling star of clarity

Cookies and Pink Propinquity

Cookies have recipes people do too
Some recipes include ingredients
Which fly in the face of obedience
And make one hate to be told what to do
But count them many if count them you must

A sparkling sprinkling of the fairy dust
Though beautiful quite natural and true
Is one ingredient which you can trust
To put the fun in fundamentalist

Love always seeks its dream and makes its vow
Some people seek a pink propinquity
Whatever one might or might not allow
And in spite of our great variety
One is just like one with a little twist

Cookies have recipes people do too
From dust to dust some sparkle in between
Though beautiful quite natural and true
The sparkling sprinkled best know what I mean

Our world is big enough for us to share
Pink for some people and cookies for each
If God is there then God must hear the prayer
Of everyone with no one out of reach
Love always seeks its dream and makes its vow

As if it were not obvious by now

Lotus

We come and go before we know what we came or went for
Even as in the shrouded silence there waits something more
A sad sense of disquietude descends upon the mind
To think about it too much or to fear what one may find
It hurts to find how small our voice how little is our say

But the lotus unfolds as if for the first time today
And we each have a lot to say if only we knew how
But we have been hurt and misunderstood by so many
We have trouble believing we create reality
Especially having hardly experienced any

Could you go to the kitchen and cook up a bunch for me
Or must I figure it out alone at night in my bed
In those prisoned paralytic hours by the telephone
Which (quite apart from creditors!) abandons me alone?
By the time I create reality I might be dead

I think I will just have to muddle through at least for now
Since while seeking to be wise I became a fool instead
And I never could create reality anyway
Being too polite and passive to strut about like God
Though God would never strut and just the thought of that seems odd

We come and go before we know what we came or went for
A sad sense of disquietude descends upon the mind
To think about it too much or to fear what one may find
Even as in the shrouded silence there waits something more
As the lotus unfolds as if for the first time today

Twice Winner of the Breadline Milk Lottery

I have been to the breadline and I have returned
I was patient and polite while waiting but stood
Secretly hoping to win the milk lottery

Like I did last week with a purple stick of wood
Which this week was orange and yet I won again

One thing about the milk lottery I have learned
Is those who win it are the patient ones like me
Those in whom civility somehow survives pain

I saw a lot of friends in the breadline today
The most interesting people are all out there
And the few who will talk have the best things to say

The ones who are worst off are the ones who most care
For those with lighter loads on better roads than they

All of us who stand in the breadline learn to share
As suffering transfigures us and breaks the day
Just as hopeful in the breadline as anywhere

Past the Puppet Show

Here in this place it is the shadows we see
This world of confusion is an illusion
Demanding we embrace it desperately
A drama-queen illusion of confusion

And if it is real what does real really mean?

All I know is it never seemed real to me
Therefore I now find myself locked out of doors
Which were opened once for me respectfully
Or held for me on the way out of pity

I wonder if I could come knocking on yours

If I ever escape this unreal city
We could share the illusion of poetry
Wherein every word has been put in its place
So at least the confusion is orderly

I see something real in your heart by your face

Look past the illusion to see it in mine
We understand each other is all I know
I take our empathy as a hopeful sign
We might yet find meaning past the puppet show

Let us pull on their puppet strings as we go

They think they are the bosses bigshots and kings
These privileged pooh-bahs who reckon they rule
But they are only puppets dancing on strings
Looking important when the telephone rings

And each and every one of them is a fool

Here in this place it is the shadows we see
Shadows which would overshadow living things
But the spark in the dark is our empathy
Past the puppet show past the shadows we see

We might find in patches of light in between
What we mean by real and what we really mean

Running in Place

    I

Part of me never became an adult
Having died and returned to life nineteen
And now I am fifty-three the result
Of being myself all these years between

Nor would I want it any other way
Because all I have lived and loved and seen
In a place I went while running in place
From a place I remembered to forget
Makes me the man I know so well today

A quite familiar face in any case
Although you might not quite have met me yet

    II

I do better if I lay off the booze
And there are better options heaven knows
With so much to gain and so much to lose
I wake up each day to see how it goes
It seems to be going at least for now

As the windows open and the doors close
I muddle through as well as I know how
Some say it will never go well enough
But I have gone through much worse long before

I know how it can get when it gets rough
I can get through this and a whole lot more

III

The dirt is still there swept under the rug
Secrets lie buried out in the backyard
At the bottoms of grave-shaped holes once dug
To be forgotten although they died hard

Leave the rug alone and be careful where
You dig when you plant your garden in spring
No sense in digging up old troubles there
We have enough new ones for anything
From a place I forgot how to forget

A quite familiar place in any case
Although I might not quite have met it yet

NOTHING LESS THAN EVERYTHING

This all-consuming
Silent suffering
Is to be a part
As blessing and curse
Of the heart of art
This which pays nothing
And which costs nothing
Less than everything

For better and worse
We are made to make

What we will fight for
More than anything
In the universe
Is just to be free
And to dream awake
As we ask for more
Quite simple really

What we want to do
Is make it better
Creating a door
Brushstroke by letter
From false into true
Breaking our fetter
To get through to you

And we may disperse
But we never break

We live in the dark
As misunderstood
Or live in the park

In your neighborhood
Each of us a part
As blessing and curse
Of the heart of art
This which pays nothing

And which costs nothing
Less than everything

The Unanswered Question

I know it could be the humidity
The lunar phase or the temperature
My biorhythm or my horoscope
Or maybe only my stupidity
That somehow I can feel something like hope
Here in the crosshairs of this aperture
Where the deathwatch is being kept for me

And yet I hear the sound of my own voice
Cry out from this my crucible of pain
"Though I have fallen I will rise again!"
I choose life now and must live with my choice
But can feel how my hand is unsteady
As my heart since how can I be ready
For what lies ahead where no one can see?

The sun has fallen too but now the night
Though we are fallen urges "rise again!"
As time comes for us both to lend our light
To rise from this my crucible of pain
Having chosen now to live with my choice
That somehow I can feel something like hope
(Or maybe only my stupidity)

The deathwatch will be frustrated (for now)
That I can feel something like hope somehow
As eyes adjust to unaccustomed sight
And as neglected wings start to unfold
The lotus blooms for always young or old
But as it blooms will I see I was right
Or maybe only my stupidity?

A Silent Song of Solidarity

Only one has the power to destroy me
No one else is strong enough for such a task
Except for me but I want to enjoy me
I need a miracle now and so I ask

And I know it will be granted unto me
That I can fly blind into the future now
To a new and unfamiliar destiny
I believe it will be glorious somehow

I have a good reason to embrace my fate
Good reason to be happy and not look back
I was a late bloomer but I have bloomed late
With all I need now and with nothing I lack

I can be extremely persuasive daresay
And I am alive to survive and to thrive
I am here to stay and will not go away
My being alive makes the world more alive

There is hope for me and I can see the day
When the sun comes up and my troubles are gone
In a truly encouraging coming dawn
For which until it comes I stubbornly wait

God is not nor would be finished with me yet
I seize my future with hope without regret
With a silent song of solidarity
Arising when my poems are read by you

And you do read them (thank you) I know you do
It is you who give me the ability
To be able to survive and make it through
Only one has the power to destroy me

No one else is strong enough for such a task
Except for me but you seem to enjoy me
So I will fly blind into the future now
To a new and unfamiliar destiny

I will be luminous and transcendental
And above all else I will always be free
To explore the primal and fundamental
Archetypes of this our shared humanity

Since I have been judged I am not judgmental
All I want to do is share the empathy
Which I have learned the hard way over these years
Love and lift you up and dry away your tears

I can do this since I know about crying
I know what it feels like to be all alone
With not enough living and too much dying
But let us rise up and make our world our own

If it is not for us then who is it for?
Those rich and rapacious monsters out for blood?
We know what is right and we are asking more
For people less for profit: the greater good

The concept today is little understood
We poor are poorer while ever before us
The rich are richer and smirking at us all
They will be surprised when they fall in the fall

No matter how hard they try to ignore us
Because above all else we are always free
To explore the primal and fundamental
Archetypes of this our shared humanity

This is how we are and how we have to be
All we have to do is share our empathy
Our overwhelming human propinquity
Will call to us always to rise and be free

Shrapnel

Not from the golden age of radio
Just from the baseball games and from the beach
But after forty-some years I still know
Annoying jingles from just out of reach
Which seem to annoy me less than they did
At that time at this time since they are part
Of that part of me I cannot get rid
Of (that part sequestered within my heart)

Pieces of shrapnel brought back from a war
Of hearts and minds which was lost from the start
It was not clear what we were fighting for
We had an idea but were not so smart
About the secrets of the radio
And we never knew like we never know

Dust

When the sun shines I want to get outside
To feel it warm me and to escape from
The artificial boxes where I hide
Where light is limited with only some
Stray shadows sneaking round the shrouded glass

I want the sun to kiss me in my face
And as the boxes where I hide must pass
So must I too but as I do embrace
This shining sun too bright to understand

Life has been a bitter disappointment
But the kiss of the sun strengthens my hand
To feel able to keep its appointment
With what it is supposed to do for you
For me and for all to do what it must

At last the sun shines! Now what I must do
Is find the diamonds hidden in this dust
For each one I find a dream will come true
Or so I must believe and hope and trust

And if this dust is all I ever find?
Shake it from my shoes ...and leave it behind

BREADLINE SOLIDARITY

Fresh-scrubbed bright-eyed corn-fed blonde-haired girls make
A special breadline box for the poet
And boys who look just like them bring it out
They offer absolutely everything
But there is only so much I can take
Since I walked down and the grownups know it
So a volunteer volunteers to bring
Box and poet home having brought about
An eye-opening confirmation class

We pass a hobo lying on the grass
He is already tired and has no place
To go with his Saturday breadline box
But he got a good one in any case
And I see he holds a new pair of socks
Too clean for his feet until later on
When he can step into the fountain's pool
Tonight when the out-of-towners have gone
He knows what to do is nobody's fool
And illustrates the central paradox
Of homelessness where hard knocks go to school
Wherever he is is his place to be

The kids have had their eyes opened today
Their confirmation class taught them to see
That hobos and poets look the same way
At least when hobos are poets like me
Standing in the breadline on Saturday
Thanking God I still have a place to live
If perhaps only temporarily
To put away what opened-eyed kids give
With love in breadline solidarity

Hear it Ring

Are you almost ready for your freedom yet?
That word you heard something about at school? Or
Would it be better to silently regret
And not resist forgetting what to fight for?
(Do we have any freedom in any case
Or is that just one of the lies of this place?)

Change is coming and cannot come soon enough
Two stolen elections toward dictatorship
A soft-bellied junta of mendacity
Helps the rich get richer while they ream us rough
And they waterboard you for a little lip
So now I suppose they will waterboard me

What I want to ask you is do you feel tough
Enough to strike back at the oligarchy
Or are you just going to sit there and fret
About the big lie and huge hypocrisy
Which would keep you a slave right into your grave?
Are you ready to assert your right to be?

Is your dignity worth your trouble to save
Or have you forgotten about being free?
Do we have any freedom in any case
Or is that just one of the lies of this place?
Hey fat cats! I want you to know what I see
As you loot the coffers and leave in disgrace:

The land of the free and the home of the brave
Will survive you and your pirate's-pillaging
But if freedom is …you will soon hear it ring

Having Come This Far

a little song for Laura

You were so hurt so scared
So small so unprepared
To go down the dark road
Beneath your heavy load
With very few who knew
And fewer still who cared
How it felt to be you
When nobody else dared

Your now is my again
I know and I care too
I would have understood
As lonely now as then
And know you know I would
But I just saw you when
You rose a butterfly
Having fallen a star

New wings caressed my face
Turned upward to the sky
By this uncommon grace
You chose to share with me
To fly across the years
Though broken straight and true
Already dried of tears
Though I might shed a few

Apparently somehow
We are in the same place
My hand is in your hand
We know what words to say
Though we will never tell

Nor want to remember
What we have seen of hell
Back in deep December

But look how strong we are
For having come this far

And since we are here now
Where we are meant to be
Arriving where we are
Having come the hard way
We might as well feel free
To be and have our say
Past the indignity
Of wounds which will not heal

It almost hurts to see
Someone as hurt as me
But look how strong we are
Sharing this strength we feel
Seeing how much we learned
And knowing it is real
With these wings we have earned
For having come this far

The Finding of Easter Eggs

Thinking better to be underestimated
Than to be a disappointment to anyone
I privately enjoyed what I had created

But now I see some discovery has begun
Of all those hidden Easter eggs of poetry
Which I had decorated and then hid around

I always wondered what people would think of me
And what I left behind should it ever be found
I thought I would have to wait until I was dead

And until then live quietly so poor and small
That posthumous success would not go to my head
Success might not be posthumous now after all

Out practicing my poetry al fresco here
Like Whitman juxtaposing his antipodes
I thought I was anonymous wearing this beard

But either I am known now or I just look weird
Suggesting Santa or summoning Socrates
Because at least here my identity is clear

Given this and my other specificities
Word travels by word-of-mouth and can travel fast
Yet I seldom seem to meet with disapproval

People make me feel like someone nice to be near
Though my fellow wanderers face forced removal
I need not wander anymore but simply be

Of late when I read to them people seem to hear
With interest mingled with curiosity
Word-of-mouth smoothed and rounded like stones from the sea

This suits me fine since I would like to stay awhile
As I begin to believe it will all work out
And that I might not disappoint myself at last

I look back on my life with a bittersweet smile
To think that what the fuss of it was all about
Was the finding of Easter eggs hidden before

That I would bloom in age and that this thing of mine
For hiding things would in the end work out just fine
A secret no more now having slipped out the door

My future my present to lift me from my past
Perhaps I might not disappoint myself at last

Four for Four

St. Valentine's Day MMVIII

    I

The eye in the sky
As it passes by
Observes and illuminates
Us here as we go
Where we never know
Before and behind our fates
A sign of the real
Designed to reveal
Celestial coordinates
By which we will find
Before and behind
There are no walls only gates
Context to context
Through one to the next
Where light behind darkness waits
As shown to us by
The eye in the sky

    II

Mother Earth I hear you sing
Hear me sing in harmony
As I bring my offering
Knowing that you sing for me
And the rest of humankind
Those who see and those still blind
Out of sight and out of mind
Soil and soul and everything

Only those who serve are free
Fashioned as we are to be
Forged by fire and suffering
Coming out the other side
As refined and clarified
To live past where others died
Mother can you hear me sing?

   III

Apocalyptic people
Strike me as suicidal
Should lightning strike their steeple
They would forget the bridal
Baptismal confirmation
Or other celebration
Of life as God might send it
As some sort of lesser thing
Preferring God just end it

Time to hush and hear life ring
Within like their steeple bell
More of heaven less of hell
And what of the rest of us
Who still have some things to do
Love to give and life to live
People like me and like you
Who live and have love to give?

Apocalyptic people
Think they are the best of us
Are the strong but they are wrong
Strong people are those who stay
Who never find life too long
Nor aspire to slip away
Keep them to the west of us
Toward sunset as we turn east

Apocalyptic people
Come and partake of the feast
Of life on its wedding day

Baptismal confirmation
Or other celebration
For no matter what you say
You will find out you were wrong
When lightning strikes your steeple
Come and see then who is strong

Apocalyptic people
It might be awhile: go long

   IV

The rose called Sterling Silver blooms
In crystal in sequestered rooms
Where ivory meets irony
And ebony knows agony
Reluctantly but far too well
Decapitated and full-blown
Where nothing really can be known
And everyone only assumes
That life must be endured alone
While outside in sparkling weather
The sun and moon laugh together
As the roses bury the tombs

Our Own Reality

When what-if and then how what-if might be
As effect of a cause no one can know
Keep me awake I try to keep in mind
The future we dread ahead as we go
Becomes the past when we leave it behind

But if you need ask you need not ask me
We each must find our own reality

The past goes fast the future comes too slow
So no one notices the present now
Slip out through a crack in the back nor how
The longer we live the clearer we see
That we are trapped within a tragedy
Heroes and villains as fate will allow
Protagonists of this dying dumbshow
As agonists often in agony

When what-if and how what-if might be then
Beyond the cause and its effect between
When all has come and been and all has gone
Dreams dreamed life lived love lost and found again
When eyes must close to bear what they have seen
Night shades itself in shadow from the dawn
Our time will come though I cannot say when
We come to go and so our life goes on

One thing alone is known and satisfies
All existential questions with a thump
I am not very good at prophecy
But I can tell you everybody dies
So rather than sit on the fence I jump

You want as much as I do to be free
We each must find our own reality

Happy Birthday

This is the day you came to join us here
Whose yearly anniversary we mark
Remembered as when a comet came near
A close encounter with a scythe of spark
As welcome interruption of the night
By something more important than we knew
This is the day of the coming of you

Sometimes you wonder about all the fuss
How much of it is heat how much is light
And if you ever gave permission to
Anyone that you should be sent to us
Yet now we would not be whole without you
And so we know in our hearts it is right
That you came as this shooting star we see

To burn through the sky your own answer why
A bridge of light marks your trajectory
Your fireworks blazing a trail of day
Where customary cloud has burned away
To show you really are a shooting star
Something far more important than you knew
This is the day of the coming of you

STRAWBERRY

Hear in the sound of fresh water flowing
Smell in the steam rising from today's bread
See in the round of a young womb growing
Taste in the strawberry luscious and red
The world turn once again to hope today

The waves crash home and cannot be turned back
The tide has turned and will not turn away
Diamond stars ice the night's velvet black
Only to melt into gold with the dawn
When the stars wink out with the moon to play

While there is life hope will never be gone
Despite disappointment dare to believe
The law of love is cause to celebrate
The universe laid for us to receive
As paradise presented on our plate

And if you can make an angry man smile
Just for a moment and against his will
He might come to think about this awhile
Minding the miracle of being still
And life might find another pair of hands

Unclenching from fists embracing to love
Reaching from a heart which now understands
His hand is meant to fit yours like a glove
As yours is meant to fit mine like my own
The world turns all and none need turn alone

Hear in the sound of fresh water flowing
Smell in the steam rising from today's bread
See in the round of a young womb growing
Taste in the strawberry luscious and red
The world turn once again to hope today

Everywhere

An infinite variety of weather
Unites in fragmentation we who wander
A constancy of change to bring together
Those of us shut outside here left to ponder
Our situation as those who do not fit
Within so find without our when and whether

Liberation for those who are used to it
The challenge of freedom for those who are not
Both ready to soar on tried or untried wings

Our task is to remember what we forgot
As the living epistles of hidden things
Forced to root for our truffles under the sky
We have found what some less adventurous sought
Intuitively in life's interlocked rings
The keys to the cosmos are kept in the heart
Where we found them and keep them by asking why

Not everyone can see such important things
But to embrace their existence is to start
To be embraced by the magic of the day
Which though it surprises comes with a warning

Yet that which is closest seems furthest away
A thousand dimensions in front of our nose

If tomorrow comes it will be that morning
About which this night has had so much to say
When at last we might learn the name of the rose
And we will be ready because we were there
Out under the sky in a change of weather
The further we go the closer together
Without but within nowhere yet everywhere

Forgotten Awhile

    I

"Never use that fine end of your pocket comb"
Grandpa cautioned me as we were walking home
While not doubting his admonishing intent
I nonetheless have no idea what he meant

Perhaps he feared those tiny teeth injurious
Though I may never know now I am curious

Should I ever see him again I might ask
Beyond such misunderstanding as might mask
This mystery of the fine end of the comb
Should we meet again having found our way home

    II

I am new to the zoo but here I am now
Wet behind the ears wearing short years long
But scheming and plotting to escape somehow
As I will do when I finish my song

Why do those old lions look at me that way
With something which looks for the world like pity
Not for the lifers but the daytrippers they
Who are swept each night from this unreal city?

Come and wash off the stain of me with a hose
The zoo is the zoo as (now) everyone knows

    III

This is a snapshot of your existence:
You will get there despite your persistence

And then when you get there you might arrive
Where Charlie surfs and you come home alive

You saddled up and went out on patrol
Without knowing what you were looking for
So they got your body but not your soul

The time returns to saddle up once more
And should you spy me aiming from a tree
Just know that I am not your enemy

    IV

I combed with the wide end for all of those years
Until my hair went grey and my whiskers white
I combed and I combed but did I get it right
(I guess maybe not if I still have these fears)?

I finally have to use the fine end now
(Duly admonished) out of necessity
I could never follow anyone but me
There was no one in front of me anyhow

Deep in the jungle forgotten awhile
Walk in those boots if for only a mile

Out Here

Being homeless is a hell of a way
To take the air or get a tan or stay
Attuned to the inside-outness of things

Along with the upside-downness this brings
To the perspective of the indoor-bred
Forced thus to think about each night each day
When a bench in the park becomes a bed
And no one gives you orders anymore
Where a lost life becomes a memory

You have to forget to ever be free
So fight to forget what you once fought for
Which is easier than remembering
The shame clinging to you like dew all night
Forgetting seems the most important thing

Being homeless is a hell of a way
To live but more popular every day
There is more to it than just being poor

And although often caused by addiction
Sometimes some existential conviction
Makes someone feel called to go wandering
In search of inscrutable destiny
Blow with the wind and leave nothing behind
But traces which few non-homeless can see

No roof but the skull which prisons the mind
(And maybe that bottle under the tree)
I never want this to happen to me
Yet there are those who come through it all right
If you are home stay in and lock the door

Lest you end up out here remembering
Forgetting seems the most important thing

Two-for-a-Dollar and One Free Song

to honor my friend Sarah

    I

I have not become what I am to be
(I mean to be better moments from now)
But I am becoming gradually
Such as the limits of spacetime allow
Unto those of human mortality
Which limits I have embraced as somehow
That individual sufficiency
Of what I need and what I would ask for

So I will become what I am to be
Beyond which limits I may ask no more

    II

Hot dogs seem made of such horrible things
That two-for-a-dollar or not it brings
Me to eat something else for lunch instead
(They are grey where they once used to be red!)

In my heart I am not a carnivore
But in the most basic necessity
Two-for-a-dollar has worked out for me
I will eat less even as I pay more
If you will forgive me those moments of
Life interfering with the law of love

    III

I am starting to look like Howard Hughes
Not the young daredevil nor the old boss

But how you hear about him at the end

Looking like that thanks for being my friend
Sharing your victory with me (in loss)
Shown openminded by the friends you choose

But what am I going to do when all
Of the money has been burned through at last
So that I have to fall hard when I fall
As I cling with all my strength to the past?

   IV

Mere strength does not matter anymore now
We have become so sophisticated
Our strength sublimated to style somehow
By fashion we are fated and mated
Two-by-two as we dance aboard the ark

Not quite as we had anticipated
In our curiosity (in the dark)
But these are shining moments of our days
The ones we live to remember always
As only now forever undated

   V

This is that which can never be rated
When we come together to strike a spark
And feel something nobody could deny
Some think they know life although they do not
(Especially if they need to ask why)

I remember some magic some forgot
Or which perhaps some never really knew
How life should be heaven before we die
If you feel unloved (too?) I could love you
(There is no answer to that question why)

We have forever right now for as long
As two-for-a-dollar and one free song

Private Mass

Sunday morning: I could feel religious
But then again too much so to join in
Manhandling the miracle of the mass
So I will just sit with the homeless now
Panhandling for miracles on the grass
Like finding a quarter somebody lost
Writing as honestly as I know how
While keeping to myself how much it cost

Here as everywhere that white-collar sin
Of the influential and prestigious
Redeems the rapists of the ruling class
Wiping their smug souls clean within the hour
With minimal inconvenience to all
So they can rush back to wielding the power
Which binds us in the darkness one and all
They own everything including the priest

We pass no protestant collection plates
But velvet alms-bags stuffed with envelopes
Unrattled by the loose change of the least
By these our masters would control our fates
And since they own them freely dash the hopes
Of those who only ask that they might live
But the best lives now are sold for money
The rest of us just want God to forgive

The joke is on us no longer funny
The priest just another snout at the trough
If they could they would not let me be there
I cannot pass the means-test given here
Nor could my Lord so we have taken off
But I think he is with me everywhere
Except back there with those people I fear
We will stay where life is free and sunny

Out among the broken where the wind blows
While the fat and lazy priest goes to brunch
To root out any crumbs which got away
His snout smells money and he has a hunch
That the swine will be first on Judgment Day
They have theirs now but someday I want mine
"The first shall be last" I heard Jesus say
And it is he who gives the bread and wine

His body and blood unite with my own
His priest went to brunch and we are alone

LISA

2 March 1980

You wore spring daisies in your hair that day
What was it and how did it slip away?

The Christmas cards
And
The whole nine yards
Hand
In hand in hand

Neither of us will ever understand
If there is understanding to be done
Today as yesterday you were the one

Not "were" but are
As
If a bright star
Was
Is and will be
Though veiled awhile by my insanity

Whatever it is we knew what it was
And did it matter? Yes it did (and does)

We might not know where
It went
Nor want to go there
If sent
Back (since the clock went clockwise and we knew)
But I was there (and might be still) with you

Mother of my children wife of my youth
Maria and Stevie and Teddy are

The proof of the existence of that star
Reflected in their eyes it looks like truth

Finish Line Blues

When you are at the end where do you start?
When you have nothing left what do you use?
When the race is over should you still try
To reach that finish line before you die
Exercising futility to choose
To go down with dignity in your heart?

So many questions with answers so few
And if an answer comes it terrifies
Nobody cares about you except you
No matter how they seem to sympathize

I can feel my life bleeding out slowly
With precious little hope of getting through
This obstacle course of indignity
Which is not the race I entered at all
I can see death waiting impatiently
But I mean to make my mark where I fall

So I live alone with my loneliness
And a houseful of people who mean well
Not one of whom could ever know nor guess
That I am no longer there but in hell

Exercising futility I choose
To go down with dignity in my heart
And though the race is over I will try
To reach that finish line before I die
Though I am at the end still I will start
When you have nothing left what can you lose?

Emblem and Anthem

Honk louder for our protest than for theirs
Gliding on grease and plastic on pavement
Scream "woo-hoo!" at your TV from the stairs
Emblem and anthem of your enslavement

Big brother as you know is watching you
With one eye on his applause-o-meter
In the form of millions of well-fed drones
Hoping that you will be a repeater

The volunteers are standing by the phones
Rank on rank and ready with smiles of steel
Though they are not actually volunteers
But those sworn to make this unreal life real

So they must be strong social engineers
Though unsung unloved and quite classified
Who listen so well since they are all ears
And are immortal because they have died
When they gave their lives for your liberty
To teach you that freedom is slavery
Mechanical slaves of the agency

If I knew what to tell you why would I
Presume to preclude your own exploration?
And if it were my secret why should I
Not keep it for my own edification?

Yet if I knew what to tell you I would
Should I find an extra answer to share
Though so far I have never understood
Not even close though I hope to get there

Something good might happen to me today
Though it started off depressing as hell
At noon I feel almost hopeful (daresay)
That my tragic comedy might just sell

"Plaudite amici!" Jingle all the way!
When it comes to "commedia finita est"
Gliding on grease and plastic on pavement
Remember to applaud but then forget the rest
Scream "woo-hoo!" at your TV from the stairs
We never got ours but they sure got theirs
Emblem and anthem of our enslavement

THE BRINK OF NEVER

If I speak in riddles it is only because
It hurts too much to tell you how it really was
And even though I was there I never quite knew
What to think of what my young self was going through

Such thoughts as I have are visual memories
Which resist translation into words such as these
By my old self today looking back on it all
Some parts of which appeal while most others appall
An unfinished memoir better left unbegun

A long and hard and painfully protracted fall
In suicidal spiral through the bright spring sun
But I fall free as you will see when I have done
What I came here to do and that it was better
Spoken in riddles than written in a letter

Neither sage nor salesman I am not so clever
As to think I could describe the brink of never

Trajectory of Tragedy

On a trajectory of tragedy
Or else on an ascent to angelhood
I map out the matter of martyrdom
A concept imperfectly understood
Especially by me applied to me

I am not now nor have I ever been
A man of a mind to worry about
Other minds understanding what I mean
I speak when spoken to but will not shout
These things people shout at me constantly

Perhaps they are warning me to watch out
Perhaps they can see what is happening
That horrid inevitability
Which so darkly dominates everything
When dream is run down by reality

It is not that I need to be a saint
It is that I must do my uttermost
Impractical improbable and quaint
Impossible in the end as a ghost
On a trajectory of tragedy

This Fountain of Us

for Mike Escobedo

The fountain in the spring belongs to anyone
Who needs it in this bright midmorning of the year

We approach this embodiment of memory
Its waters emblematic of our presence here
As through a looking-glass of hope in which to see
What we might do arising from what we have done

And over and under it goes as we wonder
Where we might be next spring and what our days might bring
Just like our parents did and all who came before

All we can do is hope and maybe make a wish
For our kids and us and better understanding
While other people's wishes sparkle in the dish
Which holds our hopes to be drawn up to dance once more

This fountain for all seasons is for everyone
Who needs a penny-wish or wants a memory

The pennies of our memories shine in the sun
Reminding us that we are here and not only
That we are here but also that we need to be
For our kids and us and better understanding

The wishes of all of us sparkle in the dish
Which holds our hopes to be drawn up to dance once more
Wherever our spring whatever our days might bring

What we feel today is what will mean most of all
When we feel confused by the chill of November
The fountain in the spring is what we remember
This fountain of us: winter summer spring and fall

SHE WAS A STAR

"here's looking at you, kid"

She subsisted on beer and cigarettes
Never ate a bite as far as I knew
But lived better and had fewer regrets
Than me sure as hell and probably you
Living on love and a liquid diet

Dying young and living life black and blue
The good way as she used to wink and say

Back then if you knew you just kept quiet
And no one knew anything anyway
Certainly not what had nothing to do
With canasta nor the horse race at hand
Or shopping or swapping a tale or two

One day they would find she had lost her mind
But I found her easy to understand
And I loved that way she played her guitar

I loved her to death and she knew I knew
As she blew that kiss then left me behind
That she was some-bod-y: she was a star

Existence Without an Apology

Is it just our being human to wait
For some to become like a caution sign
Warning each morning on the breakfast plate
Of fate? By theirs these represent the fate
Of many as represented by mine
For example as I depreciate
In value to me but I hope not you

I deviate from that conformity
Where what is brightest is not what is best
But chosen frozen and waiting for me
Predestined to death by love and by hate
Deranged by dystopic deformity

The time is as short as the hour is late
As we consume ourselves unconsciously
And wonder why we do the things we do
I wonder about the bad and the good

I wonder as I watch them watching me
As though spectators for some sport of blood
The entertainment of an afternoon
Embracing catastrophe fire and flood

Can they not see it come for them? That soon
They may not be secure behind their gates
When vengeance arises red with the moon
In its existential enormity?

Revenge is as impotent as the rage
Of the doomed who just do not know it yet
It seems to animate this angry age
For those who have forgotten to forget

A bottle of courage bottled-up for
Those made too afraid to fight anymore
By hurt upon failure night after day
By day who wish night would take them away
But who by night never got very far
And who never know how lonely they are

Some go on to become so I have heard
Raw-meat volunteers for the thought-police
Those who caution against the written word
And who fold spindle mutilate and crease

Those who fear the writing of poetry
As symptomatic of insanity
And never mind all of that music then
On which I fixed my young years fixedly
Which turned out to be the ruin of me

A cautionary figure of how when
We give our all to something still we die
But by dying live to embody why
We have to do our cautionary best
Why we must do no less to be content
To bless at our last as first we were blessed

As many have cautioned many have meant
There is no escape from the now for we
Who live this game and make these moves as pawns
In black and white chessboard eternity

Like a lifetime of disappearing dawns
With one great dusk coming when none may see
Less judgment than simply the close of day
Now is the forever of destiny

A candle winks out in infinity
A prophet writes of God and has him say
"Vengeance is mine" he says "I will repay"
A caution finds the best revenge to be
Existence without an apology

THE SECRET

for the Laughing Daffodil

Is it ever too late
To enter a gate
Of a garden which encloses
A fountain which discloses
Whatever secret it should choose to show?

All it would show is what you already know
You could only see it as you see fit

What I propose instead is that you be "it":
Gate and garden fountain and secret too

You have everything you need to succeed
With all of the universe inside of you

It is never too late
To become a gate
Of a garden which encloses
A fountain which discloses
You are the secret should you choose to know

Breakthrough

Ultimately how it will be is you and me
Little else really matters anyway
I have waited for you as you tried to break through
And you have broken through at last today

Congratulations my friend

Let us celebrate the end
Of what we both recognize as the beginning
Of an endgame we know is ours for the winning

Ultimately how it will be is one great we
Across the world and through the universe
As we transcend ourselves into eternity
We hope for better since we have known worse

All we ever have is hope

We never have enough rope
With which to hang ourselves nor restrain anyone
From hanging us as we shine flashlights at the sun

When the sun goes down our beams will shine forever
Though small and weak to shine for all to see
As we wait here on the brink of never
Alone with hope and with our lonely will to be

Ultimately how it will be is you and me
Little else really matters anyway
I have waited for you as you tried to break through
And you have broken through at last today

As we begin at the end
I celebrate you my friend

Then and When and Now

We might not have been happy when
We thought so since we were
Posed to be as supposed but then
Supposed is never clear
So squinting unsurprised we see
Life squinting back a blur

And this point of infinity
Is what we know as here

So here we are half through the night
Half sleeping half awake
Our day half dark our night half light
And in this give and take
We end up getting only what we gave
And then we disappear without a trace
Except the dust of us at best a grave
Yet warm in someone's heart our smiling face

I believe we are happy then
At first and last and best
The sun will hatch a new day when
It nestles in the west

Then is the time for us to see
What when would not allow
And this point of infinity
Is what we know as now

Good-Looking People

Good-looking people have easier lives
They seem to have less trouble than I do
With good-looking houses cars husbands wives
Children pets collectibles and treasures
And then when they want to try something new
Friends with whom to seek forbidden pleasures
Just be good-looking and good things ensue

Sometimes they get in trouble but so what?
When they get out of jail they can go back
To a soft place in a good-looking rut
In their good-looking world as sweet as pie

I wish that I could be good-looking too
But that would be the least of things I lack
I would like some health care before I die
(Do I even dare to dream of dental?)
Though sick I cannot afford to know why
I look pretty bad and I have mental
Quirks (for example: writing poetry)

Is it too late for plastic surgery?
And even if it is not I forgot
That half-a-million figure is in red
Which means not what I have but I have not

So I will just take a shower instead
And be glad my three children look so good
The good-looking genes skipped right over me
My parents looked like models cool and tall
But for reasons not clearly understood
All their good looks passed right over my head
I look like a walking catastrophe

Yet sired good-looking people after all

Embraced

The usefulness of a window or door
Like an empty pot or the hub of a wheel
Lies in the absence these things manifest
Where to be is not to be there less is more

Wherein emptiness is put to the test
Of utility in an absence as real
As a wall or what might go into a pot
And where the spokes converge the wheel is not

The best things ever said are those which never were

Embraced by silence love speaks eloquently
In communication curvilinear

Our emptiness is filled by our propinquity

We find ourselves here where little is clear
Except that it is useful for us to be
A window or a door which opens near
A pot to hold all potentiality

Toward the hub of a wheel we know well but
Only as hope yet our hope no matter what
Of coming together convergently
Here at the clear hub now where the wheel is not

Epitaph

My life has not been as I thought it would be
Having known much more of bother than of bliss
I have never amounted to very much
Except for this and this is not very much

At the height of my powers within a few hours
I nevertheless will get depressed again
Having hoped to leave a mark and not a stain

But for the moment I will riddle you this
Little word puzzle and hope you smile awhile

I never was out nor ever was in style
Both of which have worked out pretty well for me
As I have attempted to find equipoise

I made some music and I made some noise

The Hand You Feel Within Yours

to welcome Darlene to the family

A barking lunatic who learned to howl
I mean to mark my moment of the moon
By meditation and my notation
Of what I might find without and within
The poetry of our situation
And share it in an avuncular growl
With chosen ones who have chosen to be
My relatives by human relation

As I like to be especially me
And now is the only time to begin
So now I encourage you to be too
Especially you as the rose is blown
Where something happens out of our control
We unfold petals we have never known
There where the lotus blooms inside the soul
Unfolding an ever-evolving we

No human being has to be alone
But for the great aloneness we all share
As sign and seal of our humanity
Worn round our necks as long as we are here
Along with philosophy faith and fear
Sharp shards of curiosity of where
We are and how as whom and even why
We are at all if we are born to die

We think about fortune drink about fate
We mean to do good and hope to do well
We try pretty much whatever we can
We scratch about heaven cringe about hell
And end up feeling like an also-ran

Like someone cheated at the starting gate
Where no one sees across the finish line
But the hand you feel within yours is mine:

No human being has to be alone

Incarnation

for D. L.

At which point in the song does one begin
To sing? Since I forgot the beginning
My memory of the middle is thin
And what I know of the end is thinning
Into one silver syllable of sound
Spun by a spider as a filament

If there is to be a next time around
The sun for lonely denizens of space
I hope those who come after know I meant
To sing it as they say from end to end
With what comes in the middle in its place
But one end and the other were the same

The song internalized me like a friend
Wearing my face and going by my name

So now the song and I are only one
Whereas one used to think of us as two
Where time and space combine in unity
When the song is done then it is begun
Complete when it is only halfway through
I made the song because the song made me

Here in this overlapping of our sun
My song and I are one and all for you
And all for one great synchronicity
In which we find we finally belong
The universe embracing you through me
Your voice the incarnation of my song

Someday When We Look Back

Someday when we look back on all of this
Even if only in heaven by half
Or God forbid only in hell by whole
The only thing to do then is to laugh
To see this from above or from below
Instead of in the middle of it all
And to know we shared a very near miss
Prevented from falling even as we
Spun in the spiral of our fatal fall
Seen from the future of a frightened past

Where we stumbled through a shadowed valley
Of death where breath is never known to last
Past where heartbeat stops when then we must go
From darkness to where they say we can see
The whole of things (but then they may not know)
A perspective change from vain to so vast
It took life to get that fast from that slow
Up to see meaning in its entirety

They say it waits there on top of the hill
A truth so true that no one can control
What seems an improbable climb to me
Although I never was a mountaineer
To climb by blind faith believing that day
Will dawn at last after our night spent here
But I need the exercise anyway
If anyone can see something we will
If not me then you (as you always do)
And if you see it first then show me too

Our climb in any case is underway
We only took what we needed to be
Ourselves our way no matter what they say

The part we never part with is our soul

The only thing to do then is to laugh

Stardust

Come reader on a little ride with me
A magic carpet journey just for two
Let go a little while to come along
And what I show you no one else can see
Unless they see it through that second sight
By which I saw it and now by which you
Will find it spelled out in the stars tonight
A pattern in the pieces of the sky
To map the treasure buried in your heart
Which is the point and purpose of my song

If you are ready now the time is right
For something which need never stop nor start
Or something which can only always be
If you prefer to think of it that way
By which the young bud wise the weak bloom strong
Set free by captive curiosity
It takes some getting used to but you may
Enjoy what is without a reason why
Not needing to know why this is that way
No reason why not (while the iron is hot)

What I would like to see is you be free
So like a grizzled little wizard I
Am here to sprinkle stardust on your day
Until the moon has waned and I must die
When I have lived a long time anyway
And celebrated specificities
Of mysteries I never understood
Except that life is sweet and it is good
To map the treasure buried in your heart
Which is the point and purpose of my song

Night Lights

for Darlene Lance and Christie Torgerson

Is anyone else as disappointed as
I am? Somehow I thought I would be all right
But what the cruel tyrant known as time has
Left for me as legacy seems only night
Without day: origin without destiny

Somehow I dreamed that I might be the one to
Undo such damage as could be undone to
Crushed flowers like us one petal at a time
That maybe I could heal the world by singing
And planting songs I hoped would be understood
Gathering the harvest then in reams of rhyme
With the hope my best would be judged to be good
As it was and is by those who have seen it
In papers they found around the neighborhood
Who never have any money but mean it

And so I have made some friends a lot like me
People who have nothing but will have their say
The songs I planted sprouted and are bringing
Sparks in the dark across the night back and forth
Where my night lights seem to dawn on some as day

Only love can know what a poem is worth
The kisses the poet receives for his pay
But there are few who love and many who wait
For money I owe who will not go away
And no one ever wins who opposes fate
Except for someone as disappointed as
I am who somehow thinks we could be all right
Though what the cruel tyrant known as time has
Left for us as legacy seems only night

Since we are day: origin as destiny

If anything good is to happen then I
Like a spark in the dark from a falling star
Must embrace my origin as destiny
Holding on for dear life to the comet's tail
And do it myself or else die asking why

If anything good is to happen then we
However separated however far
Who seem to have been left here all alone
But surely must not have been left here to fail
Must overcome our fear of the unknown

Circles

The circle is the shape which satisfies
It shows us the beginning as the end
Symbolic of departure and return
The shape to borrow or the shape to lend
Of new life being born as old life dies
The shape to return by the shape we send

A young man goes on his journey to learn
And if he comes back home again he brings
A lesson learned the hard way home with him
And when no longer young an old man sings
About it gravely though it was a whim
Of a young man who was curious to see
If he could do it and who found he could
I know this because he used to be me
And if I could remember more I would

The circle is the shape to harmonize
Our coming and going the gain and loss
The up and down of both ends as the same
Of our departing and our arriving
The shape which joins the credit to the blame
Of being fired and of being the boss

The circle is the shape of surviving
All the pain of getting back home again
Where gold is gleaned from detritus and dross
Where souls are lost their circles still remain
As ruts worn in the earth by the striving
Of the limited for the limitless
The temporary for the permanent
Like a dog who chases his tail unless
The dog knows it is his and where it went

Change Your Mind

I have been a busy beaver
An overachiever
And I want and need to believe
Sometime before I leave
There might be meaning to be found
Through me by those around

Where would I go what could I do
Except be here with you?
Life may not be an answered prayer
But here means something there
Or so we have been led to say
So they say anyway

Though an uncertain believer
I hope it might be so
And that someday I know for sure
We will be who we were
If only outlines on the ground
But then we never know

And our not knowing is an ill
For which there is no cure
Since the only way to find out
As soon enough we will
Is death the end which leaves no doubt
But leaves the skull grinning

A doubtless and a primal end
Or final beginning
For those who give life for a friend
Who lay it down then rise
Together through shared open skies
Losing and yet winning

We might as well embrace mortality
The better to taste our time as it flies
We might as well be friends here you and me
Together to separate truth from lies
The beast released is what is left behind
When we let go of ego: change your mind

Close Encounter

for Katy Conrad

What is this in the mirror?
Could this shadow really be
The image of the existential me?
More confusing when clearer
My surprised eyes start to see
Not just themselves reversed but otherwise
This is an epiphany

These eyes of a stranger to whom surprise
Would be as alien as is this face
Of alien familiarity
Familiar once yet unfamiliar now
This face not of what is but what could be
This face of otherwise which wears my eyes
Seeming to bear them more confidently

My conjoined twin separated at birth
When it fell to me to fall to this place
To stumble around without knowing how
To live life first from and then toward the earth
Feeling from and reeling toward fromness of
And towardness of this place where time and space
Move in place here as though from and toward love

The motions of the heartbeat and the breath
I assume now as I assume these eyes
Which comprehend even as they consume
Their parallel existence at a glance
Somehow more like orgasm than like death
And unpresumptuous nonetheless presume
To deconstruct this structure known as Lance

From two sides of the mirror
Face two halves of the whole
As near evolves to nearer
I see into my soul

Soul

It is the ghost within which haunts the faces
Of certain people in uncertain places
As the outside is affected by the in
So the spirit is revealed beneath the skin
The animus itself the animation
Which distinguishes the living from the dead
And whether dignity or indignation
The soul or whatever one calls it instead
Is there to be easily read on the face
Of the certain within an uncertain place

Let this be our sign of solidarity
A reminder to both of us that we live
That I can read you just as you can read me
Where we so often feel such isolation
Though certainly we are denied certainty
We remain to take what existence might give
In our take-it-or-leave-it situation

Though we bet it all and they say we will lose
Let us dare each other to rise up and choose
To do something about it before we go
Perhaps be remembered for something we make
And since we are certain of uncertainty
If we never try how can we ever know?
Where certainty bends there uncertainty breaks
The human race survives on the empathy
Which I share with you and which you share with me
Life is held together by a few handshakes

And one thing of which I feel certain is this:
Life gives no greater certainty than a kiss
The ghost shared within the soul beneath the skin
Shared certainly (even in uncertainty)

Stranger

Doing my best to quest my destiny
Without asking too many questions of
A force which I could never understand
I am willing to bear the loneliness
Of being the way I am since I see
That the consequence of my onlyness
As a stranger lost in a stranger land
As one unable to assimilate
As such an unwitting contrarian
Such that I stick out like a sore thumb here
As a quite-possibly-dangerous-man
Is that while I flounder with the hand fate
Has dealt me here where the jokers run wild
I run across other strangers to love
Who found me because I was a lost child

I will always be lost and always found
Know who my friends are and where they are too
Know strangers who like to see me around
No strangers to each other (me and you)

How ironic becoming iconic

Especially as an iconoclast
Wearing a tall pointed hat on my head
In perfectly balanced absurdity
Acceptance seems a general tonic
And icons (as we know) are made to last
These portals of improbability
Where opposites can be reconciled once
They are given the opportunity
Where one can be a wizard and a dunce
Who knows to know nothing is everything
That winter releases the death of fall

Wiping the slate for a new question in
The time when planted questions sprout in spring
I never get any answers at all
But I enjoy it when questions begin

If anyone asks I was just asking

Unanswered questions being ironic
Of something I could never understand
A once-a-dunce becoming iconic
As a stranger lost in a stranger land

Sparrow

The rose-tips are topped with sucking insects
The buds despair to blossom with them there
Tipping with the weight of infestation
Ripped roses unspool disappointedly
And through the disappointment in the air
A hungry sparrow happens to hop by
As welcome as if by invitation

She gobbles up a few but soon rejects
These bloated bugs for fast food on the fly
She satisfied her curiosity

A sparrow can look for lunch anywhere
She finds the flotsam and the jetsam of
A bite of a burger and flung french fry
Part of a taco and a gummi bear
And some of yesterday's peanuts from me

Yesterday's causes are today's effects
As yesterday's hope becomes today's love
Today the seed sprouts planted yesterday

Those insects though they looked sweet from the sky
Were not what a hungry sparrow expects
Their exoskeletons were extra dry
But hungry sparrows always like to be
As scavengers the last ones to survive

She shrugs then flutters away fleetingly
And I understand because so must I
Still nobody gets out of here alive
So I turn away as I must and sigh
How this sparrow is fortunate that she
Is not to blame as these ripped roses die
She is just as she is supposed to be

A hollow-boned creature whistles goodbye
As much of the sky as I am earthbound
She leaves me by myself to wonder why
Roses like people so seldom seem free

While the hungry sparrows adapt and thrive
Seeming to live their lives effortlessly
We deal with our demons and diseases
As innocents experience has found

Juggling woes like bloated bugs in the air
We mumble through the liturgy of life
And giggle to encounter answered prayer
When it wells up within us suddenly

Then when a blossom or poem pleases
The rose is or I am redeemed to share
Since we know neither husbandman nor wife

I wish that sparrow could have saved that rose
Both were busy and had to bloom today
One was born to survive and always knows
That unlike the rose she can fly away
So she is always ready to surprise

A sparrow bloomed today if grey and small
She flew to find the freedom fate denies
Which I have never tasted anyway
Arising from ripped roses where they fall
To wipe the unbearable from my eyes
As all I am and all I have to say
A sparrow said it best though silently

I feel like I am a sparrow today

And Yes: When Broken Too

Conventional society deserves
Its own company: it gets on my nerves

But I avoid it pretty well somehow
With nerves preserved and pickled from the pain
Of being unconventional all day
Some nerve preserved to go against the grain
And then (cross-granular and squared away)
Some pickled nerve reserved to come again

Experience picked and pickled preserves
A sense of perspective and saves the nerves

This back-and-forth dialectic of now
Is the wonder of our wandering walk
The passage and the process of it all
Learning when to listen and when to talk
Learning when to listen especially

But I hate to listen to the cocksure
Like when proselytizers come to call
A convention for which the only cure
Is when the cocksure get knocked down like me
Here where cocksureness never could endure
To be cheek-by-jowl with its destiny

Our hearts will speak someday when they speak to
Answer the questions we ask of ourselves
Nobody knows these questions like we do
And so our hearts answer straight from themselves
When spoken to (and yes: when broken too)

You

Matters of imagination matter
The matter of dreams is what matters most
As at the end when certainties shatter
The body gives up life to free the ghost

I will not believe in reality
As some do and say I ought to believe
It may look real to them but not to me
My soul knows even when my eyes deceive

They ask each other how they are and say
No matter how it hurts that they are fine
They question their answers then turn away
Before their lines and leashes intertwine
Screaming inside they chirp have-a-nice-day

Some things are real past our ability
To understand them or to bear their weight
And these are those things which could only be
Only as they are as the points of fate

We go through the motions and do the best
We can though it is not enough we know
Praying we will not be brought to the test
Finding the test brought to us even so

And what about us now at last my friend
Here at the crossroads of the universe?

If not my imagination the end
Of reality for better or worse
Here at the end where certainties shatter
Is as good a time as any is to
Admit the matter of my dreams is you

Matters of imagination matter
You ask me do you matter: yes you do

Imagining the Unimaginable In

I have seen the unimaginable begin
To seem imaginable and something like glad
To help me unimagine what I imagine
Imagining the unimaginable in

What is unimaginable need not be bad
Perhaps a family friend as familiar guest
Not invited nor welcomed but nonetheless here
Before my face in any case ready or not

I can imagine some parts and forget the rest
But I will always recall the absurdity
Of madness as the reason for no-matter-what
And for the madness done no-matter-what to me
(How to have been used is how to have been abused)

If the curtain must fall I remember its rise
The first and last become one in the memory
I wonder if anyone can see in my eyes
That I have seen the unimaginable now

I will imagine muddling through the day once more
I think I can make it but could not tell you how
I will keep imagining until I can soar
My fall my rise the birth of hope the death of fear

An unimagined figure waits and holds the door
To a dark hallway leading down to dark-knows-where
(This is the adventure everyone else refused)
He smiles at me a little as I enter there
Because he knows this game is one I have to win

Imagining the unimaginable in
I have seen the unimaginable begin

BAD HAIR DAY?

Let the wind arrange my hair how it should be
If tousling is required by a universe
Which knows best (in any case better than me)

Poets look better when the weather is worse
Like Robert Frost when he read for Kennedy
Like Longfellow out at midnight all day long
Tousled in his mural at the library
(Or of course like Whitman any time at all)
Some wind through the hair makes a poet look... strong

The wind of the spirit the breath of the heart
The rising and then the falling of the breath
Signals to the drums for the parade to start
So the marching band can march to life from death

Shining Sousaphones now stand at attention
To strike up sudden and subterranean
Ready to root rainbows from bottom to top
Like a geyser or inverted waterfall
With colors too bright and many to mention
Except to recall them again and again

I feel the wind and never want it to stop
If tousling is required by the universe
Poets look better when the weather is worse

Heaven Knows

for Stephanie

So hard to believe but heaven knows we try
Since faith is a gift and few are so gifted
Such a rush to get it done before we die
The tide goes out before our boats get lifted
And so we are left to wait here high and dry
Sitting in the sand to watch the seagulls soar

They say the tide might turn in a tidal wave
And break our boats like it broke our hearts before
We stay by our boats not because we are brave
But because these are all we have and no more

And we always seem to feel so far from where
It seems possible to have a soul to save
From where we thought we ought to be while right there
Before us the angels adore us as we
Who try to make the best of a thing not fair
Surprise each other to feel like family

Not based on baked potatoes but earth and air
Not on life insurance but water and fire
The universe belongs to us if we care
To embrace it as the heart of our desire

We let go to get the desire of our heart
Nothing more nor less than pleasant company
Forget the real and let reality start
Close our eyes and dream we are able to see
Stop rushing and learn to live before we die
So hard to believe but heaven knows we try

CONFLUENCE

These are the moments when our two lives touch
Like the confluence of underground streams
Little things which in the end mean as much
As big things because these things are our dreams
These are the moments of life lived as such

Without the mirror of another soul
Reflecting the me another can see
My perspective is only half the whole
And lacking in complementarity
To be my brother's keeper is my role

We reflect each other but we are two
The better to see another can be
The best thing for whatever might ail you
As you are for whatever might ail me
We dream and think and talk but then we do

With a friend like you can I get through this
And come out laughing on the other side?
Just make the pain stop never mind the bliss
Or other blessings we have been denied
(When I pull the trigger I never miss)

The moments of life must be lived as such
Bright rainbow-falls fed by underground streams
Little things which in the end mean as much
As big things because these things are our dreams
These are the moments when our two lives touch

Mirrors

They live in glass houses: mirrors for eyes
An entirely different breed of cat
Always supposing themselves to be right
My meetings with them have suggested that
If they could they would wear boots to their thighs
And quite possibly have it in for me

All these years I have stayed out of trouble
By staying in with my portion double
To the kind of trouble mirrored eyes see
More for the doctor than the officer
Not worn outside but treasured inwardly
Though probably neither would understand

Mirrors and I agree to disagree
About troubles which are but never were

I live in a dark place: shadows for eyes
An entirely different breed of cat
It feels like where I am is always night
Your meetings with me have suggested that
If you would I could help you realize
There are many forms of reality

All these years I have wondered about things
Jumped in with both feet to find for myself
Places where the bird of paradise sings
Observed in the wild not stuffed on some shelf
To hold the important things by the hand
Treasures of the heart for eternity

Mirrors and we agree to disagree
About triumphs which are and always were

Robert Frost and Me (Like a Chimpanzee)

"Diabolically intelligent"
Is how I read my cousin Robert Frost
Was and how he looked like a chimpanzee
In his great age (one thing by two things meant)
Mortal yet meant for immortality

I would buy my cousin's books if they cost
Less but can get them from the library
"Diabolically intelligent"
Sounds a wonderful way to me to be
(Even if he looked like a chimpanzee)

If younger cousin still an older guy
But lovely ladies love my poetry
And this has always been enough for me

I am celibate not quite knowing why
Which seems more mere habit than anything
Holding me back from having one last fling

Yet I wonder if Aristotle flung
Or old Homer having sung ever swung:
What of the love-life of the man of mind?

I want to come to life before it goes
Like Yeats I bloom within my heart a rose
But roses like hearts must be left behind

The one thing I can take will be this soul
When I must return (as we all must learn)
My piece out of the puzzle of the whole

Could it Be?

Here I am and there you are
Alone as we can be

Each beneath a far blue star
In the solitariness
Of the arbitrariness

The extraordinariness
Of our separation here
Together you and me

Across the darkened universe
Sad eyes opening start to see
A stitch in the fabric of time
Where as in poems people rhyme

Do you believe in magic?

It is far but it could be far worse
In the starlight of a night so clear

And I believe in magic

Could your star and mine be the same?
Could what we think is far be near?
Could here be there and there be here?

Could it be?

Reach out your hand with all your heart
Believe we are neither to blame
And I will too

Two beneath one far blue star

Together you and me
There I am and here you are
Waiting for the magic to start

Of loving you

Up in the Trunks of Elephants

Smuggled up in the trunks of elephants
And over the smoky mountains far away
Then all the way to me: I tried it once
And decided to try again every day

I enjoy a coffee in the morning
(Unless I hear of a new cancer warning
Of course) and keep a constant pot of tea

But what has helped most in times of trouble
Is the universal herbal remedy
Prescribed and administered respectfully

Medical marijuana: a constant pot
Blooming beautiful buds of the cannabis kind
To adjust attitudes altitudinally

It keeps me from going out of my mind
Releasing what I forgot to memory
While expanding my consciousness to double
Whatever it was before I forgot

Snuggled up in the trunks of elephants
Where mother ganja rocks me to be free

Human Being

Muscle into metal flesh into plastic
The fading of feeling to twilight of touch
We were so much happier when we were weak
But they tell us happiness is for the strong
The past would prefer that the future be bleak

So they lie to us though they know they are wrong
And gears grind our hearts down until life is such
Heaviness the disappointment so drastic
It becomes nothing less nor more than too much
To bear anymore before we have to speak

If only to recall how it felt once to
Forget about hoping and simply to be
Forget about trying and simply to do
Forget about pleasing them and pleasing me
Yet never to forget remembering you

I exist within my imagination
Imagining myself into existence
A shadow reflecting on its creation
As a web of perspectives held in suspense
A contradiction called a human being

In defiance of the mechanization
Of our once-celebrated fragility
And a past which prefers the future delay
Or else never come at all but if it does
Tomorrow is expected as yesterday

They say we cannot remember how it was
But only the way we imagine it now
We can only see in the present because
This is our human being way of seeing
We have eyes but for what our eyes will allow

I have seen enough to know I want to see
A little peace and quiet here at the last
Not of the rocking chair but of the rocking
Of the womb of life itself and not too fast
So I can hear such wonders as come knocking

The future comes looking a lot like the past
Without of course coming because it does not
There is no escape from this moment somehow
Except to no longer exist but that way
Is closed to me down a dark road I forgot

Blinded for now to momentary seeing
I see all I have is this humanity
Which frustrates those who would control by freeing
The soul increasingly until it is free
A contradiction called a human being

Wake Up and Scream

We speak of secret weapons yet secrets themselves
Carried close to the breast are both simplest and best
As the most potent weapons life has on its shelves
If you can keep secrets you can keep all the rest

My father was the one who kept the secrets and
Kept them better than anybody I have known
As casual as the gun beneath his pillow
As much a part of him as the gun in his hand
He traded for a silent deathbed all alone
And (although I do not want to) I understand

He left this world knowing things are not as they seem
Because of people like him and of what they do
Which must have seemed still stranger to him than to me
As well as his last wife (the one I never knew)
When after his silence and the thought of it he
Died with his nightmares as I was trying to dream

Knowing only shadows of the secrets he knew
Some stories of former lives from some former wives
(Although not from my mother who would never say
One way or the other since she was my mother)
I remain secretly proud of his derring-do
His swash of the buckle and all that sort of thing
From a gun for hire to the keeper of a king

If they wanted it done my father was the one
To pull the trigger or make bad things happen but
Then he turns out to have this poet for a son
Although I was a secret and nobody knew
Except for him except for me one life for two

Looking back I can see how his friends kept an eye
On my result of his youthful indiscretion
Dark men in dark clothing at dark hours of the night
Presents of his absence to watch (no matter what)
The son of an oak grow up to be a willow

Alone as he was on the knife of madness I
Can see how he was wrong now yet how he was right
But I wish he had told me life would be this way
His love was denial as mine is confession
My father is a secret his son cannot keep

Still waters run red and deadly as well as deep
His nightmares are mine now as I wake up and scream

Just So

Though the day grows long and late
This unique ubiquity
Calling us together here
Personal propinquity
Stretching out from far to near
"Diesen Kuss der ganzen Welt"
Human solidarity
Always (if not always felt)

This is what I celebrate
Even though I know we go
To where we have never been
Sooner than we ever know
When the cycle turns again
Cloud above and smoke below
The fog of the world between

Time is neither fast nor slow
Time is only now
Overlapping you and me
As now will allow
All its pleasure all its pain
Felt (not knowing how)
In this moment of this day

Never mind the past
Forward is the only way
(There is no reverse)
Never mind what others say
(Theirs was even worse)
Now is neither slow nor fast
But the universe
Just the way it is: just so

Falling Stars Mistaken for Landing Airliners

I feel like I am utterly at sea
And that I might go down now with my ship
If you have any idea what to do
Some notion of what might become of me
Then I will shut up and listen to you
But until then I might very well scream

Smothered to sleep unable to waken
From nightmares of an American dream
I believe in though my faith is shaken
By post-traumatic stress of yesterday
Links in the chain of the past forged to last
Still stressful and still traumatic today
Connecting with new and holding me fast

I have to slip away before I slip
Beneath the sea of consciousness and go
Into the quiet embrace of the dark
Where no one will wake and no one will know
(I would not go quietly even so)

Though it is not often that dreams come true
It has happened to me and might again
Even when the dream seems to be taken
Even when there seems no end to the pain
(I am the tinder and you are the spark)

I hope to arise when I awaken
Sadder but wiser if worse for the wear
And tattooed with a bloody heart-shaped stain
Having learned the hard way how much I care
After this madness to find myself sane

But when I awaken will you be there?
I believe you will be as you have been
Because you have always understood how
I feel and have always known what I mean
Always and ever (never more than now)

Down here where falling stars are mistaken
For landing airliners out at John Wayne
New houses and new people look the same
While at our old house some want us to lose
But they are just jealous and not to blame
Since they know that we know that was no plane
We see what we saw and saw what we see

I am a falling star and you are too
Fortune dealt me this hand and I refuse
To play for less than the ultimate game
One you and I together now can win
The clock ticks louder then strikes to begin
To deal where only two players remain

A CALL TO REVOLUTION

All over the world the children learn to hate
By traditional means unspoken and still
As part of the rest of the rust of their fate
Then some seem surprised when they grow up to kill

The children are only following orders
Like their parents did and their grandchildren will
Each generation gives blood for the borders
Since that is how they have been posted and drawn
In the dirt with the blood of the human race

Until the madmen in their maprooms have gone
To wherever the madmen of maprooms go
Children will be trained to be ground in the mill
To keep the blood fresh so the borders will show

That blood in that dirt once wore a human face
But the brain behind that face would never know
The answer or even what question to ask
Their blood was required to draw lines in the sand
Unspoken and still they were bred for the task

So they never had a chance to understand
The machinations of the maproom madmen
Only that the time had come to bleed once more
Fellow humans are you not weary of war?

It will end when we end it by saying when
Too much is enough and by asking what for
And why they need our blood to mark the border
Keep our blood in and let our souls out to soar
Past maproom madmen to a higher order

No license to kill no license to steal
No license to grind our children away
The madmen in the maproom are not real
But ghosts to scatter by the light of day

In our evolution we found revolution
If once did not suffice then we must do it twice

Franziska's Song: The Return

Your skin is copper and your heart is gold
Your soul is priceless so that it is free
To belong to God and not be for sale
As you shine and share it sumptuously

Your eyes are like a tiger's and as bold
I feel them as they penetrate and see
Like probing unknown tongues of primal flame
To burn me back to where I want to be

The young learn from yet also teach the old
When love returns (if by another name)
And the most surprising thing I have learned
Is (with all my heart): I want you with me

A tiger looked at me and I got burned
As if I had been branded in the heart
Or was it your heart (since we feel the same)?
Let the fire fall free: let the magic start

A lion in winter now roaring once more
A circle completing below as above
An after which proves to be more than before
The return (if by another name) of love

GRANDMA

I carry in my heart a little light
A diamond in a secret pocket there
A tiny star to follow through the night
Kept close and carried with me everywhere

And this is my Grandma actually
A spark in the dark she left here for me

Start at the End

I start at the end of my beginning
Surprised to see it come for me so soon
But past losing now I could start winning
Even as I wax to a waning moon
Awakening on the road not taken
Because the road from which none may return

Since I have always been a late bloomer
Here at the end of beginning I see
How a seed of truth gave root to rumor
Then grew up to be this reality
Which is not real but is absurd humor

I try to enjoy my absurdity
And having begun to end know I won
A present which my past would not allow
Such good as I have done is not undone
But spreads throughout the universe to you

What has been done and has been one with me
Survives only up to the point of true
Whichever end of beginning might be
End is beginning whatever I do
Presenting me the sharpened edge of now

And the lotus unfolds aright somehow
Preventing me from ruining it all
By taking it all too seriously
As a shrouded speck on a clouded ball
Which despite its depression keeps spinning

Despite this digression I am winning
Whatever it is I win at this game
If not a good number then a good name

Some of us take a good shaking to learn
As I was shaken so I awaken
To start at the end of my beginning

Lucky

Actions have consequences some have learned
For better or worse in this universe
Having played with fire having gotten burned
Things change for the better then for the worse
But the best things stay still steady and small
And to be forgiven is best of all

In order to ever learn anything
We have to make a series of mistakes
And put up with a certain suffering
But almost everyone has what it takes
To be able to hit bottom and bounce
Or get some help by the eighth of an ounce

Some play with fire and yet seldom get burned
And one of these lucky ones might be me
Nor am I certain if I ever learned
Anything anytime actually
My life has been a series of mistakes
Preserved by a series of lucky breaks

Keep on Dreaming

If you ask me to explain life to you
I suppose you might be disappointed
To find I left my explaining behind
When I looked for an explanation too
But found mine fragmented and disjointed
Since each who would explain had lost his mind

Then is when I realized how few knew
That what is worth knowing cannot be taught
What cannot be taught can only be learned
And what is worth having cannot be bought
What cannot be bought can only be earned

Dreams live to be lived so that ours may be
Illuminated lives where dreamers see
Circles above us reflected below
Where we catch what we might never pursue
But has pursued us here for all we know

Dreams are what create us as they come true
After giving us nightmares for so long
Becoming the essence of who we are
Having not killed us they have made us strong
Enough anyway to have come this far
So keep on dreaming whatever you do

Captain Fantastic

I always like to read the comics first
And have dessert at any time I please
Appreciating life's gifts and graces
A little of the best before the worst
Enjoying my health despite my disease
And through these rose-colored glasses I see
This half-empty glass looks half-full to me

No one believes me but soon I will win
This race (which while absurd is not so bad)
No time like now to be and to begin
To do such duty destiny demands
As scary as it is as it places
The possible in improbable hands
Which have not learned the concept of defeat

I want to be Captain Fantastic now
The time has come for me to rise and soar
And although lacking laurel leaves to be
If not the laureate of the elite
The Laureate of the Mad anyhow
Who has lived a lot to live a lot more
And to bring smiles to serious faces

The spacetime fabric stretches elastic
So that an old dog might yet have his day
As Laureate of the Mad anyway

Look out world: here comes Captain Fantastic

Egg and Stone

Life is fragile as an egg and hard as a stone
But I think with you I can get through it somehow
My old friend you and I have always been alone
Before we knew the word it meant what we are now

Since to be alone seems to be our destiny
And since I always like to be alone with you
I wonder would you like to be alone with me
Or is that how we are now or have always been
Through all of our trials (and what then does this mean)?

Some people just get along better than others
Not talking much but by parallel existence
As strangers get married and friends become brothers
With the point of contact something like persistence

What would we be and what would our existence mean
If we missed the point of human propinquity
No me-and-you but only empty space between?
Alone together sharing the absurdity
Of being we are seeing at last what is shown

It is written through the universe everywhere
In the star of the sky and the sand of the sea
In the fingerprint and in the strand of the hair
That we not only are but we are meant to be

Together not whether but when and here we are
My old friend you and I have never been alone
Here we are together (if only we had known)
The space between two human beings is so far
But I think you and I can get through it somehow

Life is fragile as an egg and hard as a stone
Before we know the word it means what we are now

THE QUESTION OF DESTINY

The answer to the question is out of the question
Because it is out of the question the answer grows
So if by my saying this I make the suggestion
That I do not know it is because nobody knows

I am willing to admit the pieces do not fit
Or fit in some way other than the way they appear
But I have long since seen this and become used to it
And the jumble of it all is the place we call here

The question to the answer is the answer at last
And so on in a dialectic which never ends
Between the answer and the question present and past
And the tumble of it all is the time we call now

I would rather share questions than answers with my friends
Because none of us knows any answers anyway
Although not sure of anything we get by somehow
And the here and the now which we share we call today

I feel less confused here than I might some other place
Nobody here pretends to know anything at all
It is something like heaven (or whatever you call
It) here where the question meets the answer face-to-face

I do not know because nobody knows
And not knowing has never bothered me
But out of the question the answer grows
To answer the question of destiny

Through the flood and through the fire
Through the deluge and the flame
Drown the guilt and burn the blame
Leaving only pure desire

Source and sense and suffering
Ego mind libido name
Talent time and treasure bring
To the All in offering

I do not know
And neither do you
But neither need we go
In search of what is true

The question to the answer is the answer at last
And so on in a dialectic which never ends
Between the answer and the question present and past
And the tumble of it all is the time we call now

You are here with me
I am there with you
This I know is true
This is destiny

Interior Spacescape

As much appreciated as little understood
I am surprised to be cared about
But what I care about is caring makes me feel good
And forget what I was scared about

Every one of us has a reason to feel alone
But to be cared about is to have your reason known
(We smile at one another while stupid people shout)
I have my reason known now and am always surprised
Although alone to have my loneliness realized

Where my loneliness goes the rest will have to follow
Although it can only be unique
An interior spacescape beautiful but hollow
Cared about (surrounded) as we speak

The Consequences of Resurrection

A star once exploded inside my head
From the inside out it blew up my brain
And though then I was supposed to be dead
After a few weeks I woke up again
To be not what I was but this instead
And this instead has been all right with me

The consequences of resurrection
Are functionally like insanity
And include a craving for perfection
Having tasted it however briefly
Which to me would seem better than never
Because it gave me something to reach for
But nobody has to wait forever
Our days have a number and not one more

A Love Song Actually

Unlikely friends and likely enemies
Who are misunderstood unlikely friends
Since everyone should have a few of these
And for those who care for both means and ends
The pure joy of the process on the way
Life gave us this along with all the rest

We hid it in our hearts like yesterday
Alongside secrets never yet confessed
To learn we were lucky enough to be
Likely friends and unlikely enemies
And everyone should have a few of these

I have always gotten along with you
Just as you have gotten along with me
And if anyone asks me what is true
I answer magic and how love is free
To say I love you right out of the blue

When my eyes close my open heart can see
Of all the gifts life gave you were the best
So this is a love song actually
To say I love you and I know you knew

Hummingbird Reality

Have you ever heard the buzz of a hummingbird's wing?
A hummingbird hovered close and I heard its wing-buzz

I believe I wanted to be before I was born
And insisting on existing I remain as sworn
To be and to endure transcending such wear and tear
As those of us who insist on existing sustain
Where in the end like Cheshire cats only smiles remain
This is how it always is and this is how it was:

A hummingbird hovered close to me buzzing in the air
And this was and this is as real to me as anything

LET ME KNOW

Utility and futility
Usefulness and uselessness

One being used is probably me
But no one is useless with hope I guess
And if I had anything it would be
Some hope and a sense of utility
To be a spark in the dark if I can

I need to be useful without being used
To win the approval my father denied
And have always tried (even since he died)
To win the approval my father refused
But the monster and the myth consumed the man

I want to open my eyes and see
Hope start (small: so it has room to grow)
And life as worth living even though
Utterly uncertain as I wait for
A miracle (just one miracle more!)

To win the approval denied and refused
I seem to have to work harder than others
I need to be useful without being used
If only to honor my murdered brothers
And if anyone could love me let me know

Uselessness and usefulness
Futility and utility

TWILIGHT

With my left hand I beckon to the night
To just return my greeting anyway
While reaching with my right hand for the day:

Why must one hand be left and one be right?

I am not one of those people who must
Be right and if I were how would I know
Since I come from and must return to dust
Sooner or later? And yet even so
An ember in the ashes flashes flame
Out of the dust where the fire-rose must grow

Life out of death to keep alive the name
Of one who cannot really ever go
Because he never really ever came
But who exists and who persists upon
This isle of grey between the black and white
This land between the hand of dark and light

The night drops by before the day has gone
Its purpose to prepare the promise of
An hour when left and right embrace in love:

When twilight joins the hand of day to night

The Unruined Movie

If we could know the future would we panic
To find ourselves carried inevitably
Along a circuitous trajectory
The knowledge of which humming hypomanic
Might ruin the movie revealing its end?

I think I would rather not know what will be
So I can be surprised by what life might send

If we could remember the past would we find
Ourselves overwhelmed by the weight of it all
To live again these risings before this fall
Living less in our before than our behind?

Both future and past should be shared with a friend

But there is no future as everyone knows
They say it will come and yet it never does
And as for a past we can never recall
I just hope that now is better than it was

All anyone can do is see how it goes

And then there is the question of where we go
Which is balanced by the question of where we
Came from in the first place if we really are
Something like present here for something like now

I would ask someone but how could someone know?

Wherever it is I am going somehow
And somehow I sense it is not very far

I know no future and I forgot the past

But I really think life is better this way
And I am no saint but a sinner can pray
To be present for something like now at last
To find my present and share it with a friend

The unruined movie reveals by its end
The here of life is now and temporary

Spell (for You)

Though I feel confident to spell
And do such things as words demand
To draw my dreams before they die
One thing I never understand
But notice how and wonder why
I find my fingers feel all thumbs
And I feel stupid truth to tell
Facing figures summoned by sums
Beyond what I can count by hand
As syllables of poetry
Which soar yet never seem too high

These are the figures I can face
They seldom are more than fourteen
Or less than four or in-between
Fourteeners and in-betweeners
Pentameter and ballad-rhyme
If you know me you know I mean
I count these all day all the time
With my self-confidence in place

Yet when such mathematics comes
As figures the fiduciary
I hide and wait for it to go
Since it could not have come for me
Avoiding like an evil spell
No matter who thinks what is true
That which I have no hope to know
In favor of that which I do
To draw my dreams before they die
Whose numbers lift me to the sky
To speak these words I spell (for you)

KAREN SMITH

At this late hour and this great distance of
Forty years later I find Karen Smith
In my memory where she lives now with
A few other girls I will always love
And saw again the reason why it was
The way it was was simply just because
The way it was was how it had to be

But I wish Karen Smith was here with me

(And should you insist I should have said were
Then you did not know no did not know her)

Our Flexible Selves

Do I have to be home for fate to knock on my door?
How specific is this metaphysical visit?
What if I get in trouble out here looking for more
And miss its knock? Would fate unlock my door and come in
Anyway to take what I lose and leave what I win?
When I do not believe that fate is real then is it?

Given the choice I would rather not deal face-to-face
With one who bears a scythe to cut down those of my race
Which is only part of being human after all
And I wonder if such cutting bears a sense of place
Or if those who can no longer stand it take the fall
For those who cannot stand it but stand in any case

If not at my door there might I miss the whole affair
Or wherever I go might fate (and its scythe) be there
As well? Neither heaven nor hell but purgatory

If I am anywhere at all I am only where
(Without so much as knocking) fate has tracked me to be
A free human being (at least temporarily)

The history of humankind is a sad story
Though a tale told by the victors you can see the cracks
In the walls by which we see the blood and cruelty
Inflicted on the victims which fate silently tracks
We see the winners never really won anything
Fate does not discriminate and this should dull the ache

We are judged by neither what we take nor what we bring
If we are judged at all it is only for the sake
Of ourselves since there is nothing we can bring nor take
But our flexible selves which bend and yet never break
And what this flexible self of mine would like to do
Is to give fate the slip and then to skip out with you

Empathy in the Afternoon

The consolation of my age
Is to at last find truth
Beyond the futile fists of rage
So ready in my youth
I see in someone else's eyes
The truth I know as you

To my surprise I realize
That you are my friend too
Shrinkwrapping problems down to size
Discerning false from true
For one who grew up in a cage
And never really knew

The thinking-over of it all
Heads my heart home to peace
The way a leaf must in the fall
Learn to embrace release
As all who live must learn to die
Just as we learn to live

As most by my age learn as I
Have had to so I give
An idea which could be advice
Were I to give such things:

All we need to do is be nice
To rise upon such wings
As given any commonday
Song sparrow as it sings
Get off the floor and score some more
Empathy in the afternoon

Whatever someone else might say
My consolation brings
Me out once more to dance the moon
Which though it wax and wane
Will always be up there and soon
As empty fills again
The moment of fulfillment shines

Nor does it shine in vain
Thousand-faced on moonflower vines
As we forget the pain
Of strangers here in stranger-land
Who need not be told twice
Still strangers but who understand
All we need to do is be nice

Wait

I will wait here for you until you come
At such a time as you can be with me
And be content with nothing as the sum
Of what I know of hope and destiny
The sole exception being my knowing
My heart and feeling the feelings within

I feel the hope of destiny growing

Though all I know of what might be called real
Is just this hope of destiny I feel
Still this is enough for me to begin
We only have beginning anyway
With every heartbeat life begins again
And when the end comes then no one can say

Then only the works of our hands remain
When the spirit is far away from here
Yet never more present never more near
Because it is ever and always now
In cross-dimensional immediacy
Where spirits like thoughts will always be free

And we will be together then somehow

EXISTENTIAL MAGIC SHOW

Death is chasing us but life is running too
Though we have been so far behind for so long
We became far closer than anyone knew
Sharing certain feelings of uncertainty
And uncertainty certainly made us strong

The lotus unfolded and there I found you
Where you made me feel like a summer love song
Wearing uncertain feelings of certainty
And I knew by the time that summer was through
It would be that summer forever for me

So you are and you will be as you have been
My love and my summer forever for now
And you know I know you know just what I mean
As you saw me in half and then take a bow
Posing as the third half in the space between

Prestidigitators the both of us for
As long as there have been magic tricks to do
And I saw my lovely assistant in two
Who told me the story and swore it was true
We did our full act but the public wants more

No encore prepared and nothing up my sleeve
We reattach ourselves take our bows and leave

The Time of My Life

As I waited for the telephone to ring one day
All the while hoping the mail might bring me some good news
I realized it mattered nothing what they might say

My poems work for me (and I hope they work for you)

We each have an opinion but what matters is whose
Is the one I choose to care about and listen to

Chimpanzees comfort each other with hugs and kisses
I only wish we could be as kind as they would be
Stumbling alone through hits and staggering through misses

I guess I wish I were as kind as a chimpanzee

Because no one leaves here alive I was born to lose
I must just do it graciously whatever I do

Because no one comes here in vain I was born to win
Whatever I do I must just do it graciously
Now as I wait for the time of my life to begin

Maybe

My poems are not about anything
What I like to say about them is they
Do not represent but they simply are
(Although not about anything) something
Like crossword puzzles in The New York Times
They are puzzled over from near to far
Frustrating some entertaining some more

I like to try out unusual rhymes
Before the tide of time can wash away
These strings of syllables counted and squared
By which I am always asking what for
And why (as I question reality)
No one has answered and why no one cared
But maybe one will eventually

Manifesto

The pattern of the past becomes a pattern in reverse
Like zebras walking backwards in a mirror at the zoo
As we pass by best and worst to slum with better and worse
In a universe which seems an existentialist joke

If I feel it has failed me does it feel I failed it too?
I seek but fail to find much as my life goes up in smoke
But our failings not withstanding this is my universe

I may not understand it but I know it like the hand
Which comforts me and challenges my need to understand
With a feeling of unsettling familiarity

Do immortals watch us with amusement and do they laugh
At us as we play beat-the-clock here in the other half
(The dark side of the moon as it would seem to me to be)?

The hand which comforts me assures me that I need not know
The answers just the questions and that hand goes where I go
Though I have the questions now the answers may not be known
Until I understand the hand which comforts is my own

Thanks

I am embarrassed to look as I do
And be as I am my life having come
To this after all this late in the day

Am I a hobo or am I a bum?
Will this pain I feel ever go away?
You say I never disappointed you
That you believed in me no matter what
I used to remember that but forgot
Out on the screaming streets of nowhereland

I am embarrassed but you understood
That I held on for as long as I could
You understood because you understand

Lonely if Only

Lonely if only the way it must be
Actually we are all looking for us
Cruising for some chance encounter with who
We want to hang around with me and you

This is the business of us and the fuss
Which flusters us forward here day by day
And makes us search the faces on the bus
As I look for you and you look for me

Lonely if only the way it has been
I wonder why it has to be this way
But when we find ourselves we get along
Doing our part to keep humankind strong

It feels pretty good when it works out right
We just move along when it works out wrong
The light at the end of the tunnel may
Not be at all or be too far away

The light I care about is in your eyes
I might even have a little in mine
If that were all there were that would be fine
It took awhile but now I realize

Lonely if only you know what I mean
We need each other though we hate to say
It right out loud as lonely eyes see light
And hungry mouths taste hope however slight

ONE SPARK OF HAPPINESS

The promise of tomorrow yesterday
Becomes a disappointment one day on
Today has only tomorrow and then
Just before it gets here it gets away
And we are left with nothing but the when
Of this fleeting present soon to be gone

But this is how it is and this remains
The only payment we can depend on
The present is the profit of our pains
A penny-candle given to spend on
One spark of happiness one moment long
Like you might find in a line from a song

The present is the promise of today
The only time we ever understand
Because all other time is meaningless
Except this gift for which no one can pay
Regret and apprehension nonetheless
Forget all time but now and hold my hand

And when we come together as we must
After having come through meaninglessness
The best of our coming will be the trust
In life and one another we will feel
When finally we are able to say
The present came for us and it was real

Like you might find in a line from a song
One spark of happiness one moment long

Existential Satisfaction

We are picky in the pink of propinquity
And we like to be able to feel respected
If not quite accepted at least not rejected
The closest we let respect get to you and me

Self-banished by blandishment for a blandish while
To the indifference of anonymity
With its enigmatic subcutaneous smile
Its grin beneath our skin our bone beneath its stone

We dream our days invisible but side by side
We fret ourselves about who lives about who died
And those who did (oh God forbid) were all alone
Leave hope behind who enter here: be satisfied

I Mean to Find Some Meaning

Is the way I feel the way I am or am I the same
When I feel proud of myself as when I wallow in shame?
If only for the sake of convenience I wish I knew
Is who I am or who I feel I am the one to blame
For the manifold absurdities attached to my name?

Though I know nothing I am comforted that no one knows
And everyone should be in solidarity with me
As we try to hold on to what may come yet never came
But the sad part is that there were dreams which never came true
And there were nightmares which woke into dark reality

If I ever found some meaning I would share it with you
Though from my past experience I seem unable to
Hold on to what may come for very long before it goes
But if I could I really would whatever else I do
And I mean to find some meaning here before I get through

Found Meaning

I found meaning in painting a protest sign
In heavenly colors (which took sky to dry)
In the sunshine to hold at sunset last night
And in doing my best because it was mine

Then I felt as though I were lifting up light
By bearing witness as the warm hours went by
And a meaningless day turned meaningful night
By moments of clarity suggestive of
A galaxy whose each star is a firefly

I gave to my town and it gave back to me
Meaning came to meet me and it became clear
That it means to belong that I belong here
And the word I painted on my sign was "Love"

SNAKES ON A BUS

The python gesticulated
She wanted me to see
Her skin was reticulated
But her eye was on me

Had you to kill the cow yourself
You might decide not to
And eat (from boxes off your shelf)
Things not at all like you

Reticulated pythons might
Enjoy some bites of us
If chickenless some summer night
While waiting for the bus

An omnivore near fifty-four
Who now eats plants by choice
Cows need not feed me anymore
And chickens can rejoice

Reticulated pythons though
In search of lunch feel free
To eat some cow some chicken or
Some omnivore we know

Metabolism running slow?
Best think fast if you see
Reticulated pythons go
To university

They like to ride the bus and take
Their classes in the cool
Of evening with a dinner-break
Since they eat more at school

Snakes on a bus are not the kind
Of subject one might like
But out of sight is out of mind
So I just ride my bike...

To Herpetology

Only Love

I wonder as I blunder out here under whatever
This is these days which passes for the sky
And have been looking up for a long time but I never
Noticed how it seems to smile when asked why
This or why that or why anything I wonder about

It might as well look pleasant since at least for the present
There simply is no point explaining things
Which no matter how I figure I cannot figure out
But I had just never noticed before
How the universe appears to enjoy my questionings

An educational process is what this would appear
To be in the teachable moment of
The lotus of consciousness as it unfolds within me
And whatever else it is it is love
The sky and I might change but we are both smiling somehow

What was or will be however pleasant or unpleasant
Whatever this is which passes for now
Is as good a time as any to fall in love again
And if I fell already fall some more
Because when all this is over only love may remain

Though I hope as we grope toward togetherness
I would not presume to tell you what is true
But I love you and write these poems for you
And the love of love itself as nothing less
Than the best I can (which is all I can) be

Eating the Moon

There may always be Monday morning
But there will always be Friday night
To slide by a cop with a warning
And to make it all turn out all right
Like the best movie you ever saw
Where the sights you see are out of sight
I like to live by natural law
Pick forbidden fruit and take a bite
Just as I please and then eat it raw

And who is to tell me I am wrong?
All I want to do is sing my song

If you want to know what I think of
This situation which we are in
I will tell you I see only love
Where some other people might see sin
But how can it be sin for me to
Be the person I am and be free
To scare up some love to share with you?
I choose to live life naturally
Love is the heartbeat of what I do

You who love me more when I am wrong
Sing your song and let me sing along

When we suffer Tuesday afternoon
We think about Thursday at twilight
And how Friday night is coming soon
When we will be beautiful and bright
I lick my whiskers and kick my heels
In anticipation of the moon
Even now to feel how good it feels
To sacrifice haste and slowly taste
Our slice of moon we share with a spoon

Feeding each other getting along
Eating the moon and singing our song

Just Sitting Here with Fred

My disco ball my tiger skin
(Which is a yoga mat)
My everlasting refill cup
(Left unrefilled at that)
Are things I see when I wake up
From last night where I sat

As where I end there I begin
And right here is my cat
In his feline fidelity
Persisting to be fed
But he would never hurry me
He likes it on my bed

My disco ball my tiger skin
(No dancing tigers harmed)
My everlasting refill cup
(As charitied as charmed)
And best of all of waking up
Just sitting here with Fred

Sister on the Line

(For the incomparable Heather, who tap-danced without stopping
through all the hours of the protest today
while holding her "Live and Let Live" sign over her head,
standing next to me with my "Love" sign
and blowing my mind by reciting extended passages
of my own poetry to me from memory.)

+ + +

I met her on the protest line
And right away I knew
Someone would be a friend of mine
And that someone was you

I feel the grace of meaning start
To settle like a dove
Then rise a phoenix in my heart
And I will live by love
As I once did so long ago
When you were far away

But we knew us then even so
Until we met today
As we have known us everywhere
Forever and always
In hope and love and answered prayer:
That which has meaning stays

I look at you and recognize
The God I serve in your dark eyes

O Mother Soul

More felt than heard the heartbeat of the earth
Our constant music seldom listened to
Strikes up in utero well before birth
To keep the beat of everything we do
Through the progress of day through night to day
Through the process of you through me to you
The heartbeat of the earth to mark the way

O heartbeat of the earth O mother soul
Join my heart to the heartbeat of it all
My puzzle piece pictured into the whole:
Before I learned to walk I learned to crawl
I learned to run to the pulse of your love
And having run now I would like to fly
To see what I saw below from above

O heartbeat of the earth O mother soul
Eternal why not to my question why
Picture my puzzle piece into the whole
And teach me that to live before I die
I had to learn to be before I do
And having done now I will only be
Through the process of me through you to me

THE LOTUS UNFOLDS

for Heather (together)

Two hearts make a revolution under
Sunlight and starlight as we stand out here
With each light we grow a little more strong

The lotus unfolds as people wonder
How the thought of love caught has brought it near
How rainbows can bring lightning and thunder

And we sought above but we found it here
Now as lightning descends from the dove's tail
To warm these two hearts having come this far

If they think they can stop us they are wrong
We bear witness out here and will not fail
Because we know now what they never knew

What this is could never be kept in jail
Because this is the love of me and you
And anybody else who happens by

Thousands of people are singing our song
Because love is truth and truth cannot lie
I see in your eyes the birth of a star

You: who have stood with me here all along

LUCKY

Your middle name is Lucky but it also could be mine
Since I feel lucky too to have you holding up your sign
Here next to me as I hold up the one I made before
I met you and thought I knew love (until you taught me more)
Here as a tree in a forest of my own creation
Anchored by the taproot which becomes my liberation

You are me as I am you
Past and future meeting now
Which leaves nothing we can do
But be (together) somehow

In

I have found my bliss
And my bliss is this
To love you more than I can say
But then to say it anyway
Lucky me and you are we
Welcome to the family

The lotus will unfold because it does
And when the time comes later to reflect
I will remember and you will respect
It was what it is and is what it was
Lucky me and you are we
Welcome to the family

THE LOVE REVOLUTION

All hesitation falls away from me
As I grab life with hungry hands to hold
And welcome you to my insanity
This story which must be shown and not told
Since telling is only for vanity
Nor would I conspire to be vain in vain

So I will make this place a sacred space
Where the now will always be the somehow
And bloom like the rose where everyone knows
The lotus unfolds in a public place
Where secrets of the somehow are the now
And right in front of everyone: love grows

I turn to you and will not turn from pain
The lotus is here to unfold again

The Existentialist

for Lucky

The existentialist always laughs last
Because he has nothing and all the rest
Is his

The existentialist always laughs best
Because he has no future and no past

The existentialist need only be

Which is
The hardest part of being one for me
Or another being being has kissed
Looking for meaning or reality

Like this

A momentary existentialist
Startled in a moment of existence

A kiss
From the universe for my persistence

The existentialist always laughs now
Because he has no future and no past
And having had nothing and all the rest
I can have as much as I will allow

My momentary existentialist!
Startled in a moment of existence
Like this!

A kiss
From the universe for your persistence

ALIA

I never knew
How lonely I was
Till I met you
And only because
I was supposed to

WITHOUT FROM WITHIN

If my eyes should open what would they find?
Until I have opened them I stay blind

If I want to live at the tip of the spear
And to feel how sharp and how cool it can be
I will have to let go of all but one fear
And that is the fear of disappointing me
It will have to be now and has to be here
That I open at least two eyes out of three

Is it the third eye which as illusions die
Is opened like the petals of the lotus?
Whatever it is before it has gone by
I will become all eyes and I will notice
Now as the focal point of eternity
And how what I once thought too far was too near

So I open at least two eyes out of three
And I see that I am now and it is here
That I will create my own reality
In blazing new brilliance as old shadows clear
And I feel how sharp and how cool it can be
If I want to live at the tip of the spear

Beyond pain and pleasure blessing and sin
Paradise is found without from within

I Love You More

They photograph me constantly
Flash flash flash
You can see a picture of me
In the trash

You love me more than I love you
Because my heart is cold inside
Where I gave up and where love died

But I blow bubbles in the square

I hold a "Love" sign I made there
Asking for love and finding some
Where out-of-towners always come
And photograph me constantly

Flash flash flash

This picture of me found by you
In the trash
Makes me admit since it is true

I love you more than you love me

BUBBLES IN TRAFFIC

what I think God does

Worried people on Friday
Hurried people decide they
Will begin the revolution later than
They had anticipated: but I began

Man is born to bubbles as the troubles fly upward
And nothing quite answers the question like the absurd

If my stony-pop specificity
Is lost on everybody else but me
At least I have not eaten them in vain
That tan the homeless never meant to get
Is also mine now though not homeless (yet)

Now as I begin revolution again
Worried people on Saturday
Hurried people stop by and say
Thank you for the bubbles and the magic of
My crazy little revolution of love

Worried people on Sunday
Hurried people for Monday
Stop worrying stop hurrying just for now with me
Come contemplate these bubbles I create to set free

Which is what I think God does (or at least it could be)

Freddie's Song

He was not like Garfield but like Noodles in Mutts
He was big and fat and cool but most likely nuts

He could have been carried up into the sky (they
Say) by that hawk we saw hanging around that day

Still he seems a thing to me far too solid for
Some snatching of such existential either / or
As talons of this interloper from the sky

And why have they spoken of "was" and not of "is"
When the most present of lives I have loved is his?

That fat cat Freddie Noodles is too tough to die!

Except... now he is gone: so I have to accept
That he ran out of luck now though always adept
At dashing out of difficulties twelve years long

Cats avoid large birds and were never meant to fly
Except... this one this time: but he lived to die strong

Whatever happened "you should see the other guy"
Is what people say if they had rather not say

He left me here alone: now how do I move on
In order to find him wherever he may be?
This moment he is more in this moment than me

He lived and loved and lost: so this is Freddie's song

Except... I know he won because he won my heart
No matter what happened no matter what or why
In death as in life we will not be far apart

That fat cat Freddie Noodles is too tough to die!
Except... (accept) this time: so this is Freddie's song

Unreturnable Now

It hurts to lose a cat
But it hurts enough that
I never need to have a cat again
To lose

It hurts to lose a wife
And hurts to find a life
But nothing is more pleasant than the pain
I choose

My past futility
Future utility
Now nothing but the present I remain
To use

The soil of tomorrow is the corpse of yesterday
As I happen somehow
And I will bud to bloom here if only for today
Unreturnable now

Like a Knife

On the knife
Of this life
I live on the blade
And not the handle

My light on
Until dawn
My burning candle
Both ends unafraid

It makes it hard to sleep
When you live where
The drop is sheer and steep
And when you care

I want to stay awake
To burn both ends
My mirror does not break
Because it bends

My light will be on
As long as it takes
All night until dawn
Bends mirrors and breaks

My map to the stars
Drawn in battle scars
My burning candle
Both ends unafraid

Love is like a knife
The sharp edge of life
And this knife is made
Without a handle

Thin Green Line

A gram a day
Keeps the madness away
My thin green line
Holds (and I stay just fine)

Popularity
Is a rarity
But if it happens it can be great fun

Every now and then
You never know when
(But save your soul for after it is done)

It happens to you
Sometimes when you do
Whatever you do the way you do it

Then somehow you find
Yourself on the mind
Of one in your life to help you through it

A gram a day
Keeps the sadness away
Our thin green line
Holds (and we stay just fine)

Though I never meant to be popular
If I were not I might not have met her
And it all just might have been different when
Somehow I found myself on the mind of then

But now I find myself on the mind of this
Anticipation of a long-denied kiss
The game is not over until someone wins
But it never starts until someone begins

Though I never meant to be popular
The thin green line holds (almost... as if... I were...)

Passageway

The process of life seems a passageway to me
A birth canal between one life and another
From earth to earth through earth as daughter and mother
And as son and father simultaneously

Along this passageway where no one came alone
I came connected to remain connected still
Though the ends of my connections remain unknown
I have to be a link in this chain so I will

Because of the ones who came before me and were
Because of the ones who came after me and are
Because of my mother who shines now like a star
Because of my daughter and everyone like her
Because of my sons and the sons of everyone

Whether some reality or only our dream
The process is doing what will never be done
That which has no ending can only be begun
Things are so much more interesting than they seem

As my father and son simultaneously
The process of life seems a passageway to me

Forget About You

I am sick of writing how somebody cares
When it is as plain as the nose on my face
That the cold plastic one in question does not

I am an altruistic martyr who bears
The killing burden of family disgrace
Which she never understood and I forgot

Was she ever abused as a child? I ask

Of course she was not but I was anyway
She cannot see me crying behind this mask
But perfect perky people poison the day

No one like that could ever understand me
And I was just a Goddamned fool to ever
Misunderstand everything so stupidly

Never say never turned into just never

Impossible dream which will never come true
Baby I have got to forget about you

This Hand Which Meets Me Rising

for Heather

Bonfires of my vanities prove unnecessary
The gentle dishonesty of hoping to impress
Yields to realizing it is hopeless more or less

And impressing is unnecessary anyway
Since you have thought about it and have come back to say
That for some strange reason you care about me (as me)
Which makes me happy but which I hardly understand

To hardly understand is better than not at all
Especially at the hand of someone else's hand
This hand which meets me rising is the spring of my fall

THE LUCKY ONES

I want to lie in some lilies with you
And find out who I am or who you are
Watching the sun slipping undersea too
Would also be nice with a falling star
Falling still farther in a waning moon

When we could see the universe at night
The spine of the sky and numberless suns
Of infinite other worlds far away
Where what is present presently is right
Where now is never too late nor too soon

And presently we are the lucky ones
Who have the night to spend and then the day
To bathe together in the golden light
Of answer to the prayers of those who pray
Who knew the words but then forgot the tune

At last we know the only answer then
The question not of whether but of when

Turns Out

What turns out to have been our destiny?
Who knows what relationships mean except
Human propinquity shared and enjoyed?
Secrets to treasure through promises kept
By moments which can never be destroyed
Becoming the meaning of memory

The sharing of the wearing of the flesh
The bearing of the caring of the soul
Where love speaks freely because lives are fresh
Each life lived as part of a greater whole
This is what relationships mean to me

So here we two are now and having one
Adventure in human propinquity
After another as day follows night
Follows day and we continue to be
Two creating one shared reality

Out looking for trouble I found the light
In you and in me here under the sun
Taking time and making eternity
Taking wrong and making it turn out right
Taking and making until we have done
What turns out to have been our destiny

(True)

The Gordian knot untied
The strands which strained to struggle free
As diverse as unified
Unified in diversity
So it is and so it was
Is means is and no because

You mean a lot to me
More than I understand
With electricity
Between us hand to hand

So I suppose by now you know
You probably will always be
The only one who makes me so
Excited in spite of myself to see
You
(True)

Is means is and no because
So it is and so it was
Unified in diversity
As diverse as unified
The strands which strained to struggle free
The Gordian knot untied

The Family Goes On

This everlasting refill cup
On which you wrote my name
Emptied now and again filled up
Yet somehow still the same
Is not quite the same as we are
Who only grow more strong
Now this cup is a fading star
Which might not shine too long

I like my coffee now and then
But much prefer the taste
Of family on mornings when
This cup has run its course and gone
Into recycled waste:
The family goes on

They say it is corporate anyway
Even though I get my coffee so cheap
But I never listen to what they say
And I never have time to talk that fast
Their ears are too shallow to hear too deep:
Our paper cups wear out our families last

Though everlasting might not be
We always have right now
Which temporary you and me
Know how to do somehow
If temporarily:
The family goes on

Rebellion

My country is no longer what it was
It seems no longer as it seemed before
It bumbled by through the days of my youth
Mismanaged by mere mediocrities
But lost its way in its hypocrisies
Falling further and further from the truth
Until we forgot what we came here for

If there is truth for lies as big as these
I want to go and look for it awhile
If only to somehow escape this rush
To descend to deeper idiocies
Where the numbers crunched are of those they crush
Those who sold souls for a handshake and smile

If only to reach for a reason why
I rise up now in rebellion because
My country no longer cares about me
And I am determined to do what I
Am destined to do here before I must
Like heroes and cowards rejoin this dust

I rise up now in rebellion because
I have decided to do what I please
To make it what it could be or it was
I rise up now to see my country free
If not for me at least someone someday
My country is no longer what it was
But it is mine or once was anyway

And Along with These to Sniff Beneath Trees

When dozing hobos roll over and pee
Into the grass I hope it will not be
Right in the spot where you might sit today

You might have to sniff beneath every tree
And then end up getting wet anyway
Which is pretty much what happened to me
I just hope that never happens to you

Now as we baby-boomers keep aging
We are starting to learn about staging
From all of the drama we have lived through

Blocking and lighting and all sorts of things
Like dialogue and throwing wedding rings
And along with these to sniff beneath trees
Where we wonder what we should feel or say

When dozing hobos roll over and go
Into the grass just make sure that you know
Right in the spot where you might lie tonight

Life goes too fast when we live it too slow
And goes too slow when we live it too fast
A lifetime of balance lifts up at last
That not to haste nor waste is to live right

Hobos pee there where hormones are raging
Now as we baby-boomers keep aging

Choristers Assembling at Evensong

I suppose I should be disappointed but
Instead I feel something almost like pride
And if people were to ask me proud of what
I would have to invite them to step inside
If they could climb inside of me as I
Step in on a regular basis these days

Here anyway I might as well stop by
To see it all in motion where nothing stays
But the pattern of motion has meaning to
The one who understands where it is moving
Its clarity of motion becoming true
As true as anything at least improving

Now the pattern becomes clear as it comes near
And instead of being disappointed
I feel something almost like proud of the clear
And patterned motion of these once-disjointed
Elements as they combine to be strong
Choristers assembling at evensong

Say Good Night Little Hitler

I lift my voice now in a song of stubbornness
I can do nothing more strong than to be myself

All of the words in all of the books on my shelf
Books which I have written and which may curse or bless
Now join into one mighty word which I will say
Today and tomorrow and every single day
With which I have the privilege of having been
Entrusted as (disgusted) I prepare to rise
With no in my mouth and yet with yes in my eyes

You have hurt me once but will not hurt me once more
As anyone who has hurt me knows what I mean

I break free of you now as I should have before
And did not because of something like sympathy
But you never had any sympathy for me

Say good night little Hitler: you are no one now

Your nightmare is over so your morning must break
But to hell with you and I would do well somehow
To forget about you and your little mistake

My Magical Life

I want to take my life in a new direction
And for that I am going to need to be alone
So I hope no one will take this as rejection
But now the time has come for me to be on my own
And if you would like to understand me
What you should know is I have to be free

Is it really possible to love another?
Does otherness clarify? Is it terrifying?
I have just survived someone's attempt to smother
My specificity between living and dying
Which if you would like to understand how
Important that is try to find me now

I have withdrawn to emerge as a butterfly
And when I do I will only reveal myself to
Those willing to respect my need to soar the sky
Unhindered by what those earthbound caterpillars do
Who never understood and never will
My magical life is magical still

Perspective

If I ever have any enemies
Or if there ever might be any fuss
It will all be the fault of things like these
Stupid little things which come between us

And I mean all of us people as we
Fail to communicate day in and out
Hurting each other spontaneously
Losing the light to the shadow of doubt

So it is and was and will always be
I know it better than I hope I do
The best friend becomes the worst enemy
I never want this to happen to you

It makes me wonder about having friends
Or having them keeping them anyway
When love twists itself into hate and ends
But night forgives the trespasses of day

As when we die we remember it all
The love the hate the enemies the friends
And things which seemed so big once seem so small
When everything and everybody ends

Admitting It

for you-know-who-you-are

Whoever I am whoever you are
Whatever we might have been supposed to
(Or expected to) be in any case
I think I have already gone too far
To find my way back now successfully
Back to whatever imagined safe place
I might have known before you looked for me
Maybe my place after all is with you

Some say there are no accidents and they
Keep having their accidents anyway
But it never felt accidental when
You sought me and found me in spite of my
Resistance although it was futile then
And even after admitting it I
Kept looking for better ways to deny
I love you in spite of myself:

I do
Love you

Parallel

for my friend Tiffany Bridgman

We are alone but alone together
Suns of our parallel solar systems
Seeing each other as though through a glass
But seeing each other nevertheless
Regarding each other respectfully
Where wariness is taken for respect
Since nobody ever knew what that meant

We are alone but we wonder whether
While our flowers fade as we clutch their stems
And stand on parallel peaks with a pass
Between us we have learned is bottomless
To reach across this space of you and me
Where we are not suns but only reflect
As moons do a light both borrowed and lent

Someday When You Remember

goodbye and hello

I remember you from before we met
Near November across from April or
December on a distant shore and yet

Both future and past form connections here
Where here can only be descibed as now
Which cannot be described while happening

But not knowing why at least I know how
Two parted make one part of everything
A sum of which one part might be regret

I might see you again some other year
Older and wiser or else maybe not
But one thing we do not do is forget

And if out of pride we say we forgot
Then you will know to come back when you go
To warm the here of now till it gets hot

When you are ready then we both will know
That we were well worth waiting for daresay
Remember me then when you go away

Because you might not see me anymore
But in the gallery of memory
I hope you find what you were looking for

Someday when you remember it was me

In the House of the Dead

My only limitations are the ones I place
As impediments myself artificially
In an arbitrary contravention of grace

I know no one can limit me except for me
The soul which sees through these eyes animates this face
Only as effectively as I dare to be

I care enough to dare to be effective when
I live to die a blooming fruiting seeding flower
And anyone like me who doubts should see me then

Unfettered by convention I rise past my hour
When those with faith no more have crucified themselves
To join their ancestors on mausoleum shelves

In the house of the dead I lift my left hand
Turning ever eastward and returning still
Not needing nor expecting to understand

I expect if I need to understand I will

SEE

Some say we have a third eye by which we
May see the things we may not see because
We are looking less for mind than matter
Which would not matter if we could not mind
Two for the former one for the latter
Which eyes though without seeking always find
Matter over mind to fit and flatter
Addressing less before and more behind
Finding that behind has gotten fatter

Some are still searching for a promised land
As if it could be found if it could be
And though I too have searched I understand
That my promised land is inside of me
As it has always been yet never was
It is only present in the present
And not in what the doer did but does
Matters of mind are not always pleasant
But my third eye is open as my hand

Open your eyes and tell me what you see
With two eyes I am blind but not with three

Not for Me

If a link in the chain should break may it not be me

Not for me the disappointment of the family
Not for me to be the one on whom the house must fall

I am the embodiment of my family now
Because I am all that is left of it after all
And there is a limit to what my time will allow
Although I have very seldom felt limited to
Anything except myself no matter what I do

Whatever I do now has to be both for the chain
And for contemplation of "to thine own self be true"

If I lose hope now I may never find it again

Mindful of it all as I am mindful of how small
My life is knowing this is the only life I know
As short as it is and as difficult as it was

While still small and short it is better lived mindfully
Which is not to analyze but simply see the cause
Of the effect and to reject the heedlessness of
Hurrying this small short span without seeing how love
Forged these links of family and adds them as we grow

Not for me the disappointment of the family
Not for me to be the one on whom the house must fall

If a link in the chain should break may it not be me

ONE BRIGHT STAR

God: what does it mean and how can it be
That when I hear your voice you sound like me?

This cause has had the effect that I find
Myself remapping the map of my mind
Where you have been misunderstood so long
Your words confused and my syllables wrong

But when you sound like me how can I know?

If not today then maybe tomorrow
When I remember who you really are

You are me as I am you: one bright star

Like Living Until

How I will die and if it will mean much
That I once lived or at least what once seemed
Like living until the curtain was torn
Need not apply since life has still been such
A lot more than I had hoped or had dreamed

If only the hopes of a martyr born
To live the nightmares about which they warn
Of genius as of insanity too
A couple of shady characters those
With both of them no telling what to do
The thorn as remarkable as the rose
And in the event the two are the same
The heavens part with only God to blame
For a dance with fate which neither one chose

But now the heavens want to part with me
And veil the veil withdrawn again in shame
So I am glad to share the earth with you
A lot more than I had hoped or had dreamed
Like living until the curtain was torn

These Steps of My Own

My eyes are still good enough I can see
That the lotus unfolds if not for me
Then some other brother of history
And if it unfolds for him then it must
For me before it enfolds me in dust
To embrace the ultimate mystery

There are things I feel like I need to know
Like the holiness of humility
And how meaning is found in mindfulness
Forgetting goes fast as learning comes slow
And it all comes out in the wash I guess
But I want to be within deity
I would like to go with God as I go
Keep my eyes open and see what I see

Religion has disappointed my heart
I like what it says but not what it does
It seems to have forgotten about God
And if I were part of something which part?
An uneven part left out with the odd
Yet I am still out here waiting around
As disappointed as all of us are

But I tread a path wise wanderers trod
Whose steps combine to make this holy ground
With these steps of my own beneath this star
As far away now as it ever was

To the One I Love

No one has ever understood me but
For you the exception no matter what
Which proves the rule that I would be a fool
Not to love you all these years as I do

All I ever wanted I find in you
But where do I find you when you are gone
When you are as far away as a star
And not our eastern visitor at dawn?

I feel inside of me and there you are
As enigmatic as ever and yet
No one has ever understood me but
For you the exception no matter what

Which proves the rule if only by regret
Our eastern visitor knows what I mean
Who visits me here in my loneliness
Departing westward with what might have been

And a sunset here is a sunrise there
Tomorrow is already yesterday
But now is the sunrise of everywhere
What you give me no one can take away

So I give you myself and nothing less
You have already done the same for me
And would a thousand times just as I would
If not this then what is reality?

I feel the real in you and it feels good

THE OTHER

Struggling with my sanity I have to wait
Distracted by these deep waters below me
For the outcome of an internal debate
As to might I know God or might God know me

Yet cannot help but perceive and yes believe
That there is something other in the dark there
And the other is none other than me where
The line disappears between give and receive

Because this is the highway nobody knows
This byway I travel wherever it goes
Into the unknown and always alone except
For the other who knows where the secrets are kept

E IS FOR EMPATHY

Empathy is something I believe in:
Nothing feels better than to receive in
Giving by living mindfully in touch
The love we need to give and take so much

A Lot Like Being Born

Death seems a lot like being born to me
To stand on this side of the veil withdrawn
From the birth canal of mortality
By the banks of dusk to embrace the dawn
Of what an unknown day might hold in store
Or an unknown night like this only more

Either way it seems a passage through pain
When we leave or stay as we come and go
After it happens no one can explain
The second time and the first time we know
What all of us do twice each in our way
At dusk as at dawn as night follows day

I stand on this side of the veil withdrawn
From the birth canal of mortality
By the banks of dusk I embrace the dawn
Of what an unknown day might hold in store
On an unknown night like this even more
Death seems a lot like being born to me

Fall

Looking up into this green of these trees
And watching green turn red and yellow now
I am happy to be on days like these
No matter why and no matter why not

And I will do what I have to somehow
To remember all those things I forgot
From a long time ago I ought to know
But I always thought I knew better then

I will remember them all someday when
The time is right for looking back ahead
Watching green turn red and yellow then dead
Like things I know from a long time ago
Watching dead turn yellow and red then green
Those who have fallen will know what I mean

Fall is the motion of dying season
But is only spring in another light
The heartbeat of life itself the reason
Birth and death dance: to keep the balance right

Pink Pets and Pills

That distinctive Pink Pet eraser smell
The flag halfway down when Kennedy died
That instinctive rush at the final bell
When insiders finally got outside
To find the world spun out of our control
A sense of unease and not feeling well
But going through the motions anyway
While asking hard questions about the soul:
If ours could speak what should it have to say
Of life thought as heaven but felt as hell?

I grew up under duck-and-cover drills
And the influence of Ritalin pills

I suppose it was propaganda when
They taught us as they did tendentiously
I felt it if did not quite know it then
And it sounded good about being free
But there is no national holiday
For me then or now here or anywhere
And if God knows I wonder does he care
Or even if there could be somebody
Who might prefer not that I leave but stay
And if I do I wish I knew how to

Here at the threshold of my age I wait
To approach the moment I meet my fate

At Present

The past does not exist and memory
Is reconstructive as we come to see
That what is supposed to come never does
When how it should be should be how it was
And how it could be would be just because
The past does not exist but memory
Reconstructs how it was supposedly

I see the future but choose to believe
It must not exist and my eyes deceive
My mind into thinking of what is not
Of what might have happened that I forgot
Because it simply has not happened yet

So I will just stay where I am right now
At present in the best place to forget
To remember if I remembered how
If to remember reconstructively
And if you remember I hope that you
Remember too because I know I do
Though it be only how it was for me

We can only remember how it seems
But what are memories if not our dreams?

When I Awaken

for Franziska

The pain in my side when I awaken
At first surprising then remembered for
The rib by which my lover was taken
The missing part of me which makes me more
Asks if pain and pleasure are mistaken
For each other in my sojourning here
Or if they are in fact one and the same
If the always far is the always near
And if Franziska might just be her name

My heart is broken but my soul can fly
And soar on love over above it all
My broken wings bandaged embrace the sky
To rise again the autumn of my fall
Where lost paradise beckons to believe
At last I am ready to love again
To share with Franziska pleasure and pain
To be with her as Adam to her Eve
With love at my side when I awaken

Platinum Diamonds on Black Velvet Sky

for Franziska

My chosen one we have begun at last
As we have begun enjoying as one
Living love here between future and past
Two sudden starbursts to flash through the now
Platinum diamonds on black velvet sky
As farflung as forever might allow

I am free when I am embraced by you
To ride time and space like waves of the sea
With space for time as much to be as do
I know we have always been together
Golden goddess eastern promise of sun
Just as we are neither when nor whether

My chosen one we have begun somehow
And what has begun (may it never end)
Insists I be with you no matter what
As chosen one as lover as best friend
The other half of me which time forgot
Now rediscovered to be timelessly
Aswirl in the whirlpool of destiny

Just a Little Dream Away

for Franziska

I dream of you at night
(Of course) but also during the day
And though far from my sight
You are just a little dream away

Wherever you go here you remain
Tucked snug inside my heart
To spark my dreams again and again
Together though apart

And when you come to me
To comfort me in my loneliness
You are reality
The flesh of my dreams and nothing less
Than all of everything
The dream and the song the dreamers sing

Be

I want my love to be the means of grace
By which you are gifted to spark a smile

I want to be the one to see your face
When you come to see life not as a trial
But a process of joy in journeying

I want my love to be what you embrace
When you realize you are not alone
And then I would hope you could embrace me

I want to love you more than anything
You have ever seen or have ever known

Eight limbs like branches entwine into one
Root into now: the one eternity

Which unlike time may not be measured nor
Anticipated cannot be planned for
Because the only thing now does is be

How it Hurts to Heal

My body is broken and yet I breathe
The pain reminds me how it hurts to heal
My mind is shattered and yet I believe
In what I lived and learned which I bequeath
To you in love now that you might receive
Me at my uttermost as we reveal
The brokenness which makes us who we are
(Shyly at first because it hurts so much)

I would be healed if you could be with me
Our healing comes through fitting from afar
Our jagged edges trembling at the touch
Each of the other to combine to be
The spark which gives birth to a double star
Where nothing lasts except eternity

Somebody

That I mean something to someone
Means everything to me
But for me to mean something to
A person such as you
Makes it a joy to live to see
My moment in the sun
And see it before I am dead

If it goes to my head
It only goes as champagne does
Or the ganja I toke
But it keeps me humble because
Before my life goes up in smoke
I am able to be
Someone to someone: somebody

Throughout the Velvet Universe

Throughout the velvet universe tonight
Infinite alien worlds wink awake
Multifoliate stars bloom cold and bright
And if by accident not by mistake

Or maybe this is all inside of me
What is outside might be just what is in
This simulacrum of reality
Might only be what I have mistaken
For something unapproachable and high
When it was just the I and not the sky

Since I am unable to leave my head
To see what is unshadowed by the skull
I will live this life like a dream instead
Where bright stars bloom so nights are never dull
And tomorrow never comes anyway
Where moons on oceans and emotions pull
But never pull away and so I stay
My half empty glass soon to be half full

And if by accident not by mistake
Multifoliate stars bloom cold and bright
Infinite alien worlds wink awake
Throughout the velvet universe tonight

To Journey Mindfully

for Kyle Gaulke

You might as well be headless as be heedless
For all the good a heedless head could do
Unseemly haste scorns mindfulness as needless
But heedlessness would have you hasten to
No-one-knows-where including heedlessness

A heedless head forgets it ever knew
And this is how you know when you get there
Where getting ahead is getting behind
Ahead of your body out of your mind
And no-one-knows-where can be anywhere
Except the place you are supposed to be

A heedless head could be the death of you
As it has nearly been the death of me
But whatever happens to us passing through
This passage in which we find ourselves now
The passing through makes us better somehow
If we embrace the passage after all

The mindful pass the place the heedless fall
Reminded as they pass to journey mindfully

LIKE BIRDS

I am dreaming about you my faraway friend
Can you feel me?
The only cure for loneliness comes at the end
Can you heal me?

If only you would
I know how you could
And yet
We remain unknown
Both of us alone
With only
Regret
Too lonely
For words
Like birds
Of a feather
Not together

I am singing about you my faraway friend
Can you hear me?
The only cure for loneliness comes at the end
With you near me

Paradise

When I hold you I can hear your body sing
So I give you myself as my offering
And hope and trust that I will be enough for
You since it is you yourself which you give me
Nothing less than everything no less no more
Than the real meaning of that word "reality"

The only thing I know about things like this
Is I love how you drive me mad with your hair
How you blast me off into space with your kiss
To search the night between the stars and find you there

Born once although I want to be born twice
I want to go back where I came from within
The universe of you beyond pain and sin
Where I make love to Eve in paradise

Woman oh woman oh sister of my soul
Take me break me make me the mirror of you
Defeat me complete me in shared victory
I need you since only you can make me whole
You it is inspires me to do what I do
Woman sweet woman sweet sister of my soul

For Now

These leaves turn red before they fall
The redder leaves the colder days
Now in this time of turning
To turn to soil then that is all
Or else they flame out in a blaze
And slip decay through burning

I turn but do not turn away
I want so much to stay with you
But I am just a dying leaf
No matter how I want to stay
Whatever I might try to do
And fall seems something like relief
Somehow

So I will celebrate today
For now

I wish that you could be with me
Before I have to go
But what I know of destiny
Is what I do not know
I turn but do not turn away
I want to be with you

But shadows lengthen as today
Admits tonight as true
And it is over after all
The red the turning and the fall
And fall seems something like relief
Somehow

So I will celebrate today
For now

This

for my family

Some leaves as they fall turn around and spin
On the free flight of death they get to be
So beautiful that as they lose they win
This is how I want it to be with me

A leaf which though falling still seems to rise
And spinning sails on silently away
So beautiful it makes me realize
That today is as good as any day

No time like the present to give the slip
To gravity on a spiraling trip
And if the direction is downward then
Make this count since this will not come again

Tragic Magic

The path of life is tragic
Endured by weed and wine
But its process is magic
Diabolical or divine
As muddy waters settle and come clear
Death everywhere with life nowhere but here

So forward then I stumble
Though I aspire to dance
As trouble keeps me humble
I know I get just this one chance
To see the light and get it right somehow
Since all is lost with nothing left but now

The path of life is tragic
But its process is magic

Your Other

can you handle the truth?

That erstwhile ecstasy of being me
Makes present life worth present agony
And births the hope my former happiness
Having gone could come back nevertheless
And that presently something might go right

But something has always been right I guess
Rising in the dark while sinking from sight
Just as the sun has always come and gone
From day through night to day from dusk to dawn
The vessel overflows its emptiness

I live as me so you can be
The star which you believe you are
My old makes possible your new
But I knew how to be a star
Before you ever met you
And I will not forget you

I may be an extra in your movie
But I am a star in mine
An image beyond your reality
But yours is no heaven mine is no hell
I enjoy how I can see
I rock your world a little: I can tell

Yours is flashy mine is fine
Unseen therefore underestimated
And those who will not see will find it strange
This is my movie released unrated
In which I smile my silent threat of change

From day through night to day from dusk to dawn
The vessel overflows its emptiness
I may be an extra in your movie
But I am a star in mine
I live as me so you can be
The star which you believe you are

I will not be your mother
But you seem to have that covered just now
So I will be your Other
And you just have to deal with me somehow
So be mindful what you do

This is my movie released unrated
In which I smile my silent threat of change

The vessel overflows its emptiness

Keep

stars over Studio Lance

I fall back to the keep
Of my castle to sleep

With love to all the homes within this house
I fought for and won while losing my mind
In the fight but that seemed part of the plan
When lions were silenced by the roar of a mouse

A solitary yet a lonely man
Determined to leave it intact behind
As it was set before me long ago
When nobody knew they would come to know
That I was more stubborn than all of them
Together and whether or not I knew
This is my Zion never mind Jerusalem

This is my somewhat worldly paradise
My home and that of many very nice
Somewhat worldly paradisians like you
And I will see you again tomorrow my friends
As another mouse-roaringly mindful day ends

I fall back to the keep
Of my castle to sleep

All Right with Me

Somehow everything is going to be
Though going through these many twists and turns
Now as it always is: all right with me
Since this is just one of those things one learns
In the course of this turning and twisting

Like we learn it is pointless resisting
This twisting and turning of what some call
Fate in winter yet destiny in spring
Like love in summer cools to hope in fall
What is it then but the name we give it?

But it is nothing less than everything
My life is what I name it after all
And it is mine to embrace and live it
With all my heart believing it to be
Now as it always is: all right with me

www.ingramcontent.com/pod-product-compliance
Lightning Source LLC
Chambersburg PA
CBHW021303240426

43669CB00041B/46

From day through night to day from dusk to dawn
The vessel overflows its emptiness
I may be an extra in your movie
But I am a star in mine
I live as me so you can be
The star which you believe you are

I will not be your mother
But you seem to have that covered just now
So I will be your Other
And you just have to deal with me somehow
So be mindful what you do

This is my movie released unrated
In which I smile my silent threat of change

The vessel overflows its emptiness

Your Other

can you handle the truth?

That erstwhile ecstasy of being me
Makes present life worth present agony
And births the hope my former happiness
Having gone could come back nevertheless
And that presently something might go right

But something has always been right I guess
Rising in the dark while sinking from sight
Just as the sun has always come and gone
From day through night to day from dusk to dawn
The vessel overflows its emptiness

I live as me so you can be
The star which you believe you are
My old makes possible your new
But I knew how to be a star
Before you ever met you
And I will not forget you

I may be an extra in your movie
But I am a star in mine
An image beyond your reality
But yours is no heaven mine is no hell
I enjoy how I can see
I rock your world a little: I can tell

Yours is flashy mine is fine
Unseen therefore underestimated
And those who will not see will find it strange
This is my movie released unrated
In which I smile my silent threat of change